Through Veterans' Eyes

RELATED TITLES FROM POTOMAC BOOKS, INC.

America's Covert Warriors:
Inside the World of Private Military Contractors
—Shawn Engbrecht

Losing the Golden Hour:
An Insider's View of Iraq's Reconstruction
—James Stephenson

Iraq in Transition:
The Legacy of Dictatorship and the Prospects for Democracy
—Peter J. Munson

Claim Denied! How to Appeal a VA Denial of Benefits
—John D. Roche

The Veteran's PTSD Handbook:
How to File and Collect on a Claim
—John D. Roche

The Veteran's Survival Guide:
How to File and Collect on VA Claims
—John D. Roche

Minefields of the Heart:
A Mother's Stories of a Son at War
—Sue Diaz

Through Veterans' Eyes

The Iraq and Afghanistan Experience

LARRY MINEAR

Foreword by Sen. Richard G. Lugar

Preface by Bob Patrick
Director, Veterans History Project, U.S. Library of Congress

POTOMAC BOOKS, INC.
WASHINGTON, D.C.

Library of Congress Cataloging-in-Publication Data
Minear, Larry, 1936-
Through veterans' eyes : the Iraq and Afghanistan experience / Larry Minear ; foreword by Sen. Richard G. Lugar ; preface by Bob Patrick. — 1st ed.
p. cm.
Includes bibliographical references and index.
ISBN 978-1-59797-486-8 (hardcover : alk. paper) — ISBN 978-1-59797-490-5 (pbk. : alk. paper)
1. Iraq War, 2003—Personal narratives, American. 2. Iraq War, 2003—Veterans—United States—Biography. 3. Afghan War, 2001—Personal narratives, American. 4. Afghan War, 2001—Veterans—United States—Biography. 5. Soldiers—United States—Biography. 6. Veterans—United States—Biography. I. Title.
DS79.76.M555 2010
956.7044'34092273—dc22

2010014258

Printed on acid-free paper that meets the American National Standards Institute Z39-48 Standard.

Potomac Books, Inc.
22841 Quicksilver Drive
Dulles, Virginia 20166

First Edition

10 9 8 7 6 5 4 3 2 1

To those who have suffered and
sacrificed in the wars in
Iraq and Afghanistan

CONTENTS

FOREWORD

In 2000, with unanimous support from the United States Congress, President Bill Clinton signed legislation authorizing the Library of Congress to collect, preserve, and make available the personal stories of America's veterans and civilians. Members of Congress were encouraged to participate in the Veterans History Project because the histories of the average GI, the men and women who carried the burden of protecting our freedom, are sorely lacking. With shelves of information about generals Patton and Eisenhower, admirals Halsey and Spruance, our national history is in desperate need of these kinds of stories, just the sort of stories the Veterans History Project is providing.

In February 2002, I traveled across Indiana to initiate the Veterans History Project's documentation of the stories of Hoosier veterans. With more than 500,000 veterans in Indiana, Hoosiers have much to contribute. All of us can benefit from understanding the patriotism, devotion to duty, and willingness to serve a cause greater than self that our veterans continue to demonstrate. I am pleased to see so many young people engaged in conducting the interviews that have made their way into the Project.

Drawing from my own time in the Navy, I understand the life changing experiences that occur in the military. I vividly remember my time working in the Pentagon briefing Admiral Arleigh Burke. Admiral Burke was a true leader in uncertain times and he taught me the importance of leading well and using the proper tools to accomplish my goals. So many Hoosiers have answered the call to duty throughout our great history, fighting in battles from the Civil War to our current war on terrorism. These brave men and women have a story that should be shared so that future generations can come to understand the many sacrifices made on behalf of freedom.

Each story shared as part of the Veterans History Project provides a window into the life and service of our veterans. We are able to witness first-hand accounts of veterans who left home to become heroes at critical times throughout our history. The men and women serving in Iraq and Afghanistan continue a long tradition of American determination and heroism in difficult times, and I am grateful for their military service. I have benefited enormously from talking to many Hoosiers who have served in Iraq and Afghanistan since 2001, both in the regular military and as members of the National Guard and Reserves.

Since the beginning of this project, my staff and our many partners across the state, including high schools, Boy Scouts, and other volunteers, have submitted the memories of nearly 9,000 Hoosiers into our national history at the Library of Congress. Our history is much richer for the stories we have and are continuing to collect because it helps us appropriately recognize and appreciate our veterans for all they have done, and all they continue to do, for the United States of America.

In an era in which Iraq and Afghanistan dominate our national debate, *Through Veterans' Eyes: The Iraq and Afghanistan Experience* presents personal reflections on the global war on terror by the men and women engaged in this conflict. I am pleased that Larry Minear has provided a forum for a wider audience to appreciate their reflections. Their selfless service and first-hand knowledge of the situation are valuable additions to our national discussion.

Richard G. Lugar
United States Senator

PREFACE

During World War II, a seasoned war correspondent reported, "This war must be seen to be believed, but it must be lived to be understood." This has been the case with any war. The writers, reporters, and chroniclers of our nation's wars have written extensively about combat, a soldier's life, and the fog of battle. However, many have been unable to catch the essence or relate an understanding of the human experience of war: What are the remembrances of events by those prosecuting the action or those behind the lines in support? How do soldiers feel deep inside about what they are called upon to do? In the context of an individual's life experience, what impact did going to war have upon him or her?

The Library of Congress Veterans History Project of the American Folklife Center seeks to add to the understanding of war through the collection of the wartime remembrances of America's veterans. Veterans from World War I through the current conflicts in Afghanistan and Iraq have participated in the Project and provided insight into the human experience of war: its valor, its monotony, and its horror. From the foxhole to the cockpit, from the motor pool to the medical tent, these men and women have offered insight into what those who enter conflict have seen, felt, and been affected by. This is what the U.S. Congress intended when it created the Veterans History Project in 2000.

The Veterans History Project (VHP), with its tens of thousands of interviews backed by hundreds of thousands of original photographs, memoirs, and personal documents, has matured into a valued resource for scholars, educators, and those seeking inspiration. It has also provided the opportunity for very personal connections among generations in families, schools, and communities. By opening their hearts and giving voice to their memories, veterans have been afforded the chance to tell of experiences, often for the very first time. In the process, these men and women have been elevated in the eyes of those who love them as well as those in their communities who didn't know that heroes were among them. All of America has been enriched, because these accounts are now preserved forever in the Library of Congress, where they can be accessed and appreciated.

One goal of the VHP is to allow historians and scholars to tell the story of war through the words of those who were there. As the Project moves into its ninth year, we have been fortunate to see this happening more frequently. We have had researchers use the memories of the American doughboys who fought in the Meuse-Argonne Campaign—one of the most costly and intense battles of all time. Through the VHP collections, scholars have explored the experience of women and African American service members in WWII who fought not only the Axis, but also the perception that they were not capable of serving their country. Scholars have also reviewed the interviews of members of Congress who are Vietnam veterans as a way of determining how that experience affected their later lives of service to the nation. It is becoming clear that personal narrative, particularly being able to hear a voice and see a face as the story is being told, is becoming a source of choice by those professionals writing accounts of momentous historical events.

Now it is heartening to see someone who has used the voices of today's brave young men and women who were involved with the global war on terror. In this book, Larry Minear has selected VHP interviews taken from our most recent wartime veterans, those who served in Afghanistan and Iraq. Their voices and pictures provide insight into the conflicts we have seen every day on our television screens and in our newspapers, but may not clearly understand. They are service members who have earned our respect and our support through commitment to their missions in difficult environments, against a determined enemy, and facing repetitive deployments. Additionally, their experiences bring to the forefront questions of how the United States needs to look at fighting wars in the future, with close examination of such matters as the effect of war on the individual service member, the deployment of Reserve components, and overcoming cultural differences.

Even with the global war on terror, the first conflict of the twenty-first century, the VHP collections reflect experiences common among America's veterans of all wars. Pride in service and making a difference. Realization that going to war is a life-changing experience. Frustration in the ranks with policies, plans, and procedures. Importance of a soldier's ties with family and community. Camaraderie among those who serve together. We see, too, in *Through Veterans' Eyes*, that today's warriors, while facing conflicts in treacherous terrain with new technology and evolving doctrine, share a bond with those wartime veterans who have gone before them—they are serving America with honor while keeping hope and freedom alive in an uncertain world.

The VHP encourages all of America's wartime veterans to come forward and tell their stories. It is not only important to their families and friends, but also significant to their country, which needs a constant reminder of the price that must be paid to live with the freedoms we hold so dear.

Bob Patrick
Director, Veterans History Project
American Folklife Center
U.S. Library of Congress
January 2009

ACKNOWLEDGMENTS

Many people have facilitated the research and writing of this book. I am particularly indebted to Bob Patrick, Director of the Veterans History Project in the American Folklife Center at the Library of Congress and his staff, including Alexa Potter, Tom Wiener, Stephanie Weaver, Rachel Mears, Monica Mohindra, and Steve Winick. Janice Ramseur in the Office of the Assistant Secretary of Defense for Public Affairs also provided useful information.

This book draws on the work of a number of journalists and newsmakers, analysts and editors. I would like to express particular gratitude to Joelle Farrell of the *Concord Monitor;* Andrew Jacobs, editor of *Operation Homecoming;* Yvonne Latty, editor of *In Conflict;* Lovella Calica, editor of *Warrior Writers;* Matthew Currier Burden, author of *The Blog of War;* Deborah Scranton, director, and Robert May and Steve James, producers, of *The War Tapes;* Jay Craven, producer of *After the Fog;* and Matthew Gutmann and Catherine Lutz, authors of *Breaking Ranks*. Excerpts from their works are used with their permission, which is gratefully acknowledged.

I would also like to thank colleagues associated with the Feinstein International Center at Tufts University, including Peter Walker, Antonio Donini, Ian Smillie, Greg Hansen, and Anita Robbins. A special word of appreciation for research assistance goes to Adela Raz, a graduate student who is herself an Afghan national, and for expert editing by Joyce Maxwell.

Other family and friends who have been helpful include my wife Beth; my mother Gladys; and also Michael Craig, Gene Dewey, Jason Forrester, Lori Garrison, Barbara Gerlach, Gregory Heilshorn, Crosby Hipes, Jerry Hoganson, Emmy Huffman, Jason Knobloch, Richard Neal, John P. Reeder, Tom Tarantino, and Robert V. L. Wright. I am grateful to the staff of Potomac Books, Inc., including Senior Editor Hilary Claggett, Marketing Manager Claire Noble, and Production Editor Melaina Phipps. Most of all, I am indebted to the veterans and their families who have shared their experiences and reflections. A special word of thanks as well to the veterans who agreed to have their photographs grace this volume.

INTRODUCTION

The first decade of the new millennium will be remembered by Americans as the decade of the global war on terror. The United States responded to the September 11, 2001 attacks on New York and Washington, D.C. by launching military offensives against Afghanistan in October 2001 and Iraq in March 2003. By the end of 2008, almost two million American service personnel had served in Operation Enduring Freedom (OEF) in Afghanistan and in Operation Iraqi Freedom (OIF) in Iraq. As of January 3, 2009, 38,073 U.S. military personnel had been killed or wounded since the inception of the conflicts.[1] The official tally of the costs of the wars was approaching $1 trillion; unofficial estimates put the costs higher still. [2]

This book examines the conflicts through the eyes of U.S. military personnel deployed to the Afghanistan and Iraq theaters. The narrative weaves together commentary from interviews and other available sources. The voices of the veterans come from all military services (Army, Navy, Air Force, Marines, and Coast Guard), from all branches of the military (Active Duty, National Guard, and Reserves), and from various ranks (including enlisted personnel and commissioned officers). The responsibilities these veterans performed include combat, transport, military police, public information, civic action, and legal affairs. The veterans include career professionals as well as recent inductees, women as well as men, gay men and lesbians as well as straights, foreign nationals on a path to expedited U.S. citizenship as well as American citizens.

The composite narrative draws extensively on materials in the Veterans History Project in the American Folklife Center of the Library of Congress in Washington, D.C. Of the more than 70,000 oral histories assembled by the Project, almost 1,200 have been contributed by men and women who served in Afghanistan and Iraq. Of these, the author has reviewed some 150. The Veterans History Project, which has prepared a field kit of suggested questions for those conducting interviews, is also the source of the volume's photographs. Each photo is used with permission and accompanied by an extended caption explaining the circumstances and the importance to the veteran involved. A description of the Project by its director, Bob Patrick, is provided in the Preface.

The narrative also draws on an earlier study by the author, *The U.S. Citizen-Soldier and the Global War on Terror: The National Guard Experience.*[3] That study highlighted the experience of veterans and institutions in New Hampshire and Vermont in particular and included interviews with members of veterans' families, community leaders, mental health professionals, and the general public. The present book and the earlier study also draw on e-mails, letters, and commentary from newspapers, journals, and other publicly available sources. A bibliography lists publications in which the views of veterans are compiled.

All in all, this book draws on commentary from more than two hundred veterans and their families, communities, and institutions. The term "veterans" is used broadly to encompass not only those retired from service, but also those who continue in the ranks. Some have redeployed for additional tours in Afghanistan and Iraq or continue in National Guard and Reserve units. The narrative updates the traditional picture of veterans now that young people in their twenties bearing the scars of Afghanistan and Iraq are joining the ranks of the soldiers of earlier wars. The term "soldier" is used throughout in a broad sense to encompass members of all the service branches, not simply the members of the Army and Marines who fought on the ground as distinguished from their sea and air compatriots.

In fashioning this composite picture of the experience of U.S. military personnel in Afghanistan and Iraq, I have sought to present an account in which veterans tell their own stories in their own voices. Quotation marks are used to indicate their words; unquoted material represents the author's paraphrase or explanation. For the most part, the commentary they provide needs little explanation. Such is the case, for example, when they describe their reasons for enlisting (Chapter 2), the violence encountered in Afghanistan and Iraq (Chapter 4), and the debilitating reality of post-traumatic stress disorder (PTSD) and traumatic brain injury (TBI) (Chapter 9). At other points, however, more descriptive context is necessary: in situating their experience within the Global War on Terror (Chapter 1), in sketching the international legal and ethical framework for soldiering (Chapter 5), and in examining the response of U.S. institutions to their needs (Chapter 10). Focusing on the perceptions of veterans, the book does not attempt to provide a freestanding analysis of matters such as the Global War on Terror, the applicability of the Geneva Conventions, or the cost-effectiveness of outsourcing functions formerly performed by the military to private contractors.

Early on in my research, a counselor at a vet center whom I was interviewing injected a cautionary note. Whatever you do, she said, "don't 'spin' the experience of veterans in the global war on terror into anything positive. There was nothing positive about the war. It would have been better for the veterans whom we see every day had it never happened." Others provided the opposite counsel, believing that carnage and casualties should not be allowed to obscure the bravery and patriotism of the troops. Such conflicting instructions have reinforced my desire to make this a book in which veterans tell their own stories, with my own role limited to setting the stage and filling in a few of the blanks.

On what basis did I select the veterans whose experiences are recounted in this study? The accounts of several hundred soldiers out of a universe of two million offer a tiny selection indeed. I have made no attempt at assembling a scientific sample: taking, for example, every thousandth entry on a Pentagon roster or interviewing a precise cross-section of veterans mirroring the composition of the armed forces with respect to age, gender, racial/ethnic background, or service branch.

The veterans who appear in this study are chosen randomly from accounts available in the Veterans History Project collection, from published reflections in books and journal articles available in the public domain, and from my own contacts and interviews. My narrative does not offer a scientific poll of veterans' attitudes toward this or that, although it does make reference to quantitative studies by government and private authorities. My narrative instead seeks to convey the texture of the experience as veterans themselves describe it. An index at the end of the book lists the pages on which each soldier's quotations fall and provides details concerning the rank and affiliation of each.

Readers are encouraged to make their own judgments about the fidelity of the book's narrative to the soldiers' experiences. The materials on which much of the presentation is based are accessible to the general public at the Veterans History Project. Since some of the interviews are available in digitized form on the Internet, readers from the comfort of home or office can visit the Project online, download dossiers, and read in their entirety some of the interviews excerpted here. The published writings of veterans, listed in the Bibliography, are also available to those who wish to examine the data for themselves.

My expectation is that many readers will find that the composite narrative rings quite true to the experience of veterans with whom they may be acquainted or whose stories they may have heard. While some may be offended by the language veterans use to share their experience, I have not seen my role as that of censor or moralist. A more extended discussion of methodological issues in selecting and distilling veterans' experiences is provided in my earlier study.[4] A note on my background and earlier publications is contained at the end of the book.

The quotations this book weaves together are faithful to the interviews from which they are drawn, with only minor stylistic editing to improve their readability. I have omitted repetitive phrases and speech mannerisms (for example, throat-clearing) and have changed an occasional tense. I have not used brackets to signify alterations in punctuation or capitalization. In no instance have I altered the substantive thrust of interviewees' commentary. Persons quoted are identified by name, unless they have requested not to be.

Veterans often comment on how little is known or understood by the general public about their experience. With that in mind, the primary audience of this volume is the general public, including veterans' families and communities. The material will also interest health, educational, and other professionals and institutions seeking to respond to veterans' needs and government officials charged with framing and managing government and private-sector programs. The rich oral history resources on which the narrative draws should also pique the interest of historians, teachers, and students. Veterans themselves may find resonance with their own experience and be encouraged to share their views and needs more fully with each other and beyond. What we all have to gain from listening to the voices of veterans is the subject of a concluding chapter.

For me, the three-year process of interviewing veterans and reading and listening to interviews conducted by others has been a riveting but sobering exercise. The process began with my drop-in visit in mid-2006 to a National Guard armory in the small town of Bradford, Vermont, where the duty officer didn't quite know what to make of an inquiry from a curious citizen about how rural Vermonters assess the impacts of their National Guard unit's recent deployment to Iraq. My interest stemmed in part from having done field research on the impacts of the conflicts in Afghanistan, Iraq, and elsewhere on humanitarian assistance personnel. Thanks to that initial query, the experiences of the Vermont National Guard and those of its counterpart across the river in New Hampshire form an important part of this book. I hope that in satisfying my own curiosity, I am able to inform others as well.

The experience of fighting in the Global War on Terror on the frontlines in Afghanistan and Iraq has been fulfilling and satisfying for some veterans, searing and traumatic for many, daunting and unsettling for most. "The war is a very personal experience for everyone," noted Marine Lt. Col. Robert D'Amico.[5] "You change forever when you experience something like this," observed Army SSgt. Shawn Stenberg, whether that change be for the better or the worse.[6] Relying on the voices of veterans themselves, this book seeks to share that experience with a public that has remained largely unengaged in events in these two theaters.

Important in their own right, the voices of veterans also identify issues that run well beyond the scope of this book. These include the assumptions and conduct of a global war on terror, the high costs—personal and social, direct and indirect, financial and institutional—of the approaches taken to tackling terrorism, the need for more energetic and long-range efforts to reintegrate returning veterans into American society, and the lessons from Afghanistan and Iraq for future U.S. foreign and military policy. As these topics begin to receive long-overdue attention, the experience of veterans will provide a useful guide and goad.

Larry Minear
Orleans, Massachusetts
March 2009

ACRONYMS AND ABBREVIATIONS

AFC	American Folklife Center
AK	AK-47, Kalashnikov automatic rifle (standard weapon of Soviet Union forces during the Cold War)
Amn.	Airman
AWOL	Absent without leave
CEO	Chief Executive Officer
CERP	Commander's Emergency Response Program
CRS	Congressional Research Service
CTS	Contingency Tracking System (DOD)
DVA	Department of Veterans Affairs
DMDC	Defense Manpower Data Center (DOD)
DOD	Department of Defense
E-3	Private First Class (Army), Lance Corporal (Marines)
E-4	Specialist or Corporal (Army), Corporal (Marines)
E-5	Sergeant (Army and Marines)
E-6	Staff Sergeant (Army and Marines)
E-7	Sergeant First Class (Army) and Gunnery Sergeant (Marines)
EMT	Emergency medical technician
FOB	Forward Operating Base
FOIA	Freedom of Information Act
Humvee	High-mobility multipurpose wheeled vehicle (HMMWV)

GI	Government issue
IAVA	Iraq and Afghanistan Veterans of America
IED	Improvised explosive device
ISAF	International Security Assistance Force (Afghanistan)
IV	Intravenous feeding
IVAW	Iraq Veterans Against the War
JG	Junior Grade
KBR	Kellogg, Brown, and Root
KIA:	Killed in action
LCPL	Lance Corporal
LOC	Library of Congress
M16	Standard weapon of U.S. armed forces beginning in the mid-1960s
MBA	Master of Business Administration
MFSO	Military Families Speak Out
MIA	Missing in action
MP	Military Police
MRE	Meals Ready to Eat
MSgt	Master Sergeant
NATO	North Atlantic Treaty Organization
OEF	Operation Enduring Freedom (Afghanistan)
OIF	Operation Iraqi Freedom
PBS	Public Broadcasting Service
PRT	Provincial Reconstruction Team
PT	Patrol torpedo (boat)
PTSD	Post-traumatic stress disorder
PX	Post exchange
ROTC	Reserve Officers Training Corps
RPG	Rocket-propelled grenade
SOFA	Status of Forces Agreement
SSgt	Staff Sergeant
TBI	Traumatic brain injury
TCN	Third Country National
U.K.	United Kingdom

UN	United Nations
U.S.	United States
USA	U.S. Army
USAF	U.S. Air Force
USMC	U.S. Marine Corps
USN	U.S. Navy
VA	Veterans Administration
VFA	Veterans for America
VHP	Veterans History Project
WIA	Wounded in Action

PART I
The Setting

The experiences of veterans in Afghanistan and Iraq take place within the broader context of the Global War on Terror. Part I provides the backdrop against which veterans tell their stories. Part II describes their soldiering. Part III reflects upon the challenges of reentry and of coming to terms with what they have experienced.

— ONE —

The Global War on Terror

Through Veterans' Eyes presents a composite view of the experiences of U.S. troops serving in Afghanistan and Iraq as part of the Global War on Terror. Chapter 1 provides a snapshot of the men and women involved, outlines the historical context of the two conflicts, and provides basic information about the U.S. military forces of which veterans were a part.

TODAY'S VETERANS

The term "veteran" carries a lot of historical baggage. For many Americans, a veteran is a grizzled man now in his nineties who was drafted into the ranks and served in World War II. We imagine him catching his breath in a foxhole in France or storming an island in the Pacific. Following the end of the war in Europe and Japan, he was deposited by a troop ship on the east or west coast, welcomed home with parades in New York or San Francisco, and reconnected with his family, resumed his job, and perhaps went back to school under the GI bill.

The veterans whose mettle is being tested in Afghanistan and Iraq are different. They belong to an all-volunteer military. Many are "citizen-soldier" members of the National Guard, bringing a wide array of skills to their assignments. There is a large contingent of women who now play more extensive roles, including combat. Many of today's veterans have been deployed to the two conflict theaters several times. About one in eight has been involuntarily retained in the service after having met his or her contractual obligations. Returning to the States, today's veterans remain longer in the harness than their World War II predecessors, continuing in active-duty units, resuming National Guard training, or being assigned to the Reserves. Most veterans are twenty-somethings, with much to contribute to civil society or the military and decades remaining in which to do so.

The wars, too, are different. Today's veterans have a better chance of surviving than their predecessors, particularly if they sustain battlefield injuries. Yet they are more likely to return with serious health problems associated with the "signature wounds" of Afghanistan and Iraq: post-traumatic stress disorder (PTSD) and traumatic brain injury (TBI). The two conflicts are proving longer lasting than U.S. involvement in World War II. As of 2009, the Afghanistan war and the broader Global War on Terror are in their eighth year, the Iraq war in its sixth. Veterans from today's conflicts draw numerous comparisons between "their" wars and those of their predecessors, as noted in Chapter 11.

Veterans' organizations are different as well. Responding to a different veteran with different interests and needs than those of the world war eras, a wider array of groups is stepping forward to take a fuller spectrum of positions on matters of war and peace and to perform a broader array of services on behalf of their members. The families of veterans are also better organized and more active and vocal. In short, the wars in Afghanistan and Iraq give new meaning to the term "veteran."

SEPTEMBER 11 AND ITS AFTERMATH

This book shares the experiences of veterans from the Afghanistan and Iraq theaters of the Global War on Terror. The *Global War on Terror* is the name given by the administration of President George W. Bush to its response to the terrorist attacks of September 11, 2001, on the United States. "In the smoky, chaotic hours after September 11's stunning attacks, Bush put into motion a simple and direct policy: Terrorists were to be pursued relentlessly and given no safe haven; those who harbored or tolerated terrorists were also the enemy. Those orders spawned a flurry of diplomatic, intelligence and military activity, including the destruction . . . of Afghanistan's Taliban government."[1]

The events of September 11, said the president, represented "an attack that took place on American soil, but it was an attack on the heart and soul of the civilized world. And the world has come together to fight a new and different war . . . against all those who seek to export terror, and a war against governments that support or shelter them."[2] The resulting Global War on Terror, an American initiative joined to one extent or another at one time or another by more than four dozen countries, has had three principal theaters: Afghanistan, Iraq, and the home front.

U.S. military operations against Afghanistan began on October 7, 2001. Air attacks were followed by ground action designed to capture self-confessed 9/11 mastermind Osama bin Laden, destroy his Al Qaeda organization, and remove from power the Taliban regime that provided sanctuary in Afghanistan. On the day following 9/11, NATO declared the attacks to be an assault against all of its members.

On December 20, 2001, the UN Security Council endorsed the creation of an International Security Assistance Force (ISAF), over which NATO assumed leadership in April 2003. ISAF during its lifetime had support from some forty NATO and non-NATO member nations. Under American command, ISAF troops as of January 2009 numbered about 50,000, including 24,000 from the United States, supported by about 100,000 members of Afghan army and police forces. An additional 10,000 troops were deployed to Afghanistan under sole U.S. command as part of Operation Enduring Freedom.[3] Most of the interviews upon which this study draws regarding Afghanistan are with troops involved in Operation Enduring Freedom; there is little commentary by U.S. soldiers in ISAF or by soldiers in Afghanistan from other nations.

The Global War on Terror was broadened on March 19, 2003, with a U.S. attack on Iraq. Invoking the authorization of force provided by Congress in October 2002, President Bush sought to disarm Iraq's weapons of mass destruction, end the regime's support for terrorism, and free the Iraqi people from the rule of Saddam Hussein.[4] Iraq quickly became the second major theater in the Global War on Terror, with the conflict there soon overshadowing military operations in Afghanistan. Seeking but failing to receive the imprimatur of the UN Security Council, the United States assembled a "coalition of the willing" to support the war in Iraq. Twenty-one nations provided military, logistical, and other support to U.S. military efforts there.

On May 1, 2003, following the overthrow of the regime of Saddam Hussein, President Bush declared major combat operations completed. "In the battle of Iraq," he said in a ceremony aboard the USS *Abraham Lincoln*, "the United States and our allies have prevailed."[5] Although the United States sought to turn attention to reconstruction, fighting continued and involved a widening array of actors, described by Secretary of Defense Donald Rumsfeld in June 2003 as including "looters, criminals, remnants of the Baathist regime, foreign terrorists, and those influenced by Iran."[6]

"After a brief period of relative quiet following [the end of] major combat operations, forms of violent expression grew in variety, intensity, and frequency, hitting peaks in 2005 and 2006. By 2008, indicators of violence had tapered off to markedly lower levels."[7] The justification for the war was the subject of heated public debate from the outset, fueled by the discovery of no weapons of mass destruction and by the lack of a confirmed connection between the regime of Saddam Hussein and the Al Qaeda terrorist network. The objectives and legitimacy of the war against Iraq are a recurring topic of comment among those interviewed for this book.

In November 2008 following months of negotiations, the United States and Iraqi authorities signed a Status of Forces Agreement (SOFA) committing the United States to withdraw combat troops by the end of 2011. Coming into force at the expiration of the applicable UN Security Council resolution on December 31, 2008, the agreement placed foreign troops under the authority of the Iraqi government, effective January 1, 2009.[8] American troops, while remaining under U.S. command, would carry out operations approved by a joint Iraq-U.S. committee.[9] Earlier UN Security Council resolutions had reaffirmed the territorial integrity of Iraq, called upon the occupying powers to obey international law, including the Geneva Conventions of 1949,[10] and authorized creation of a multinational force.[11]

As of December 2008 there were about 142,000 U.S. troops in Iraq, along with some 5,000 from other countries, working in collaboration with Iraqi security forces. During 2008, a number of U.S. partners, including Australia, Georgia, Poland, and Korea, reduced their forces in Iraq or redeployed them within the country. In 2008 the United Kingdom, the major U.S. partner, announced its intention to reduce the number of troops in

2009 and change the mission of those remaining.[12] As of early 2009, only the U.K., Australia, Estonia, and Romania were providing troops.[13] A number of U.S. soldiers interviewed mention interactions with military personnel of other coalition members.

Beginning in late 2007 and continuing throughout 2008, the focus of the United States began to shift from Iraq back to Afghanistan. The "surge" in the levels of American troops deployed to Iraq, begun in February 2007, was widely credited with reducing the numbers of American and coalition casualties. Meanwhile, however, the levels of violence in Afghanistan were escalating, with the numbers of casualties per month by late 2008 overtaking comparable figures for Iraq.

In the Afghanistan theater during the latter part of 2008, major frictions emerged between U.S. and ISAF forces on the one side, and the government of President Hamid Karzai on the other. Tensions were exacerbated by several high-profile incidents in which substantial numbers of Afghan civilians were killed or wounded in situations implicating international troops. Frictions also existed with the government of Pakistan, which was seen as providing sanctuary for hostile elements in its regions bordering Afghanistan. During the Bush administration and in the early days of the Obama administration, the United States launched occasional attacks against suspected Al Qaeda operatives within territorial Pakistan. In February 2009, the new Obama administration announced its intention to commit 17,000 additional troops to the war in Afghanistan.[14] This number was soon augmented by the commitment of another 4,000 U.S. troops.

The third major theater in the Global War on Terror was the United States itself, where the Bush administration mounted a cluster of activities under Operation Noble Eagle. The U.S. military carried out operations designed to defend the homeland (for example, improving port and airport security) and to support the work of federal, state, and local agencies. Three days after the September 11 attacks, President Bush committed up to 50,000 troops, of which 35,000 were eventually mobilized, including about 10,000 from the National Guard. In a separate undertaking called Operation Jump Start, some 6,000 National Guard personnel were deployed along the Mexican border to help deter illegal immigration and enhance border security.

The Global War on Terror was framed by the Bush administration from the outset in terms of doing battle not just against Al Qaeda, but against "terrorism of global reach." Beginning in 2002, administration requests to Congress for foreign assistance funds highlighted the importance of twenty-eight "front-line" states cooperating with the United States in the Global War on Terror or themselves facing terrorist threats.[15] In October 2002, the administration extended Operation Enduring Freedom from Afghanistan into the Horn of Africa, with a taskforce based in Djibouti, in order to disrupt terrorist activities in that region. In October 2008, the Department of Defense (DOD) announced establishment of an Africa Command to coordinate counterterrorism activities across the continent.[16]

To manage the Global War on Terror, the president introduced a number of policy, organizational, and administrative changes. The U.S.A. PATRIOT Act (the Uniting and Strengthening America by Providing Appropriate Tools Required to Intercept and Obstruct Terrorism Act of 2001), which became law on October 26, 2001, and has since been extended, gave the president broad authority to protect the country from future attacks. Early administration priorities included strengthening U.S. intelligence-gathering and implementing new airline security measures. Under the PATRIOT Act, the president created the Department of Homeland Security to coordinate U.S. policies and programs across a wide range of executive branch agencies.

The Congressional Research Service (CRS) places the three-theater costs of appropriations by Congress for Operation Enduring Freedom, Operation Iraqi Freedom, and Operation Noble Eagle from the time of the 9/11 attacks through early 2009 at $864 billion. These funds underwrite "military operations, base security, reconstruction, foreign aid, embassy costs, and veterans' healthcare" for all three operations. Of the $864 billion, CRS estimates that Iraq has received about $657 billion (76 percent) and Afghanistan about $173 billion (20 percent). "About 94 percent of the funds are for the DOD, 6 percent for foreign aid programs and embassy operation, and less than 1 percent for medical care for veterans."[17]

Estimates of war-related costs vary according to what items they include, how far into the future they are projected, and what other assumptions are made. Estimates advanced by some independent analysts run considerably higher than the $864 billion CRS figure. One estimate from early 2008 envisioned total costs of some $3 trillion.[18]

U.S. MILITARY FORCES IN AFGHANISTAN AND IRAQ

The veterans whose voices are heard in this book are members of U.S. military forces that, since the end of conscription in 1973, have been composed entirely of volunteers. In the wars in Afghanistan and Iraq from their inception in October 2001 and March 2003, respectively, through November 30, 2008, a total of 1,834,760 members of the U.S. armed forces have been deployed. Of these, 725,668 have been deployed more than once. As indicated in Figure 1, the total number of deployments, as distinct from the total number of individuals deployed, stands at 2,881,783 for this period. (A single individual who has deployed four times appears in the "total deployment actions" column as four.)[19]

The narrative includes considerable discussion about linkages observed between the frequency of deployment and the incidence of mental health problems. More vulnerable than their counterparts in earlier wars, the chances of veterans returning with PTSD with psychological symptoms is estimated by one government study at 38 percent for members of the Army, 31 percent for Marines, and 49 percent for the National Guard. As discussed in Chapter 10, the vulnerability to PTSD of a given individual reflects, broadly speaking, the duration and intensity of the conflict to which a veteran is exposed.[20]

The Introduction includes a discussion of the relationship between the several hundred veterans whose experience has been consulted and the much larger universe of veterans who have served in either Afghanistan or Iraq. No attempt has been made to identify a scientific sample of individuals from the larger population. The narrative draws upon selected interviews from the Library of Congress's Veterans History Project, supplemented by interviews with veterans, families, community leaders, and policymakers conducted by the author. It also reflects the experiences of veterans who in various venues have offered their own accounts of service in these theaters. For those individual veterans who comment on their experiences in this narrative, an index at the back of the book indicates the location of service of each, whether Afghanistan, Iraq, or within the United States as part of

FIGURE 1

U.S. Military Deployments to Afghanistan and Iraq through November 2008

Individuals Deployed as of 11/30/08 264,961
Deployed Once 1,109,092
Deployed More Than Once 725,668
Individuals Deployed 1,834,760
Total Deployment Actions 2,881,783

200,000 900,000 1,600,000 2,300,000 3,000,000

U.S. Department of Defense, Defense Manpower Data Center. Contingency Tracking System

Operation Noble Eagle. Individual entries in the index also indicate a given veteran's rank, branch of service, and unit, where this is known. Veterans consulted in the process, but whose experience is not referenced in the text, are not listed.

The troops involved in these two conflicts represent a significant portion of total U.S. military manpower globally. As of late 2008, approximately two thirds (264,961) of currently active U.S. armed forces strength was committed to the conflicts in Afghanistan and Iraq.[21] In fact, by 2009, policymakers were expressing growing concern that "the wars have left troops and equipment severely strained [making] it difficult to carry out any kind of significant operation elsewhere."[22]

U.S. military personnel serving in Afghanistan and Iraq are drawn from the three components of the country's armed forces: active-duty forces, the National Guard, and the Reserves. As of late 2008, active-duty personnel represent 74 percent of total U.S. forces in the two theaters, with personnel from the National Guard and the Reserves contributing about 13 percent each.[23]

Active-duty forces are comprised of members of the Army, Navy, Coast Guard, Marines, and Air Force. National Guard forces are made up of fifty-four separate National Guard units, one from each of the fifty states plus individual units for the District of Columbia, the Commonwealth of Puerto

Rico, and the territories of Guam and the Virgin Islands. Each unit reports to its respective governor and is utilized primarily within its own geographical area. However, the president may activate Guard units to respond to needs in other states (for example, Hurricane Katrina) or abroad.

National Guard personnel represent an unusually large proportion of total forces in Afghanistan and Iraq, have been activated for more lengthy and more frequent tours, and have been more heavily engaged in combat than has normally been the case for the Guard. The fact that Guard contingents are attached to active-duty units when deployed to Afghanistan and Iraq has made for some similarities between the experiences of these two categories of soldiers, despite their otherwise different make-up and roles. The experiences of the National Guard personnel in Afghanistan and Iraq were the subject of an earlier study by the author.[24]

U.S. forces in Afghanistan and Iraq also include members activated from the Reserves. The Reserves are comprised of service members who have completed active-duty tours but have time remaining before they have fully met their commitment. While personnel normally enlist in the armed forces for three to six years, of which at least two are spent in active-duty status, "all soldiers have a statutory eight-year military service obligation which is established at the time of entry into military service (active or reserve)."[25] A significant number of those returning from Afghanistan and Iraq become attached to the Reserves, from which they can be activated as needed. The narrative comments on the particular challenge of meeting the needs of returning veterans in National Guard and Reserve units, a more difficult task than assisting those who upon returning congregate on active-duty bases and in communities of military families.

Figure 2 charts the number of casualties sustained by U.S. military personnel in Afghanistan from the inception of the conflict on October 7, 2001, through January 3, 2009.[26] The data are for Operation Enduring Freedom as a whole, which includes areas "in/around Afghanistan, the Republic of the Philippines, Southwest Asia, and other locations." Figure 3 provides comparable figures for U.S. casualties in Iraq during the period March 19, 2003, through January 3, 2009.[27] Figure 4 combines the two sets of casualty figures in order to show the total numbers of U.S. military personnel killed and wounded in both operations as of that same date.[28] Casualties as defined by DOD include those killed in action (in both non-hostile and hostile circumstances) and those wounded in action.

Of the casualties sustained by U.S. forces in Afghanistan and Iraq through January 3, 2009, 79.8 percent were active-duty personnel, 7.4 percent members of National Guard units, and 12.8 percent from the Reserves.[29] A higher percentage of casualties has been sustained by active-duty forces than their share of the total number of troops provided. The experiences of members of each of the three components are reflected in the narrative. The narrative draws on interviews with commissioned officers and enlisted personnel. The latter are more numerous in the narrative, as of course they were also in theater.

Of the total number of casualties through January 3, 2009, 70.5 percent of those killed or wounded in action were members of the Army; 25.9 percent, Marines; 2.1 percent, Navy; and 1.5 percent, Air Force.[30] The majority of those whose voices are heard in this book are members of the Army or the Marines. The Navy, Coast Guard, and Air Force have the smallest numbers of members serving, and also the fewest whose experiences are reflected in the book.

Of the casualties sustained through January 3, 2009 by veterans in all components whose ages were known, 28.8 percent of those killed and wounded were under the age of twenty-two, 25.9 percent were between the ages of twenty-two and twenty-four, 25.2 percent between the ages of twenty-five and thirty, 10.2 percent between the ages of thirty-one and thirty-five, and 9.9 percent age thirty-six or older.[31] The composite narrative draws on the experience of persons across the age span.

About 82 percent of approximately 80,000 men and women who joined the Army in 2008 were high school graduates. In 2008, in the interest of boosting lagging recruitment, "The Army provided waivers to 18 percent of active-duty recruits in the final months, allowing them to enlist despite medical conditions or criminal records."[32]

Regarding the makeup of U.S. military forces globally with respect to gender, the proportions of men and women are 90 percent and 10 percent, respectively. The narrative draws extensively on the experience of women

FIGURE 2

Casualties among U.S. Military Personnel in Afghanistan through December 2008

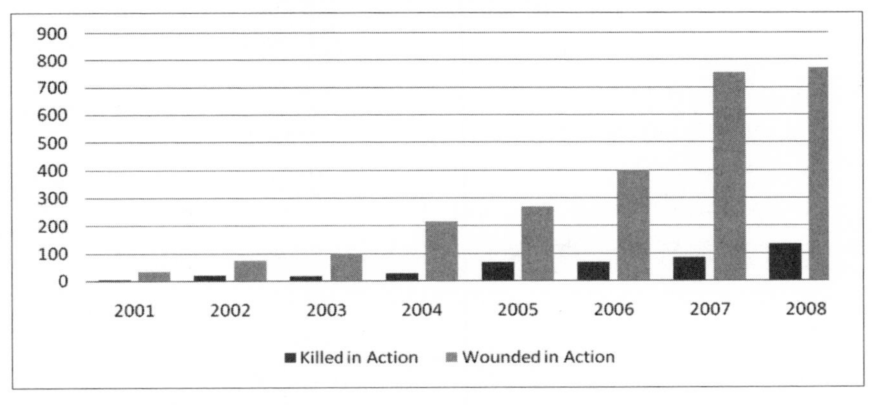

U.S. Department of Defense, Defense Manpower Data Center. Contingency Tracking System

FIGURE 3

Casualties among U.S. Military Personnel in Iraq through December 2008

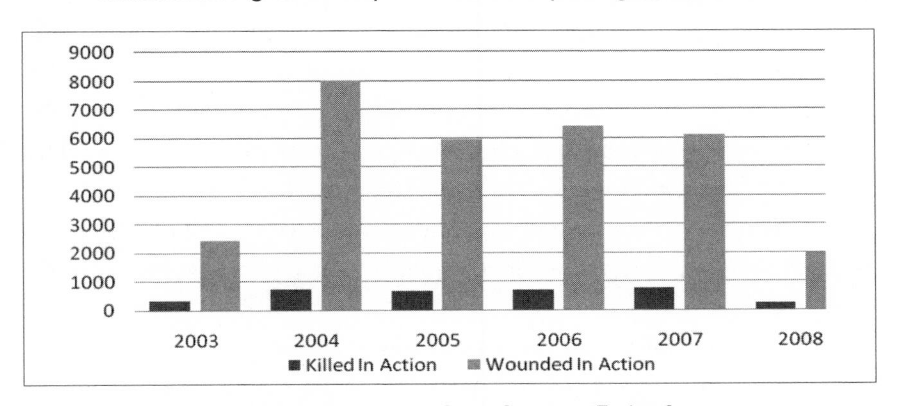

U.S. Department of Defense, Defense Manpower Data Center. Contingency Tracking System

in Afghanistan and Iraq, commenting on the presence of women in significant numbers among the deployed and on the wide-ranging roles they played. More than 100,000 women and 16,000 single parents have served in Afghanistan and Iraq. Some 55 percent of military personnel serving in these two theaters are married.[33] Of total casualties sustained through January 3, 2009, about 2 percent were women, 98 percent men. As of that date,

FIGURE 4
Total Casualties of U.S. Military Personnel in Afghanistan and Iraq through December 2008

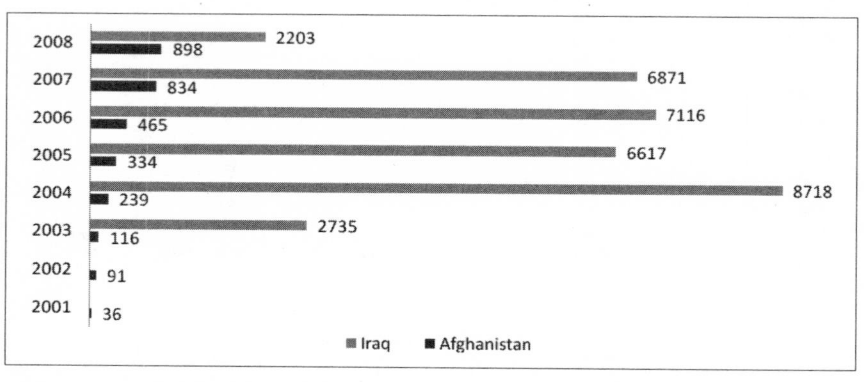

U.S. Department of Defense, Defense Manpower Data Center. Contingency Tracking System

14 women had lost their lives in Afghanistan, 101 in Iraq.[34] Globally, U.S. military losses are 10 percent female.

With respect to racial/ethnic backgrounds, the casualties sustained in Afghanistan and Iraq were roughly proportionate to the make-up of U.S. forces globally. Of the casualties in both theaters through January 3, 2009, the elements are as follows: white, 76.9 percent; black, 8.3 percent; Hispanic, 6.8 percent; American Indian/Alaskan native, 1.1 percent; Asian/ Pacific islands,1.5 percent; and multiracial, 4.6 percent.[35] All of these racial and ethnic groups are represented among the first-person accounts in the narrative.

As of late 2008, U.S. active-duty forces at the global level included some 35,000 non-U.S. citizens.[36] Members of the armed forces are not required to be U.S. citizens, unless they are serving as officers. While there is no provision that non-citizens who serve will be granted citizenship, the citizenship process may be expedited to reflect their service. "U.S. immigration and nationality laws provide special rules for the naturalization of non-citizens who have served in the U.S. military."[37] The experiences of non-U.S. nationals are mentioned at various points in the narrative.

The views of soldiers are drawn from across the full timeframe of the conflicts shown in Figures 2, 3, and 4. With respect to the war in Iraq, for example, several of those interviewed were on hand in Kuwait even before the outset of hostilities. Many served during the peak casualty periods. Still others were on the ground in the area in 2007–2008. However, the interview materials utilized from the Veterans History Project and from the author's own conversations with veterans contain heavier representation from the earlier years of each conflict.In the case of Iraq, a larger number of the voices heard were from soldiers deployed in 2004–2006 than in 2007–2009. As the casualty figures confirm, they were on the ground during the most lethal period. The passage of additional time, the return of veterans more recently deployed, and the processing of new interview material will eventually allow for the distilling of experiences more evenly across the full span of both conflicts.

In historical perspective, the demographic profile of those who are serving and have served in Afghanistan and Iraq differs significantly from that of their predecessors. The average age of a combat soldier in Vietnam was nineteen. The average age of an active-duty service member in Afghanistan or Iraq is twenty-seven, with members of the National Guard and Reserves averaging thirty-three. Most service members in previous wars were single; 60 percent of the men and women deployed in the two theaters today have family obligations. Ten percent of those deployed in Afghanistan and Iraq are women, an increase over their percentage of the troops in Vietnam by a factor on the order of a thousand. Of today's women in the two theaters, 16,000 are single mothers.[38] The voices of veterans heard in this book reflect this new demographic profile.

Many of the figures cited in this and later chapters are taken or adapted from the websites of DOD and veterans' organizations and from news and journal articles. The Office of the Assistant Secretary of Defense for Public Affairs has provided some additional data. Some information requested by the author from DOD would not have been forthcoming in time for inclusion in this study had the necessary Freedom of Information Act (FOIA) procedures been pursued.

PART II
The Experience

The stories that veterans share about Afghanistan and Iraq touch on many aspects of the experience. These include why soldiers enlisted in the military (Chapter 2), how they view politics and political issues (Chapter 3), how they have functioned in unfamiliar and violent surroundings (Chapter 4), and how they have come to terms with the carnage and their role in it (Chapter 5). Soldiers also express strong feelings about local populations (Chapter 6), private contractors (Chapter 7), and the media (Chapter 8). Part II offers a composite narrative weaving together the comments of veterans from interviews and their own writings on these themes. Part III describes the challenges they face in returning to the United States following their deployments overseas.

—TWO —

Enlistment and Patriotism

One of the initial questions suggested by the Veterans History Project field kit for interviews of veterans from America's various wars concerns why a person joined the armed forces. Other questions inquire about why the interviewee chose a particular branch of the service and where he or she was on the day a given war was declared. Still other questions explore the training received, the responsibilities shouldered, the dangers experienced, the relationships formed, and the most memorable experiences. Finally, interviewees are asked to reflect upon how their experiences have contributed to their thinking about their country and military service.

The field kit is not always followed by interviewers, who ranged from middle school students to college professors, from mental health personnel to officials of veterans organizations, from members of congressional offices to officials of state historical associations. Yet the questions provide a useful framework for organizing and examining the experience of the veterans who served on the front lines of the Global War on Terror in Afghanistan and Iraq. The interviews conducted by the author touched on similar issues.

ENLISTMENT

The fact that the United States has not drafted citizens into its armed forces since the end of conscription in 1973 means that all of the two million people who have served in the global war on terror in Afghanistan and Iraq have entered the ranks of the military of their own volition. The principal reasons for enlisting are, first and foremost, economic and educational. A sense of duty to country is expressed less often as a motivating factor, a personal response to the events of 9/11 less frequently still.

Economic considerations figure prominently in enlistments into today's military. "It's one of the few places where if you're born into poverty, you can actually get out of it," said Sgt. E-5 Terrell Spencer, who enlisted in the Army in late 2003.[1] "There are many reasons why I joined the Marine Corps," recalled Sgt. Jeremy Lima, who served in Iraq with the Provisional Security Battalion of the Third Marine Aircraft Wing. "I wanted to go to college. I was poor. I wanted to set myself up for a career, not just a job. But most importantly, I wanted to be part of something I could be proud of. Pride is what I was really looking for. You don't join the Marine Corps. You become a Marine."[2] That sentiment suffuses Lima's photographs, one of which appears in Chapter 9.

Asked why he joined the Air Force, Col. William F. Andrews, whose twenty-five-year career included service in Germany during the Cold War and flying in Desert Storm and Operation Iraqi Freedom, answered: "That was really simple. I wanted to fly, and when I was sixteen, I took some flying lessons. I ran out of money and wanted someone to teach me how to fly for free."[3]

Ryan Maloney, who spent eleven months with the Vermont National Guard in Iraq in 2004, had enlisted because of economic need. He was also continuing a family tradition. As his mother, Nancy Brown of Waitsville, Vermont, explained, two of her brothers had enlisted in the National Guard and served in Vietnam (one is still struggling with resulting post-traumatic stress disorder).[4] One of the attractions of the Guard over the years has been that members can improve their lot in life while staying connected with their families and communities. The Guard draws many enlistments from impoverished areas, particularly rural ones.

For some veterans, a combination of factors led to the decision to enlist. Asked what he hoped to gain by joining the Army, Capt. Andrew M. Wells, who entered by way of the Reserve Officers Training Corps (ROTC) program at Iowa State University, summarized his reasons as "adventure, patriotism, good leadership experience, and an overall life-rounding experience. I think it's important for Americans to serve at some point in some capacity, either their local community or their country as a whole."[5]

The educational benefits of serving in the military, both in developing skills and expanding opportunities, figured prominently in many enlistment decisions. Spec. Jennifer Schwab, who had signed up for the New Hampshire National Guard in May 2000 while still in high school to defray upcoming college expenses, used her combat bonus to underwrite college tuition costs. While based in Afghanistan, she also took distance-learning courses and completed her degree upon returning. Building on her experience in the Guard, she moved into journalism and nonprofit organization work. Many others returned from Afghanistan and Iraq to further develop skills acquired overseas, avail themselves of educational benefits, move up the career ladder, and even explore new careers.

The importance of the military as a source of economic opportunity is confirmed by the impact of the 2008–2009 recession on recruitment. "As the number of jobs across the nation dwindles," noted one reporter in January 2009, "more Americans are joining the military, lured by a steady paycheck, benefits and training." Expanded educational benefits and incentives under the GI Bill, which took effect in August 2009, were a contributing factor. A reduction in violence in Iraq, Pentagon officials confirmed, also played a role in helping meet enrollment targets for the first time since 2004. In the interim, the military had sought to attract new recruits by "increasing signing bonuses and accepting a greater number of people who had medical and criminal histories, who scored low on entrance exams and who failed to graduate from high school."[6]

Some veterans signed up for the military in search of a new lease on life. Marine Corps SSgt. Brandon M. Bass, a Colorado native who served in Iraq, told an interviewer that he enlisted "to get away and be on my own."[7] Sgt. Brian Coles sought out the Army in 1991 in response to pressure from his father, who served him with an ultimatum: attend college or go into the military.[8] One recruit, who enlisted as part of a group decision arrived at with several friends, recalled his personal circumstances at the time. "I was living a little bit of a crazy lifestyle and wanted to get things together—basically, to get my head straight."[9] One veteran confided apologetically to his interviewer that he had forgotten why he enlisted.

Numerous veterans express appreciation for what they consider the positive aspects of their service. Initially aggravated at the disruption to his work, school, and family life, in the end Army Sgt. Matthew Sean Neely viewed his military experience in positive terms. "I put my life on pause for a year," he said in words that ring true to the experience of many others, "maybe to help somebody for the rest of their life. I think it was worth it, certainly." He describes his time in an infantry division in Iraq as "a life-changing experience for sure. I view life a lot more differently. I have a better handle on things."[10]

Spec. Philip Wade Geiger of the Missouri National Guard assessed his own experience similarly. Military service "has made me a better person. It's made me more respectful and more socially conscious. Before I enlisted, I didn't care about any world events or news. This keeps my eyes open now because I'm interested in things that are evolving that could involve me or friends of mine."[11] Spec. Nicole Ferretti experienced an unexpected boon from her Army duty in Iraq. Rifts in her family began to heal as family members rallied around her at a time of peril.[12]

In a statement echoed by numerous other veterans, Lt. Ron Maloney, a home contractor who had joined the New York National Guard while in high school, noted that he had moved from "banging nails every day" to being "part of something bigger."[13] Marine LCpl. Brian Aria was forever thankful simply for having survived the war. "I appreciate things every day now."[14] However, such rewards, cited and recited, exist in tension with the negatives of the experience, including—in addition to the disruption of personal and family life—injury, loss of life, and regular confrontation with death and destruction. These will be examined in subsequent chapters.

PATRIOTISM

Judging from the interviews, a sense of duty to one's country in its hour of need figured less prominently in enlistment decisions than did economic and educational factors. Of those interviewed who signed up after September 11, 2001, only a minority acted specifically in response to those events or expressed a particular interest in protecting the United States from future terrorist threats. However, their thinking was noteworthy nonetheless.

The 9/11 attacks spurred a number of people to enlist. Marine Cpl. Stephen Wilbanks wrote in his blog that on September 11, 2001, "when the news about the terrorist attacks in New York City came over the radio . . . I immediately drove to the recruiter's office to inquire about reenlistment options."[15] "The only reason I joined the military," recalled Army Spec. E-4 Basil Cofield, who enlisted shortly after 9/11, "is because we got attacked in New York. My country called and it's my time to answer."[16] For Spec. Gregory James Schulte, "September 11 changed a lot of things. After September 11, I got tired of everybody talking—all talking and no show—so I tried to join." In December 2001, halfway through his senior year in high school, he was accepted into the Missouri National Guard and served in Iraq as part of a helicopter detail.[17] Lt. Col. Jude Ferran, who was already in the Army on 9/11—in fact, he was working in the Pentagon at the time of the attack—found it "startling" that such an event as 9/11 could happen.[18]

SSgt. Neal I. Mitchell, who by 9/11 had already served in the Marines, takes pride in having signed up for the New Hampshire National Guard after the attacks on New York and Washington, D.C. He was following in the footsteps of his father, who had enlisted in the Navy in the aftermath of the attack on Pearl Harbor and had served as a navigator on PT boats. But Mitchell the younger was not looking for front line exposure. "You have to have a screw loose," he said, to seek out combat, at the same time recalling that he "at the very least expected to be participating in some domestic security effort."[19] One Vermonter who enlisted in the Guard in 1987 expressed the view that following 9/11, the United States needed to assert itself overseas and draw the line against terrorists. He felt it was important to lend that effort his personal support.

Some who signed up specifically to defend their country from terrorism took particular satisfaction in their work. "Before 9/11," recalled Spec. Dave Bischel, "I was doing wireless communication sales and always feeling that there was something missing in my life. But 9/11 changed a lot of people's lives and how they viewed their lives, including me. After 9/11, I started re-evaluating my priorities. I wanted to be able to help if something

Sniper Duty

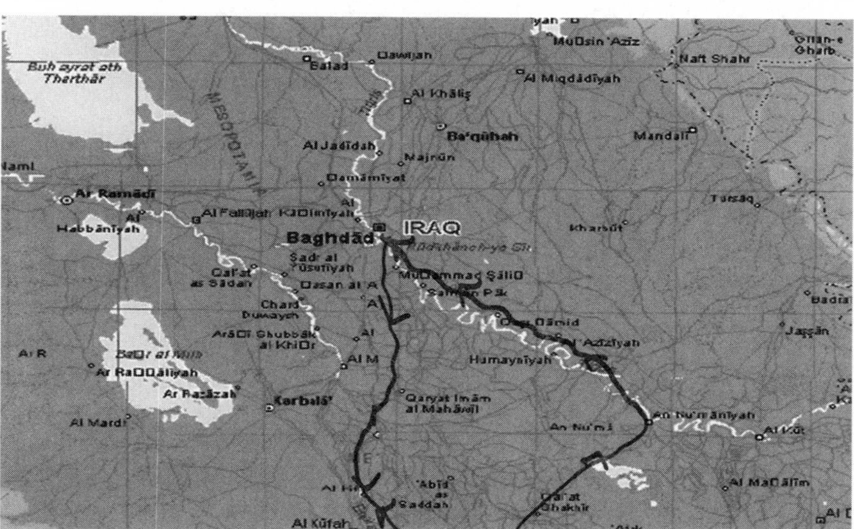

Blake Cole (AFC2001/001/62554), Photographs (PH 38), VHP, AFC, LOC.

SSgt. Blake Cole served as a Marine scout sniper from 2002 to 2008. He worked his way up from an infantry rifleman to his position as chief scout sniper in the Third Battalion Fifth Marine Regiment and eventually instructed sniper students at Quantico, Virginia. During

Sniper Duty continued

that time he was deployed to Southeast Asia and completed three combat tours, a total of 18 months, in Iraq, seeing action in Baghdad, Fallujah, and Ad Diwaniya. Wounded in action on November 12, 2004, he received a Purple Heart medal as well as other commendations.

His sniper team's assistant leader took this photograph in April 2005 outside Fallujah, in a village along the Euphrates called Saqlawiyah. While taking photographs during missions, especially in daylight, is strictly forbidden, Cole was part of a Marine convoy that had stopped in non-hostile territory. "I remember wanting to take this picture," he recalls, "because it was an area that looked like . . . a lot of places we were familiar with in the U.S." He included a map of the location in his Veterans History Project collection.

Cole is carrying about eighty pounds, including body armor and ammunition, which is standard for a rural mission; for urban missions, the load would weigh about one hundred pounds. The picture, taken shortly after dawn, shows Cole wearing night-vision goggles.

As of 2009, Cole was enrolled in the Marine Corps Enlisted Commissioning Education Program at the University of Illinois Chicago, which leads to a college degree and a commission as a 2nd Lieutenant.

Ethan Carty, a seventh grader in the Ni River Middle School in Spottsylvania, Virginia, interviewed Sergeant Cole as part of an annual project organized by Ethan's teacher, Tracie Short, in which several dozen students conduct interviews of local Iraq and Afghanistan veterans. The students hand deliver recordings of the interviews along with other relevant artifacts to the Veterans History Project in the Library of Congress, where they are archived. As Ms. Short believes, "It is important for young children to know what these people have done for us."

---

bad happened on the west coast, so I joined the Guard." Ten years out of the full-time Army, he reenlisted in the Guard and soon found himself in Iraq, where he served with a California Guard unit from March 2003 to April 2004.[20]

"I joined to wear the uniform," said Sgt. Shawn E. Molloy, who was part of an Army medical company in Operation Iraqi Freedom. "Once I put this uniform on, I inherited all the respect and all the history that all these other veterans have fought for. I wanted to be part of something like that."[21] Sr. Amn. Patrick J. McGonigle III observed, "I wear my uniform proudly. I wear it every once and a while just to wear it and say, 'Hey, I earned this!'" In his case, "September 11 hit home." His family was from the New York City area. His parents had fortuitously decided against having lunch in the Twin Towers the previous week and his uncle happened not to have been at work in the Twin Towers that fateful day.[22]

Col. Mark Warnecke, an infantry battalion commander from the New York National Guard during Operation Iraqi Freedom, had a vivid memory of seeing "those smoking holes in the ground" where the Twin Towers used to be. Against that backdrop, "The first time you're actually looking at an Al Qaeda guy in the eye made the whole year worthwhile."[23] Timothy Rieger, who had served in the Marine Corps' Judge Advocate General's unit in Afghanistan, noted: "There's an old saying that the greatest warrior is one who does not need to kill. If you demonstrate that you're prepared and willing and that you will sacrifice in order to defeat the enemy, that is a great deterrent. I think that we have to continue to demonstrate that, particularly to these radical organizations that will blow up the World Trade Center or the Pentagon or the stadium in which you or I are watching some baseball game."[24]

Family military traditions often played a key role not only in the decision to enlist, but also in assessing the experience of military service. "I come from a family of warriors," Jay Czarga wrote in his blog. "I am a product of their collective service to the nation." Czarga, who did three tours of duty with a helicopter unit in Iraq, explained, "This isn't about adventure or money or some death wish. It's about doing the right thing."[25] Marine Brig. Gen. Joseph V. Medina, who commanded a seven-ship unit in the Persian Gulf as part of Operation Iraqi Freedom, traces his family involvement in the military to fifteenth century Spain and later Mexico.[26] Army Spec. Eric James March "felt the call of duty" to enlist in June 2001 despite the fact that none of his immediate family had served in the military. On his first day of basic training—it happened to be on September 11, 2001, he recalled—"I remember the drill sergeants saying that we were getting ready to go to war. I had that on my mind and heart." [27]

Given that numerous soldiers who served in Afghanistan and Iraq had enlisted well in advance of September 11, 2001, it is not surprising that many do not identify terrorism or the global war against it as a major motivation. They often present themselves, along with Army Capt. Michael Fortenberry, as simply doing their duty, meeting the obligations they assumed when they enlisted. "I'm not a war monger—I'd rather be home with my family," he said, "but someone has to do it."[28]

Recruits for the National Guard in particular, with its traditionally domestic focus, often reflected a desire specifically not to serve in overseas theaters. When she enlisted in the National Guard, recalled Spec. Jennifer

Schwab, "I had no expectation of overseas service." A year later, when her unit shipped out to Afghanistan following the events of 9/11, she confessed with some amusement, "the joke was on me."[29] Some of her cohorts were less amused. "The only reason I joined the Guard," commented one, "was not to be deployed anymore." He and others were bitter at the diversion of Guard troops from domestic to international tasks: in effect, moving the goalposts while the game was in progress.

For Capt. Christopher Buser, a social worker in a Department of Veterans Affairs (DVA) medical center who worked with veterans back from Afghanistan and Iraq, enlisting in the Army Reserves was a matter of self-respect. He wanted to avoid having to regret later on that he failed to serve. Responding to his wife's complaint that she didn't want to be a military spouse, he said that the Reserves were unlikely to be called up. "Don't make it a career," she cautioned. Assurances to the contrary notwithstanding, Buser's mental health unit was activated on short notice. He worked on contingency planning for responses to terrorism attacks within the United States and expected thereafter to be deployed to Afghanistan.[30]

Although a sense of duty at a time of international duress led some to enlist, many veterans downplayed their involvement in any sort of global antiterrorism effort. In interviews and writings, they used the term *global war on terror* surprisingly infrequently. Even the terms "terror" and "terrorism" were rarely invoked. Spec. Mario Raymundo, a Salvadoran national who joined the New Hampshire National Guard in order to protect his adopted country "for my family and for everybody else's family," believes that the idea of terrorism "doesn't fit" the circumstances. He would have preferred, he said, the concept of "a war against extremism."[31] Such a formulation, chimed in one of his New Hampshire cohorts, would leave room for including homegrown American terrorists such as the Unabomber and the Oklahoma City bomber as threats to U.S. national security.

New Hampshire Guardsman Sgt. Benjamin J. Flanders, who served in Iraq in 2004, also had his doubts. "How does it feel to have been a participant in the Global War on Terror?" he was asked. "The 'global war on terror' nomenclature didn't really fit the situation on the ground," he replied. "Nobody stands around and wonders, 'Is what I'm doing part of the Global

War on Terror?'" In fact, the link between the terrorism banner and the boots on the ground in Iraq seemed something of a stretch. "Are the troops in Iraq fighting terrorists," he asked, "or are we babysitting a civil war?"[32]

Terrorism is undoubtedly a real threat to the country, noted one Vermont Guardswoman, but U.S. policy related to the Global War on Terror is "not serious" and has no bearing whatsoever on her interest in being in the Guard. Second Lt. Eric Giles, who served in a military police company in Iraq, viewed the war there as "very complicated." Based on his law enforcement and intelligence background, he viewed the war as an organized crime operation. Yet because it was overlaid with tribal and religious elements, he said, it's a "multi-level conflict, with [the] U.S. in the middle of it all."[33] Is the conflict in Iraq even a war? Some troops wondered. "We thought of this as war," countered Marine Sgt. Travis Fisher, even though it is somewhat unlike wars in the past.[34]

While there was a widespread belief that a citizen's duty requires service at a time of national duress, the fact that the duress was the result of a terrorist attack from abroad was for many of distinctly secondary importance. Most veterans would have responded to the call, they said, no matter what specific event had triggered it. The prevailing attitude is captured in an Army widow's description of the involvement of her husband, Sgt. Charles M. King, in Iraq. "For Charles," wrote Dana Canedy, "the war was not about 'weapons of mass destruction' or an 'axis of evil'; I never heard him speak those words. It was about leading the soldiers he had trained by example, about honor and dignity, and about protecting a country he loved from enemies real or imagined."[35]

"You don't sign up for the global war," observed Maj. Gen. Kenneth Clark, adjutant general of the New Hampshire Guard. Terrorism, he said, is a vague and nondescript term. "Even the militias who fought and won America's independence from the British would be considered terrorists." What September 11 and its aftermath has enabled the Guard to do, he believes, is to assemble a group of people, "now with their eyes wide open," who are expressing "some level of patriotism in the sense of placing service above self." It would be a mistake, he implied, to read the enlistment numbers in the Guard as some sort of referendum on the global war.[36] A similar conclusion could be drawn for the experience of active-duty ranks as well.

As noted in Chapter 1, U.S. forces in Afghanistan and Iraq contain a surprising number of non-U.S. nationals, like the Salvadoran, Spec. Mario Raymundo. Sgt. Terrell Spencer was impressed by the presence in his Chemical Company unit of a Nigerian who was studying molecular biology and a Bosnian who spoke five languages.[37] In the Iraq theater, one New York National Guard contingent included eight non-citizens, who as a result of their mobilization were put on a fast track to citizenship. A Nigerian in the same group who had sought out a recruiter in New York City following 9/11 was killed in an ambush in Iraq but died a U.S. citizen. On Independence Day 2007, "325 foreign-born soldiers who are fighting in the United States military took the oath of allegiance in two ceremonies in Iraq."[38]

As with full-fledged Americans, the enlistment of non-nationals involved a mixture of motivations, only one of which was the promise of an expedited path to citizenship. Army Spec. Nicole Ferretti, a Brazilian national who lived in Texas, enlisted in 2002 at age twenty-one to advance her educational goals following ROTC training in high school.[39] Sgt. Camilo Mejía, whose parents had played lead roles in the Sandinista revolution in Nicaragua in the 1980s, explained, "I needed a radical change. I needed to do whatever it took to be a part of [American] society. Instead of becoming a political icon, like my parents, I decided to find my own path and joined the U.S. Army." Mejía served in the Florida National Guard in Iraq for seven months beginning in March 2003.[40]

The lack of resonance of the Global War on Terror for many of those fighting in it echoed a certain confusion among policymakers. "In 2005, the Pentagon argued that the phrase 'war on terror' should be replaced by 'global struggle against violent extremism.' The shift, advocated by Donald H. Rumsfeld who was the defense secretary at the time, was overruled by President Bush."[41] The Pentagon itself devised the Global War on Terror Expeditionary Medal and the Global War on Terrorism Service Medal, but these were given out liberally and caused some confusion among the troops about the specific contributions they recognized. A February 2007 audit by the Inspector General's office of the Justice Department found a lack of clarity and consistency in the department's reporting on terrorist activity.[42]

There was also discomfort on Capitol Hill where, beginning in 2007, the House Armed Services Committee no longer used the term "Global War on Terror" in its reports.[43]

■ ■ ■

In sum, a sense of obligation to country emerges as one of several motivations in the decision of soldiers to enlist and, having enlisted, to serve, if required, in Afghanistan and Iraq. However, the concept of participation in a clearly defined and widely understood global war on terror does not emerge as a broadly mobilizing or animating force from the soldiers' accounts of their experiences.

—THREE—

Politics and Professionalism

The ground rules are clear: members of the U.S. armed forces must remain apolitical at all times. By and large, U.S. soldiers in Afghanistan and Iraq have respected that dictum, operating in theater with a high level of professionalism. At the same time, many held—and hold—strong personal views, often sharpened during their overseas postings, regarding the rationale for U.S. engagement, the strategies and tactics employed, and a host of operational matters including training, equipment, and the duration and frequency of deployments. Such concerns have generated an upsurge of political activism on the home front among veterans' families and organizations. As a result, veterans have emerged as a political force increasingly to be reckoned with.

PERSONAL VIEWS

Most veterans of the conflicts in Afghanistan and Iraq are reticent to make their political views public. In introducing "War Stories," the *Concord Monitor's* five-day 2007 series of investigative articles based on interviews with numerous members of the New Hampshire National Guard, editor Mike Pride observed, "As in all wars, most combat veterans are reticent in public. Many have had extreme experiences or witnessed frightful scenes, and they think 'rightly' that there is no way civilians can understand what they went through. Or when they do want to talk, they find that even their friends don't really want to hear it."[1] Soliciting the views of returned soldiers, a global war on terror study conducted by the New Hampshire Guard found most returnees unwilling to join such issues in public. "There has been considerable and heated debate over many aspects of the Iraq war," the Guard's report concluded, "and most veterans would rather not participate in the debate in a public forum."[2]

Interviews with veterans confirm that reticence. "Expressing professional views to civilians is part of the military's responsibility," concluded one series of discussions among senior military officials. "But once decisions have been made, continued expressions of disagreement undercut civilian authority."[3]

Soldiers throughout the ranks themselves underscore the importance of strict non-partisanship. "As far as I could see," recalled Capt. Josh Bradley of his time as a field artillery captain during Operation Iraqi Freedom, "the focus in my unit was entirely on completing the assigned mission and bringing everyone back home safely. I never heard anyone publicly express his or her opinion about the rightness or wrongness of the overall effort."[4] At the same time, there is ample evidence to conclude, as does the *Concord Monitor* series itself, "for some soldiers, their experiences on the ground shaped their political views about the war."[5] Veterans History Project interviews also contain ample evidence that veterans hold strong views on matters political.

Capt. Ralan Hill, who made his way into the Army officer corps from a ROTC program at Tufts University, noted how essential it was for officers to separate professional responsibilities and personal political opinions. "You can't be in charge of 500 people," he noted, "and be bad-mouthing the policies in general." Discipline and morale would be a casualty.[6] Army Sgt. Craig Keys, a Nebraskan who served in Iraq, described himself as "not high enough on the food chain" to worry about political questions. Yet irrespective of his personal view that President Bush is "full of shit," he was committed to playing his part in the war effort. "If they give me a mission, I do it, with no questions asked."[7] Criticism about the war, observed Petty Officer Matthew S. Smith, who served in Desert Shield and Desert Storm as well as in Operation Iraqi Freedom, should be directed at the administration and Congress and not at veterans. After all, it is not as if veterans on their own say, "'Hey, let's go over there and fight this war.' They go where they are told to go," Smith points out.[8]

"Politics?" asked New Hampshire MSgt. Michael Pascalis, who deployed to Afghanistan. "No time for politics. I can't sit here and think if this is the right thing or the wrong thing for me to do. Every man or woman decides that among themselves. However I feel about the situation, I still have a job to do."[9] Others, too, steered away from discussions of the rights and wrongs of U.S. policy. Sgt. Jeremy Feldbusch, blind and brain-damaged following an artillery attack on his position, commented, "I don't have any regrets. I had some fun over there. I don't want to talk about the military anymore." He said he has no political opinions.[10]

"I am quite happy to leave the politics to others," said a Vermont Guardsman. "Mine it is not to reason why," he said earnestly. "Mine is but to do or die." Mississippi National Guardsman Lt. Col. Ralph Riley observed, "President Bush is my commander in chief. As long as I'm in the Army, whatever he says goes."[11] Lt. Ron Maloney of the New York National Guard expressed much the same view. "I'm part of the military, and I believe in its ways. When the military says you go, I go, and I believe in it. It's the teamwork, the values, the ethics, the morals, the camaraderie. Where else do you get a job that constantly enforces those types of values: personal integrity, personal courage, selflessness? Not too many bosses out there say, hey, these are the key requirements for you to be in this job."[12]

Notwithstanding such expressions of political aloofness, soldiers in letters and blogs described political debates that heat up billets and bunkhouses. "I always find it amusing when people talk about 'the military' vote, perspective, or whatever," wrote Sgt. Sharon Allen, a driver of diesel fuel tankers with the Ohio National Guard in Iraq in 2004. "My company has 170-some soldiers, and 170-some opinions. We might have more invested in foreign policy than people back home, but that doesn't mean we all agree on exactly what those policies should be." She went on to say that "tempers can get heated, and on some days it probably isn't a good idea that we are all armed."[13] The expression of political views among the boots on the ground could interfere with the chain of command, undercut morale, and perhaps even impair military operations.

On the fundamental question of whether the United States should be conducting military operations in Afghanistan and Iraq, interviews suggest a higher comfort level with the former than the latter. "When the American government invaded Afghanistan in response to the September 11 attacks, soldiers said they were ready to go," confirmed the *Concord Monitor* reporter. "But when Bush and his administration stretched the war on terror to include Iraq, some troops had reservations."[14] Soldiers from other states as well expressed greater personal support for Operation Enduring Freedom than for Operation Iraqi Freedom.

National Guard personnel, reflecting the Guard's long-standing citizen-soldier tradition, tend to be more outspoken in expressing their views than are active-duty military personnel. Of course, once Guard personnel are called up and attached to active-duty units, the more stringent apolitical ground rules apply. However, upon returning to the United States, members of the Guard are often more outspoken in the public arena than their active-duty counterparts. Such engagement reflects the return of citizen-soldiers to their lives as citizens, the active and varied professional and personal roles they play in their local communities, and the acknowledged right they exercise first and foremost as citizens to express their views.

Political issues surfaced regularly in the banter of New Hampshire National Guard soldiers in *The War Tapes*, a documentary filmed by three Guardsmen and aired back home after their unit had returned from the field.[15] "I think that five guys out of the whole company didn't vote for Bush," speculated New Hampshire's Sgt. Zack Bazzi, "and they probably kept it low. If you're a guy, you know the whole Bush macho 'let's kick ass' thing sounds pretty good."[16] "I support George Bush and everything," his cohort, Spec. Mike Moriarty, chimed in, "but for him to say that 'major combat missions are over' kind of conflicts with what we are seeing and dealing with every day."[17] Asked by an interviewer to recall any humorous events from his own time in the military, Army Sgt. E-5 Eric Cox left no doubt about his view: "Clinton's term in office."[18]

With respect to Iraq in particular, veterans make eloquent and impassioned statements both for and against the presence of U.S. troops. "I'm not in favor of this war," said Army Spec. Tina Garnanez, who served as an emergency medical technician in Iraq. "I believe it's illegal and immoral, a bunch of lies from start to finish. It's nothing but the greedy agenda of a few who speak for the many. Now that I'm out of the service, I've made it my mission to speak out. This war is not about what they say it's about. It's not about terrorism or spreading freedom or democracy. If it were, I'd be all for it. Honestly, I feel it's about oil."[19] Even if the president conceded tomorrow that it is about oil, countered Army 1st Lt. Derek Sutton, "you are still there and you do what you have to do."[20]

Voicing an alternative view of the Iraq war with equal passion is Col. Mark Warnecke of the New York National Guard. "The vast majority of the Iraqi people want us there," he argued, and "don't want anything to do with the insurgency. It is forced on them and they're forced to live with it. The insurgents make it a policy to punish those that support any activities against them. Their goal is to establish a fundamentalist Islamic state similar to what was in Afghanistan under the Taliban throughout the entire Middle East and in all Muslim countries. That's their goal and they'll do this and maintain it by whatever terrorist means it takes to do it. We need to be there."[21] "I support the war 100 percent, said Nebraska's Joshua Townsend, as does "almost every soldier I know.[22]

"Do I think we're making progress?" asked New Hampshire's Sgt. Steve Pink in *The War Tapes*. "No, I don't know. I think any country should be allowed to have its own civil war without people getting in the way. But I also believe that there are some pretty dangerous people in Iraq."[23] Establishing the proper balance between the two elements that Pink identified—the sovereignty of adversary states and the protection of U.S. national security—is the stuff of presidential decision directives and congressional pronouncements.

The undisguised breadth of opinions on matters political was striking for Andrew Carroll, who edited ten thousand pages of writings submitted by soldiers into a single volume, *Operation Homecoming: Iraq, Afghanistan, and the Home Front in the Words of U.S. Troops and Their Families*. "There are contributors who voice staunchly antiwar opinions and accentuate in their writings the pain and destruction the hostilities in Iraq and Afghanistan have inflicted," he noted, "while others express a strong sense of pride about going off to serve and focus on the positive achievements made in both countries over the past few years."[24]

Some boots on the ground have difficulty concealing their irritation with the political debate in Washington and around the country about the appropriateness of the U.S. combat operations in Afghanistan and Iraq. "Let's stop crying about whether we had reason to go in there or not because we can fight about that forever," said Moriarty. "It's a done deal. We're in Iraq."[25] SSgt. Brian Shelton, who served with the New Hampshire National Guard in Afghanistan in 2002 and Iraq in 2003, recalled a Chinese proverb: "Those who say it cannot be done should not interrupt the person doing it." He went on to observe, "For all the people that are saying we can't accomplish what we were sent there for, we're doing it every single day."[26]

Others were more tolerant of having a wide variety of views aired, viewing public debate as affirming the very values the troops are fighting for. In the final posting in his blog before returning to the States, 1st Lt. Rusten Currie of the California National Guard, who believed that the coalition was winning the war in Iraq, thanked "those of you who engaged in healthy and heated debate with me over our political views. Soon we'll see one way or the other, won't we? Those of you who continue to question this war and why we are here, good for you; without different opinions, there is no debate."[27]

Interview data also suggest that the views of veterans on the global war and their own involvement in it have undergone changes over time. "Everybody goes through a cycle," observed SSgt. E-6 Bradley Burd. After two months on the ground in Iraq, he says, soldiers doubt the mission of the troops; after four months they're unsure; and by six months they're thoroughly persuaded in its importance.[28]

Some of those interviewed confirm that progression. A number who had been ambivalent about their mission upon deployment became more persuaded over time. "You don't necessarily agree why you're fighting," explained Spec. James R. Welch, a Toledo, Ohio, native who served for seven months in the infantry in Iraq. "But when you get over there and you see the way these people are living, and you see the way Saddam was living and his family was living, you really want to give these people a better life, because you know what you have back home. . . . Regardless of what the government says you're doing it for, regardless of what your superiors say you're doing it for, you know you're over there doing it because you're freeing these people from a dictatorship they've been under for the past thirty years. Whatever keeps you going from day to day is why you're doing it."[29]

Others became more doubtful or even cynical over time. "I was pretty gung-ho at first," recalled Army Sgt. Gregory Mayfield, who saw intense combat in Iraq. "But now, I question a lot of policies and the politics of it. I mean, you just don't go to war for any damned reason. You'd better have a good reason to do it, because it is so damaging."[30] A CBS documentary detected gradual erosion in the commitment of a contingent of Iowa Guardsmen to the Iraq mission. In one instance, two members of the same family ended up with opposing appraisals of the war. With the passage of time, however, the view that the troops were advancing freedom for the Iraqi people had fewer and fewer proponents. By May 2007, CBS found growing disenchantment. One reporter who spent time with the 82nd Airborne Division found, "A small minority of Delta Company soldiers—comprising the younger, more recent enlistees in particular—seems to still wholeheartedly support the war. Others are ambivalent, torn between fear of losing more friends in battle, longing for their families, and a desire to complete their mission."[31]

The three soldiers who chronicled their experiences in *The War Tapes* also grew disenchanted over time. Pink, who had enlisted to "test myself and make sure I could accomplish something," said upon returning, "I don't want to tell people what it was like over there. What a fucking mess, you know? I went over there and I did the job I was supposed to do."[32] Moriarty, who described himself as a "substantially patriotic person," had contacted a recruiter shortly after 9/11 and said, "You slot me into a unit only if they're going to Iraq." But front line exposure chastened him. "I'm so glad I went. I hated it with a God-awful passion and I will not go back. I have done my part and I feel like it's someone else's turn." [33]

Zack Bazzi, the third in the trio, joined the Army after graduating from high school in hopes of seeing the world. "Most soldiers," he observed on returning, "want to think they're there for a good cause, something noble.

You're fighting for freedom and everything that's right. It was tough, because you have to do some not-so-nice things sometimes." His conclusion: "I love being a soldier. The only bad thing about the army is you can't pick your war." Two of the three felt that guaranteeing oil resources had been a compelling reason for U.S. involvement. All three had medical and/or post-traumatic stress issues needing attention upon their return.[34]

Whatever their specific views, soldiers of all ranks, along with families and veterans' service organizations, are playing a much more visible role in public policy debates than in earlier wars. Family members in particular feel less constrained in expressing personal views. "Being anti-war and being patriotic are compatible," says Carole Welch, whose weekly column, "My Soldier," in the Bradford Vermont *Journal Opinion* kept local people in touch with the activities of her son, Army Spec. James Welch, and his unit. Reflecting on the negative impacts of the experience on her son, his family, and her own life (she resigned from a job in order to care for his young child), she makes no secret of her view: "War is having a big impact on unraveling the things that this country and community were built on."[35]

POLITICAL ACTIVISM

The involvement of the military in Afghanistan and Iraq over most of the past decade has led to an upsurge of political activism on the home front, with many soldiers and families deeply engaged. For many who before enlisting had lacked a sense of purpose or passion in their workaday lives, military service in Afghanistan or Iraq has provided a new sense of direction. They returned home with a new understanding of the importance of family, community, and nation. "They came back with a sense of individual empowerment from having taken on a difficult assignment and performing it well," noted Ernest Loomis, chairman of the New Hampshire Committee of Employer Support of the Guard and Reserve. Many also had "a new-found sense of the worth of our way of life and our type of government."[36] Some became leaders in the movement to bring the troops home.[37]

One veteran who attained particular prominence was Maj. Ladda Tammy Duckworth, a helicopter pilot in the Reserves and a major in the Illinois National Guard. "I was not originally slated to go to Iraq," she recalled, but

Linda McHale (AFC2001/001/47162), Photographs (PH01), VHP, AFC, LOC.

U.S. troops deployed to Iraq and Afghanistan were involved not only in combat and security operations but also in providing training and technical assistance to government ministries. In each country, the infrastructure had been destroyed by the conflict and the host government struggled to restart the delivery of services to its population.

Linda McHale, a colonel in the U.S. Air Force Reserve, came from a family with strong traditions of military service. Her father had served in World War II; her brother and a brother-in-law had been drafted during the Vietnam War. Linda trained as a nurse and joined the Air Force reserve, in part because it allowed her to remain in her rural Texas community with her husband (also in the Air Force Reserve) and two children.

In 1991, she was detailed to a base in England where wounded soldiers from Operation Desert Storm were treated. "I wasn't so much a warrior as I was an administrator," she recalls. However, her 2004 five-month stint in volatile Iraq represented "the first time I actually had

Health Diplomacy continued

to be a true warrior." Issued a weapon upon arrival in Kuwait, she recalls, "as a nurse it was very difficult to think about . . . carrying a gun." Arriving in Baghdad, she settled into her duties at the Ministry of Health, carrying her weapon but dressing as a civilian and liaising with Iraqi counterparts in the ministry, with whom she worked to devise a nursing system for the country.

She made "wonderful friends" with Iraqis, discovering they shared much in common. "They want to take care of their children, they want to send them to school every day, they want to go to work every day and be safe. So many of their desires in the nursing field were so much like ours. [Her Iraqi colleagues] just wanted to promote the ability of nurses to provide good quality care and to have an opportunity to progress in their field." She viewed her mission as one of "health diplomacy." "[We're] there to show them what it is to be an American. . . . The fact that I was military was a secondary."

In February 2004 when her daughter took the picture, Linda was departing Denver for training at Fort Bliss, Texas. Thinking back, Linda reminisces, "Not only could I not spell Baghdad, I also had no idea what I had gotten myself into. Going to war-torn Iraq was the hardest thing I did in my thirty-three-year Air Force Reserve career, but it was definitely the most rewarding."

---

when the troops she had trained were activated, "I called my commander up and said, 'Listen, please take me. I can't be one of the only aviation officers in this state standing here waving good-bye to the unit as it goes to war.'"[38] In Iraq, she lost both legs in an RPG (rocket-propelled grenade) attack in 2004 and nearly died. "I can't deny the interest in the fact that I am an injured female soldier," she commented during her bid for the House seat for the Sixth Congressional District in Illinois. "Understand that I'm going to use this as a platform."[39] Head of the Illinois Department of Veterans Affairs, Duckworth won the Democratic primary in March 2006 but lost narrowly to the Republican candidate in November. She was under consideration to fill the Senate seat vacated by then-Senator Barack Obama following his election to the presidency in 2008, and she ultimately accepted a senior position within the Department of Veterans Affairs.

Rep. Mark Kirk (R-IL), who serves as a naval reserve intelligence officer, is one of five members of Congress serving in the Reserves as of 2009. In early 2005, he took the lead in introducing the Americans in Uniform Act of 2005, a measure designed to improve the quality of life for reservists and their dependents. "In the Cold War, the Reserves were a force of last resort, rarely called to active duty," he explained. "Today they make up almost half of the forces deployed in Kosovo, Afghanistan and Iraq."[40]

Some soldiers upon returning from Afghanistan and Iraq take a new level of interest in community activities, participating in civic affairs and seeking out positions in town and city government. Ryan Aument, an Army captain from Lancaster, Pennsylvania, believed that his safe return from Operation Iraqi Freedom was God's way of giving him an opportunity for public service. He helped out first as a volunteer in town affairs, was appointed and then elected to the town council, and eventually considered running for county or state office.[41]

Upon returning to the States, several soldiers have founded organizations geared toward helping civilians displaced by the conflicts. One such group sought to provide food to Iraqis who had fled into Jordan, another to arrange medical treatment for Iraqi children abroad, and a third to raise funds for hospitals and schools in Iraq. The trend struck Anna Badken, a *Boston Globe* reporter, as noteworthy. "This kind of outreach may seem surprising," she wrote, "in a war that teaches many soldiers to see every civilian as a threat: a farmer could be a guerrilla fighter, and a woman on the street can bomb a convoy. But it also suggests a new response to the war: An idea that the troops' responsibilities don't end when they deploy back home."[42]

Returning in disillusion and ill health from a five-month tour in Iraq in 2003, Army Capt. Jon Soltz arranged for a meeting with Sen. John Kerry (D-MA), who was laying the groundwork for a run for the presidency. "I'm the guy that went to Iraq with no armored vehicles," he told Kerry. "I'm the guy that was ambushed the first time he drove in. I'm the guy who after one of my men died, I heard my commander in chief say, 'Bring it on.' I'm the guy who looked my friend and fellow soldier in the face when he was blown up in the hospital and asked, 'Is it worth it?' I'm the guy who got help at a VA hospital, and my commander said he was going to close that hospital." Soltz signed on as the Kerry campaign's veterans' coordinator for Pennsylvania.[43]

Other veterans found candidates of their choice in the 2008 primaries and elections to assist, functioning as the public's "eyes and ears of a controversial war. Informed and impassioned by their wartime experiences, they aid candidates whose views on Iraq mirror their own," wrote Irene Sege in the *Boston Globe*. [44] Fearing that active-duty military personnel would become engaged in election campaigns, the chairman of the Joint Chiefs of Staff issued a stern reminder in mid-2008. "The U.S. military must remain apolitical at all times and in all ways," wrote Adm. Mike Mullen. "It is and must always be a neutral instrument of the state, no matter which party holds sway. The only things we should be wearing on our sleeves are our military insignia."[45]

About a dozen veterans of Afghanistan and Iraq ran for federal office in 2006. Patrick Murphy, a Democrat from Pennsylvania's Eighth Congressional District in suburban Philadelphia, became the first Iraq veteran elected to the U.S. Congress. After the 9/11 attacks, he had volunteered to serve overseas and was sent first to Bosnia and then to Iraq. With assignments including the House Armed Services Committee and the House Select Committee on Intelligence, he played an active role on issues relating to the war, supporting (along with then-Senator Obama) an unsuccessful measure to accelerate the withdrawal of U.S. troops. His autobiography, *Taking the Hill: From Philly to Baghdad and the U.S. Congress*, published in 2008, spurred public debate on issues of the war.

Veterans' organizations have been a barometer of the upsurge of interest in the political arena. The nation's oldest such groups have generally continued their accustomed role of supporting U.S. foreign and military policy. With respect to the Bush administration's "surge strategy" announced in early 2007, for example, which committed additional troops to Iraq at a time when those already there were taking substantial casualties, groups such as the Veterans of Foreign Wars (founded in 1899) and the American Legion (1919) "issued pro-war position statements and lobbied skeptical Republicans to back the current Iraq strategy." With memberships of 2.4 million (VFW) and 2.7 million (the Legion), they were courted by the administration and in turn recruited others "to argue for the surge strategy at town hall meetings."[46]

But the lay of the land had been changing. Upon returning from Afghanistan and Iraq, some soldiers look to veterans' organizations to play a more critical and cautionary role. "The wars in Iraq and Afghanistan have spawned some new veterans groups, many of which are in a rebellious mood," noted National Public Radio's John McChesny in early 2007. "They have different agendas and different approaches."[47] Among the newcomers are the Iraq and Afghanistan Veterans of America (IAVA) and VoteVets.org. Iraq Veterans Against the War (IVAW), comprised of active-duty personnel as well as retirees, was perhaps the most antagonistic to Bush administration policy at the time, offering ten reasons for opposing the war, including that it ostensibly violates international law.[48] Vets for Freedom, established on Veterans Day 2007, describes itself as "the largest Iraq and Afghanistan veterans' organization in America" and is firmly committed to "success in Iraq, Afghanistan, and the overall war on terror."[49] The Servicemembers Legal Defense Network, founded in 1993, is supporting legislation to prohibit discrimination in the armed services based on sexual orientation.[50]

The wars in Afghanistan and Iraq have also generated new organizations comprised of families with sons and daughters in the armed services who have become actively engaged in the political sphere. "Today's families are less likely than those of previous generations to just accept the situation," observed James B. Peake, former secretary of Veterans Affairs and the object of intensive lobbying on a range of issues.[51] One such group, Military Families Speak Out (MFSO), counts as its members more than 3,400 military families opposed to the war in Iraq and working to bring U.S. troops home. A subset of that number is the one hundred Gold Star Families Speak Out, modeled on a similar Vietnam-era group of persons who have lost family members due to hostile action or suicide. Organizers of the new Gold Star group explain that their organization was set up not to counter other voices, but to be a voice in their own right.[52] The original Gold Star Mothers, established in 1928 to link people who had lost "a son or daughter in service to the country," has been encouraging officials to "stay the course" in Iraq.

Traditional and neophyte groups alike have joined in advocating public policies to meet veterans' needs. However, newer-breed groups often contextualize those needs within a framework of opposition to U.S. military involvement in Afghanistan and Iraq. IVAW, for example, organized "Winter Soldier Iraq and Afghanistan: Eyewitness Accounts of the Occupations," a three-day set of hearings near Washington, D.C. Testimony from some two hundred veterans shared "the bare-knuckle stories that tell us the truth about what happens at the other end of the rifle, the missile, the bomb."[53] Two MFSO members are suing the DVA for negligence in the suicide of their son following his return from Iraq.[54] Indeed, as the Iraq war has proceeded, veterans groups have increasingly come to play high-profile and politicized roles in the broader political debate about the rightness and winability of the conflict.

The Veterans History Project field kit suggests asking the interviewees, "Are you a member of any veterans' or other organizations related to your service? Why?"[55] While a large number of those who have served in Afghanistan or Iraq answer in the affirmative, it is unclear how that compares to earlier U.S. conflicts. Some veterans join and participate actively while others reject membership, wanting only to put the war behind them once and for all. Army Sgt. Craig Keys did both. He joined such a group, only to resign in protest over the annual membership fee. "I'm not going to pay you to be a veteran," he told them heatedly.[56] Without a doubt, veterans today have a striking array of service organizations across the entire political spectrum seeking their involvement.

Some interviewees express discomfort with their families' political activism because of the sensitivity of the issues or because they may not agree with the sentiments expressed. "Just make clear that you're not speaking for me, Mom," said one Vermont soldier of her mother's advocacy efforts.[57] Carol Welch's regular updates in the local paper on the nitty-gritty of her son's daily life in Iraq were also avidly read by his cohorts and superiors in the field. Persons across the political spectrum, from peace activists advocating withdrawal of U.S. troops to members of groups applauding U.S. involvement—all of them claiming to support the troops while promoting diametrically opposed recommendations—make frequent references to the experiences of sons and daughters in uniform. Perhaps the temptation of people of all political stances to put words in soldiers' mouths has contributed to the reluctance of some veterans to engage in the public arena.

The outspokenness of military families in promoting withdrawal of the U.S. military from Iraq has made it difficult for those urging the continued support of the wars and the commitment of additional troops to question their patriotism. That was clearly the case at a January 2007 demonstration in Washington, D.C., where the presence of military families (some carrying pictures of their sons' or daughters' graves) and of soldiers themselves (some in uniform, some suffering from PTSD) underscored the message that those who were expressing critical views have earned the right to be taken seriously.

New levels of political activism have also been seen among retired military leaders. In the run-up to the 2008 primaries, a group of officers met with candidates of both parties to present recommendations on the issues of detention and torture.[58] As the 2008 presidential election heated up, phalanxes of generals rallied around the candidates of their choice. In fact, both presidential candidates in 2008 staged photo-ops with top brass. Following Barack Obama's victory, a dozen retired senior military officers who had met with him earlier called on his transition team to recommend policies to "remove the stain" on the United States from its treatment of terrorism suspects by closing Guantanamo and repudiating torture.[59]

But many in the military are uncomfortable with such high-profile approaches. While retirees from the ranks are not forbidden from playing such a public role, will doing so contribute to a public perception that deep down, the military as an institution is anything but apolitical? Their active roles as analysts and commentators on talk shows raise similar issues. A series of recent off-the-record discussions among senior retired military officials confirmed a preference among their number for conveying views on policy and political issues through military or private channels or through elected representatives. "Partisan political activities of retired senior officers fueled civilian distrust of currently serving military officers," reported the facilitators of the meetings.[60] Expressing a somewhat different viewpoint, Brian Aria, a Marine lance corporal, suggests that since the views of officers such as these are well known, it is important for more enlisted personnel now to join the debate.[61]

■ ■ ■

In sum, most of those who served in Afghanistan and Iraq, faithful to military traditions and canons of military professionalism, have kept personal views of the conflicts largely out of the public spotlight. At the same time, many veterans hold strong views that are shared with each other in theater, communicated to families and a wider circle by e-mail and in blogs, and advocated by their respective organizations. As a result, veterans and their families and groups are becoming more of a political force to be reckoned with.

— FOUR —

Coping with Unfamiliarity and Violence

Soldiers deployed to Afghanistan and Iraq face numerous challenges. Above and beyond the technical requirements of their specialties—for example, infantry, military police, engineering, transport, and intelligence—two challenges loom particularly large. The first is functioning in an unfamiliar and foreign environment. The second involves coming to terms with the threat and/or reality of violence. The interviews provide an instructive picture of how veterans perceive and cope with these challenges.

UNFAMILIAR TERRAIN

The vast majority of U.S. troops in Afghanistan and Iraq describe some degree of culture shock upon touching down for the first time in their new surroundings. Linda McHale, a colonel in the Air Force Reserve, remembered vividly her "first big deep breath in Kuwait," the way-station where many of the troops bound for Iraq were given a few days or weeks to acclimatize. "I think probably everybody talks about the heat," she said, "but it was so foreign to me."[1] Others, too, mention feeling assaulted by the temperature. National Guard personnel from New Hampshire and Vermont, having trained in sub-zero weather in the White Mountains and at Fort Drum in northern New York, faced a 100-degree temperature shift almost overnight. Members of a Guard unit from the Virgin Islands, deployed to the mountains of Afghanistan, experienced the problem in reverse, from hot to cold. Julius Tulley, a sergeant in the National Guard from a Navajo reservation in Arizona, with less of a temperature change to contend with, still commented about how, upon his arrival in Kuwait, everything "looked so different. There were no deer, no mountains, all desert. It was about 120 degrees. It took some time to get used to it."[2]

Colonel McHale also found "the dress and the Arabic language" off-putting. Even though she knew that Kuwait was "relatively safe, it felt threatening to me."[3] Unease among soldiers increased as they crossed into Iraq, leaving behind the creature comforts and relative security of Kuwait and becoming live targets for enemy action. Even identifying the enemy, however, was difficult. "They all dress in civilian clothes," said one soldier from New Hampshire with exasperation. Referring to their *thoubs*, he said, "They put those dress things on—the man dresses, we called them."[4] In the circumstances, how could outsiders—and the interveners felt very much like outsiders—make the necessary distinctions between enemy insurgents and civilians?

Army Sgt. James J. Maddix from Michigan, who saw a lot of Iraq as a transport driver during his tour of sixteen months, found the language and culture confusing. "It was us who had to adapt" to the Iraqis, he observed, and the Iraqis often "pretended not to understand when asked to do things." Cultural differences notwithstanding, he welcomed interactions with locals working on the base. "It was nice to learn about them and to meet new people."[5] Spec. Aubrey Shea Youngs of the Indiana National Guard also found her encounters a positive learning experience. "We got a chance to interact with the locals on a first-hand basis. We got to see what they wanted as a country, not just: 'Oh, we have all the terrorists over here that we have to wipe the country of.'" As a result of the interactions, she said, "You're forced to figure out who you are and what your values are and what you want in life."[6]

Marine Sgt. Travis Fisher found communication with local Iraqis "tough" and "really wished he'd spoken Arabic." He appreciated the few Arabic words and expressions picked up during training back in the States but felt that having better communications skills would have improved relations with local Iraqis considerably.[7] "When having a conversation with someone in English," observed Lt. Col. Terry F. Moorer of the Alabama National Guard, "I can focus on their inflection, demeanor, gestures, and eye contact to form an impression of how truthful they are being. This was much harder to do when you didn't know the language."[8]

The situation in Afghanistan was not much more comfortable. Lt. Col. Jude Ferran, who served with the 11th Armored Cavalry, found the Dari and Pashtun languages difficult. Forced to rely on interpreters, he reported relatively little direct back-and-forth with the local population. He spoke warmly, however, of an occasional meal with Afghan leaders and he enjoyed regular conversations with merchants in the bazaar, with one of whom he discovered a common bond: they each had strong mothers-in-law. Once you meet and get to know local Afghans, he observed, you discover that "they're no different than anyone else."[9]

Many soldiers found the cultural complexities of the two countries unnerving. Variations in religious beliefs and practices, both within Islam and between Muslim and Christian sects, political factions and tribal and ethnic distinctions, complexities of language and customs—all seemed daunting. The perceived unreliability of some Iraqi soldiers and civilians with whom the troops were working also contributed to a sense of apprehension. In one incident in early 2007, U.S. troops killed a man planting a roadside bomb who, it turned out, carried papers identifying him as a sergeant in the Iraqi army. "We're helping guys that are trying to kill us," observed one of the Americans, wrote Michael Kamber in the *New York Times*. "We help them in the day. They turn around at night and try to kill us."[10] Lt. Col. Ross Brown, with the Army's 3rd Armored Cavalry Regiment, contrasted the situation in Iraq, where "there is nothing black and white—it's all about gray," with the simplicity of the Berlin Wall and the Cold War.[11]

The challenge of familiarization with the local scene was not one that the troops could carry out in a vacuum. That U.S. soldiers were outsiders whose presence was contested by armed groups in Afghanistan and Iraq alike added an element of danger. To be sure, the initial American contingents deployed to Afghanistan in October 2001 to battle the Taliban and track down Osama bin Laden had the support of wide segments of the population. Similarly, the widespread unpopularity of Saddam Hussein ensured U.S. troops who invaded in March 2003 a welcoming reception in many quarters. Yet in each instance, the liberators soon found themselves ensnared in situations with deep historical roots and great political complexity and came to be viewed by significant elements of the population as unwelcome occupiers. In Iraq, some of the weapons they had expected to have handed over were soon trained on them.

While most of those deployed considered themselves in danger, some contingents were more exposed than others. Some Vermont National Guard units, participating in Task Force Saber in central Iraq, found themselves on the front lines. Other units, managing a supply and transport depot in Kuwait at the Iraq border as part of Task Force Green Mountain, faced comparatively little risk. Similarly, the experience of the New Hampshire Guard in Iraq featured a daily diet of danger while New Hampshire cohorts providing support for operations at the Bagram Air Base in Afghanistan encountered only the occasional stray mortar or the odd detainee protest. One soldier who spent an entire year in and around Bagram noted that on only a dozen occasions had she and her unit ventured "outside the wire," referring to the more risky areas beyond the protected confines of military installations.

Even those who did not consider themselves directly in harm's way sensed the prevailing insecurity. "You have to be a little scared," said Sgt. Shawn Molloy, who served with an Army medical company. "I was scared the entire time I was in Iraq. I was always in danger,"observes Sgt. Mike Moriarty in *The War Tapes*: [12] "You almost have to have a false sense of security to do this business. You almost have to convince yourself in your head that it won't happen to me. . . . If you didn't have any faith, you'd probably have a very hard time leaving the wire everyday."[13] In the words of another New Hampshire soldier, the experience of serving in Iraq "fucking changes you. It doesn't mean it changes your personality, and change doesn't have to be all bad. But this is a huge, life-altering fact."[14]

A chaplain in the DVA hospital system, himself a veteran with a long résumé of frontline assignments, described the wars in Afghanistan and Iraq as involving an inescapable feeling of "living 24/7/52 with the fear, inside the wire, of artillery attacks and mortars and with the question, outside the wire, 'Is it my turn for my jeep to get hit by an IED?'" One observer wrote,

"For some, becoming a soldier means surrendering the past and the future. In war, soldiers live breath by breath, each minute another that could have been lost."[15]

"I lived in constant dread," recalled Sgt. Benjamin Flanders, who was based at a transport hub in Iraq. "I had to contend with an imminent threat. It was an extremely stressful environment in Camp Anaconda. It was prone to attacks. You were not safe on the inside or the outside."[16] A compatriot confirmed this view: "This is the most helpless feeling I've ever had. I have no idea if I'm going to wake up tomorrow."[17] "On a day-to-day basis you try not to think about it, but when you get woken up by a mortar shell coming in, it's hard not to be afraid," recalled Col. Ralph Riley, who served in Iraq with the Mississippi National Guard as a dentist in early 2005. "It keeps you up at night. After a while, you just get used to it."[18]

The invisibility and elusiveness of the enemy, particularly in Iraq, contributed to a pervasive sense of fear and uncertainty. "The whole time I was there," observed Spec. Josh Nadeau of the New Hampshire National Guard, "I never fired at anything but muzzle flashes. You never saw them. I found myself screaming at the top of my lungs, you know, 'Come out, come out.'"[19]

UNDERSTANDING THE LOCAL SCENE

The life-and-death importance of understanding the lay of the land places a premium on having persons within the ranks who speak the local languages. Some of the native-speakers were Americans who had grown up with or had learned Arabic, Dari, or Pashtun. New Hampshire's Bazzi, an American of Lebanese extraction, received a commendation for "using his Arabic language skills to question three enemy prisoners on the spot, extracting information leading to a hasty raid on an enemy stronghold [and] the capture of a stockpile of enemy weapons, ammunition, and explosives."[20] But Army Sgt. Henry Lujan, who had studied some Arabic before deploying, found that even then he had difficulty distinguishing friend from foe.[21]

Unfamiliar with local culture and relatively isolated, the troops relied heavily on local interpreters, or "terps." These were often the Afghans or Iraqis whom the soldiers got to know best and trusted most. The only Iraqi friend that Spec. Jeffrey Daniel Bartling of the Michigan National Guard made during his time in the country was, he said, his interpreter.[22] "You put a lot of faith in your translator," observed Army Capt. Ryan Aument, who served in Operation Iraqi Freedom (OIF). "He lived and worked with us. He went with us into the most difficult conflict situations." Interpreters, Aument pointed out, operated "with tremendous risks to themselves and their families."[23]

One American soldier whose task was to train members of the Afghan National Army, however, sounded a cautionary note: "Every Afghan that you talk to has an agenda. They may like you, they may be nice, they may even be loyal to a degree, but every single one of them has their own agenda as well."[24] The reliability of local interpreters was indeed an issue. In a documentary shown on U.S. television, *America at the Crossroads*, an Arabic-speaking colleague of the crew that had done the filming on location in Iraq discovered on the soundtrack, after the crew had returned to the United States, what was really taking place: "Iraqi soldiers, ostensibly searching for cached weapons under the tutelage of American troops, discuss among themselves where the contraband is hidden and why the Americans won't find it." [25]

In Iraq alone, some 300 Iraqis serving as interpreters for the U.S. military reportedly lost their lives during the period of 2003–2008, whether from targeted attacks or random violence. Local interpreters are credited with helping U.S. soldiers "make sense of Iraq's streets, politics, and history," even though "these guides have been killed by snipers on foot patrols, blasted to shreds in roadside bombings and vilified by extremists as traitors." In an effort to protect themselves, many terps went to elaborate lengths to conceal the identity of their employer and the nature of their employment.[26] A decision in November 2008 by the U.S. military command in Iraq, taken in the light of reduced levels of violence in Baghdad, to forbid the wearing of feature-concealing face masks proved highly controversial.[27]

The Pentagon took several initiatives to orient soldiers more fully to the circumstances they would face. A spouse described the work of her husband, Sgt. Charles M. King, beginning in January 2002, at the Marines' National Training Center at Fort Irwin, California. "The military had built a billion-dollar simulated Iraq deep in the Mojave Desert, complete with mock operating bases and Iraqi villages, in which Iraq's exiles acted as civilians and insurgents. Charles' job was to observe recruits as they conducted simulated assaults and gauge their proficiency with weapons and familiarity with combat rules of engagement. The training," she concluded, "might one day save the life of a young man or woman who less than a year earlier had been taking their sweetheart to the prom, or that of a career soldier close to retirement."[28] Army Sgt. Gregory Mayfield confirmed that the United States had "built up little miniature Fallujahs and staffed them with Arabic-speaking people." Despite the value of such training, Mayfield noted, "deep down in the back of your mind, you know it's still training, even as real as it gets."[29]

In September 2007 the Pentagon launched a program to "assign teams of anthropologists and social scientists to each of the twenty-six American combat brigades in Iraq and Afghanistan."[30] Some of the early results of these "human terrain teams" were positive. The 82nd Airborne reported a 60 percent reduction in injuries in combat operations and a more steady focus on "improving security, health care and education for the population."[31]

DOD's human terrain team initiative however, proved highly controversial. At the 2007 annual meeting of the American Anthropological Association, supporters and opponents faced off. Some urged a boycott, arguing that embedding anthropologists in the ranks of the military violated the core principles that "anthropological research should never be used to inflict harm, must always have the consent of the population being studied, and must not be conducted in secret."[32] Others touted the benefits to local populations from more knowledgeable occupation forces. "I'm frequently accused of militarizing anthropology," responded Montgomery McFate, one of the authors of the new army counterinsurgency manual that encourages putting social science insights at the disposal of military operations. "But we're really anthropologizing the military."[33]

In early 2009, the Pentagon announced an initiative to allow immigrants with temporary visas to serve in the U.S. military, broadening the current applicant pool beyond those with green cards who were already eligible to serve. "The American Army finds itself in a lot of different countries where cultural awareness is critical," said a senior Pentagon official.[34]

Priority will be given to those with critical language skills and with specified professional backgrounds. Two weeks after the initial announcement, one report noted, "The enormous response so far highlights an untapped resource that could be critical to filling severe shortages in the military of doctors and nurses and people who speak languages such as Arabic, Hindu, or Pashtun that could prove crucial to operating in foreign countries."[35] However, for a combination of bureaucratic and political reasons, the program did not meet its objectives.[36]

VIOLENCE

The fears harbored by outsiders as they negotiated unfamiliar and dangerous terrain were well founded. One study of troops who had experienced combat found that 58 percent of Army personnel sampled in Afghanistan and 89 percent in Iraq reported being attacked or ambushed; 84 percent and 86 percent, respectively, had experienced incoming artillery, rocket, or mortar fire; 39 percent and 95 percent had seen dead bodies or human remains; 43 percent and 86 percent knew someone who had been seriously injured or killed; and 30 percent and 65 percent had seen dead or seriously injured Americans. In addition, 46 percent and 69 percent, respectively, had seen injured women or children whom they were unable to help, and 12 percent and 48 percent reported having been responsible for the death of an enemy combatant. One percent of the sample in Afghanistan and 14 percent in Iraq acknowledged responsibility for the death of a non-combatant. The study found higher rates of major depression, generalized anxiety, and PTSD among U.S. troops in Iraq than in Afghanistan.[37]

The progression from a sense of impending uncertainty and danger to actual violence was often sudden and traumatic. For a young soldier from Madison, Wisconsin, Spec. Abbie Pickett of the Wisconsin National Guard, it happened when an incoming missile struck a fellow soldier on her base. "All of a sudden I could see that he had been hit in an artery in his arm and there was blood coming out all over, and we didn't have anything to put on this guy's arm. We finally were able to scrounge up a medic bag. I applied a bandage to his wound and we set off for the hospital. When we got to the hospital, I'm covered in this guy's blood, pretty much from head to toe.

Convoy Moving Through Najaf

Luis D. Almaguer (AFC2001/001/34147), Photographs (PH08), VHP, AFC, LOC

Marine Corps Sgt. Luis D. Almaguer, deployed in Iraq between June 2004 and February 2005, took this photograph from the passenger side of an armored Humvee, part of a six-vehicle convoy providing security for a U.S. colonel on a visit to the city of Najaf.

"Most of the ambushes we got were on small streets like this," he explains. "There are many hidden dangers in areas like this one. For example, insurgents use potholes . . . to hide IEDs. They also hide weapons under [their clothing] and would use them against us when we pass through. The street is a little congested with the daily traffic of people. We had experiences in which a group of insurgents would crowd the middle of the street and slow [down] or even stop our convoys. At that point we came into contact with live firing from the top of the buildings and windows. One moment they're waving at you, the next moment they're shooting at you."

Almaguer dropped out of high school to earn money, but then returned to get his diploma. He enlisted in the Marines in 1997, and as part of a Marine Expeditionary Unit at Camp Pendleton, California, he has been deployed to East Timor, Jordan, Australia, Thailand, the Seychelles, Africa, and Kuwait. He was returning to the west coast when the September 11 attacks occurred. When he left Iraq for the U.S. in 2005, he was significantly disabled from combat-related injuries. To be closer to a veterans' health care facility, he moved from Del Rio, Texas, to San Antonio. In 2009, he spent several months at the VA hospital in San Diego receiving treatment for traumatic brain injury (TBI). Now retired from the military, Almaguer provides for his family through social security and veterans benefits. Despite his full disability status, he maintains a remarkably positive attitude. Looking back on his time in Iraq, he comments, "It has been a rough experience. War is surreal, a strong reality that I deal with every day of my life. The VA has been a great help to me and my family in moving forward."

Everything was chaotic. The hospital didn't have blood there for transfusions. They were turning their sleeping cots into gurneys."

"Bam! Another one hits," she continued. "'Cover your patient! Cover your patient!' We didn't have anything. We didn't have flak jackets, for goodness sake. The only thing we could cover our patients with were our own bodies, because we weren't hurt at this time—at least not as bad as they were. I remember how angry I was after the attack. I was out there feeding these people during the day, I said to myself, and now they're attacking us at night. I was really pissed off and just wanted to go out and find the people that had hurt that guy and hurt them as bad as they had hurt him."[38]

Army Spec. E-4 Teresa Little, who deployed to Iraq on the first day of the U.S. invasion, recalls having stopped by the side of the road next to a burned vehicle containing two charred bodies. "You can always see that car with a burned body hanging out of it," she said. "Someone in my unit actually took a picture of it," but "we trashed it afterwards because it was so horrific." Asked by her interviewer how she dealt with the emotional impact of such events, Little replied, "I just held everything inside. If I didn't, I'd be one of the crazy people. To this day, I'm terrified."[39]

On their first day in Iraq in January 2004, Marine Cpl. John C. Little and Cpl. Lucas Bollinger were providing security for an unusually large convoy of troops from the 82nd Airborne who were being rotated into Iraq. Trained for warfare in which two armies would face off against each other, the danger they confronted in Iraq instead came from small arms. The IED explosion that targeted their convoy served as "a big wake-up," they explained. Surveying the damage and anxious to counterattack, they realized, "there's no one to take it out on." They found they needed to be continually on guard. Neither the Iraqi civilian defense forces nor the Iraqi police, they felt, were trustworthy. In fact, their commanding general had gotten into hot water with his superiors for instructing his troops: "Expect every Iraqi to kill you but don't treat them that way."[40]

In both the Afghanistan and Iraq theaters, the smell and feel of death were palpable. "Today was the first day I shook a man's hand that wasn't attached to his arm," recalls Sgt. Steve Pink of an incident involving a civilian driver in Iraq for whom he provided first aid. "I looked down and he had his hand dangling from the exposed bone that used to be his elbow like a child's safety-clipped mitten dangling from their winter coat."[41] Maryland Guardsman Sgt. Matthew Miller, a paramedic back home in Maryland and a medic in Iraq using helicopters to rescue the injured, finds the contrast between venues striking. "At home it's car crashes, but their body parts are still on them," he explains. "Here there is so much blood and pieces of bone missing. We have sprayed our aircraft and have found pieces of bone."[42]

Army Spec. Nicole Ferretti expressed relief that she was not among those in her unit in Iraq asked to take dead bodies out of vehicles. "A couple of guys talked about that but they didn't seem too damaged" by the experience. "I don't know how they could do that."[43] Josh Barber, a combat soldier in Iraq, told his wife that he would never be free of "the smell of death" from an incident he witnessed in December 2004, in which a suicide bomber killed twenty-two people. Barker took his own life in August 2008.[44]

Army Sgt. Gregory Mayfield, whose first exposure to combat came in an ambush of his truck convoy in the Sadr City section of Baghdad, described the sequence of emotions he experienced. Initially, he said, "you don't think, you just act. There wasn't a lot of time to be scared. Afterwards when you have time to think about it—that is when your hands start shaking and you feel like you're going to crap yourself and you get scared and think, 'Man, how did we get through that?'" At the same time, however, "there was also a feeling of, 'Man, that was cool!' There was exuberance and a massive adrenaline rush unlike anything I ever experienced before."[45] Adrenaline rushes are featured in the Armed Forces' recruitment literature.

A large proportion of the troops in Afghanistan and Iraq were guaranteed direct exposure to violence because of the dynamics of military operations there. "The big change" in these conflicts, explained an officer in the New Hampshire National Guard transport unit, "is the front-line concept. A lot of what we do is still based on the whole World War II concept that there is a frontline and then there is a rear echelon farther back and that it's safer. That's not the case right now. We have forward operating bases in the middle of countries like Iraq and Afghanistan and it's a 360-degree front all around these bases or areas that we're operating in. You can be a logistician that typically would be one hundred miles away from the front and you could be smack dab in the middle of Baghdad. It's a totally different concept. There is no more rear echelon. Everyone's there in the middle of it and that's the current operating environment."[46]

Nowadays, confirmed Army Col. Mark Warnecke, traditional distinctions between combat troops on the frontlines (normally, active-duty forces) and support and supply troops in the rear (normally, National Guard units) no longer prevail. Most bases are subjected to incoming fire; convoys supplying them and patrols operating outside the wire encounter IEDs, suicide bombings, and small arms fire. Guard troops and other support units are exposed to a much greater incidence of military action than in previous wars.[47] This change in the choreography of warfare increases troop vulnerability and enhances psychological stress. As a result, while the study mentioned earlier sampled the exposure to violence of soldiers with combat duty, the lay of the land in Afghanistan and Iraq ensures that many noncombat troops are exposed to significant violence as well.

The risk of daily exposure to violence took its toll not only among boots on the ground, but also on loved ones back home. "My wife tried not to think about the danger," New Hampshire Guardsman Sgt. Ben Flanders recalled. "She was just missing me. I remember having a conversation with her, and she is crying, 'I miss you, I miss you.' I celebrated our first-year wedding anniversary in Iraq. We never talked about the danger I was in."[48] Some contingents wished for more action and felt guilty that they were less exposed than their colleagues. However, families were quite happy when their loved ones were not exposed. "Thank God they were bored!" exclaimed one spouse in a focus group of her peers.[49]

INDIVIDUAL EFFORTS TO REACH OUT

Faced with unfamiliar and dangerous surroundings, some soldiers sought to reach out to people near their encampments and reduce the element of peril. "I shall never forget the ten minutes I spent with this family," recalled Cpl. Michael Bautista, a cavalry scout in the Idaho National Guard who accepted an invitation to stop at a home near his base for a cup of tea. "No conversations of substance transpired, no earth-shattering foreign policy formed. Simply hospitality and gratitude; just smiles, body language, and handshakes. For a while, there was no fighting, no explosions, no terrorist possibility lurking around the corner. Even though I was in full combat gear, sharp steel sheathed, ammunition and explosives strapped to my chest, rifle slung at my front, for a moment, I was just a guy enjoying a hot beverage and some candy with the neighbors."[50]

Army Sgt. Christopher Walotka recounts a highlight of his tour in Afghanistan: slipping away from his base at night to chat with local tribal elders at a nearby roadhouse. The conversations confirmed for him the purpose and value of being there: to help "keep people like that safe and free."[51] Pursuing such contacts, however, rendered him absent without leave (AWOL). Special Forces units were sometimes less isolated from local people than were combat and support troops, renting "safe houses" in Iraqi villages and hiring Iraqi cooks and housekeepers. Nevertheless, as Sgt. Trevor Bradna, a Special Forces finance officer, pointed out, the bombing of one of those houses in Erbil proved it anything but safe.[52]

Some veterans identified similarities between their new surroundings and their home settings. Army 1st Sgt. August C. Hohl Jr., who supplied Afghan schools with pencils and paper provided by people from his native Wisconsin, wrote that "coming here has shown me that while we might all live differently due to environmental, geographical, and educational conditions, people are basically the same inside. Learning some of the history, social habits, and religion of this country has left me with a profound sense of hope that we can assist the people here. But we're not so smart that we can't learn from them, too."[53]

One innovative connection to the local scene was devised by Sgt. 1st Class Jonathan Trouern-Trend, a Connecticut National Guardsman who, beginning in February 2004, served for a year in Iraq with the 118th Area Support Medical Battalion, stationed at Camp Anaconda. "Its fifteen square miles held not only a large portion of the American military arsenal in Iraq," he wrote, "but also many birds and other creatures that shared the base with us." An avid birder, he reported the results of his walks on the base and his travels around Iraq to family, friends, and other bird enthusiasts through blog posts. "The birds gave me both the excitement of the new and exotic and the anchor of the familiar. I hope to return to Iraq one day," he wrote in the introduction to *Birding Babylon*, "armed only with binoculars and a camera."[54]

One New Hampshire Guardsman, who had received what he considered inadequate advance training at Fort Carson in Colorado regarding cultural differences, was struck by the fact that things considered odd in Afghan society were commonplace for Americans, and vice versa. Among these he mentioned praying five times a day, even in the midst of combat. "But in the end," he concluded, "aside from not speaking the same language, we were the same people."[55] Other soldiers remained more negative in their views. One Marine lance corporal deployed to Iraq was outspoken in his views. "I'm just not a big fan of their culture," he said. "They're just a nasty, unclean people."

Capt. James Sosnicky, who saw Michael Moore's trenchant antiwar film *Fahrenheit 9/11* in a theater with an Arab audience in Amman, Jordan, noted that during the scene in which an American mother weeps for her dead son at the White House, "every headscarf-wearing Muslim Arab woman around me was sobbing. The pain of a mother grieving for her dead son cut through national and religious boundaries and touched on an emotion common to us all. That compassion, the compassion of the average Muslim Arab, is hardly ever put on display."[56] Other veterans, too, discovered and articulated a sense of shared humanity.

A number of soldiers commented in interviews and dispatches home on the rich religious history of Iraq. Some took advantage of tours arranged by U.S. military officials of the Mesopotamian city of Ur, home of the prophet Abraham.[57] One soldier commented on the eye-opening experience of discovering centuries-old cuneiform tablets on a visit to Babylon. Nineveh, a city mentioned in the Old and New Testaments and an archeological treasure trove, was also a favorite destination.

Some veterans sought to interpret the history and culture to families and friends back home. In a "Letter from Afghanistan" that appeared in the *Caledonian Record*, Vermont National Guardsman Jeffrey Bitcon, sheriff of Vermont's Caledonia County and a police trainer in the Afghan Ministry of Interior, provided a detailed description of Ramadan, a holiday celebrated by "more than a billion Muslims worldwide—including some eight million in North America." After explaining to his readers in rural northern New England the elements of prayer, fasting, and charity, he remarked that the holiday "sounds a little bit like Christmas to me." His conclusion: "Our Holy celebrations are not all that different than other cultures or theirs different from ours."[58]

On occasion, family members discovered commonalities for themselves. Myrna E. Bein, whose son Charles, a twenty-six-year-old Army infantryman, had been seriously wounded in an ambush near Kirkuk on May 2, 2004, shared her thoughts in correspondence with friends as she visited him over a period of months at Walter Reed Army Medical Center in Washington, D.C. "I'm not a sage, or a politician, or anyone with answers to all the hard questions," she wrote. "I'm just a mother. I know what I'm feeling down in my soul is what countless other mothers have felt over the centuries. I know the mothers in Iraq and Afghanistan feel the same thing. It's a timeless and universal grief."[59]

The task of getting to know the local people and discovering common bonds was complicated by the limited interaction between troops and nearby communities. The constraints were often dictated by the security concerns reflected in the rules of engagement. "We were confined mostly to the main roads and weren't allowed to go to the villages," recalled Sergeant Flanders. "We were segregated from the population." Constraints on normal intercourse were tighter in Iraq, particularly in the later years of the occupation, than in Afghanistan, although troops stationed there also become more wary over time. "It would have been nice to have a little more interaction" with local people beyond those who visited his camp in Iraq on business, observed Capt. Ralan Hill, "but there is an associated risk with that."[60]

Stephanie Corcoran, an MP whose Army unit, the 988th Military Police Company, deployed from Fort Benning, Georgia, to Iraq for a year beginning in late 2005, articulated the trade-offs between important but competing objectives: reaching out to local people and maintaining troop security. "What a great privilege it was," she reflected, "to have been able to escape the fortification of Camp Kalsu and explore the Iraqi way of life. Traveling outside 'the wire' has made me gain new appreciation for things

I never thought twice about before now. I know this is true for others that have seen different walks of life. I'm very grateful to the military for this opportunity." Describing the country as "a classroom," she noted, however, "everything over here has an invisible 'approach with caution' sign on it. Not realizing this could compromise the mission and duty to protect others around you." She found herself challenged to find "an enjoyable balance between experiencing a new culture and staying as safe as possible in a war zone."[61] She also came to view good working relationships with local people as themselves an investment in security.

In a wrap-up e-mail to family and friends, Corcoran commented on "the most disappointing part" of her deployment: the "hate toward the people of Iraq" expressed by members of the U.S. military. She was repulsed by the "racist and ignorant views held by people expected to promote great things like the rights of life, liberty, and property. I've learned that it's very easy to hate everything about Iraqis if you let yourself." To guard against that attitude, she concentrated on "the simple things. Receiving a genuine smile from someone whose country we're occupying is always nice and has the power to light my day. Seeing compassion and pain through someone's eyes is moving, and really helps you grasp how tough life is for the Iraqi people. Seeing a mother hold her child with the same nurture and love that an American mother holds her child makes me understand that these people love the way we do. This is the chip that I take from an iceberg that's complex, complicated, and exhausting to understand at times."[62]

Kelly Dougherty, a Colorado National Guard sergeant deployed to Iraq from February 2003 through February 2004, expressed revulsion at having to search Iraqi women for weapons. "In their culture," she explained, "you can't touch a woman who is not your wife, and they would get upset. There was a lot of misunderstanding. What we are doing now is racist and goes beyond that," she concluded. "It's like they can't take care of themselves. The only way to live is how we tell them to live because they're not capable of doing it themselves. They are too uneducated, savage and poor. That feeling really permeates the military," including those whom she liked and otherwise respected. Dougherty sometimes even caught herself saying that she hated Iraqis.[63]

To what extent did soldiers feel adequately prepared for the unfamiliarity and violence they would experience? Second Lt. Eric Giles, who served in military police units in Afghanistan and Iraq in 2004, commented on the complexity of the wars and their settings. Given the myriad historical and political dimensions of the situation, he said, "the army is pretty good about training for cultural factors." His sixteen months of exposure to Iraqi culture, he felt, "enriched my own personal knowledge," even though he was aware that there was still much to understand.[64]

Other veterans were more critical of the lack of pre-deployment attention to cultural and other factors essential to the success and safety of their mission. "If the United States is going to be engaged in the endeavor of dealing with countries and helping reconstruct countries," noted one New Hampshire Guardsman, "then we really do need to understand them in a much deeper way than we did in Iraq." The military sought to provide advance training regarding what to expect. Soldiers carried a wallet card confirming that they had received sensitivity training and reminding them of the basic dos and don'ts. But the military, many felt, had limited success in preparing them for what they would encounter.

Reflecting upon training received at Fort Drum in northern New York prior to deploying to Afghanistan, one officer noted that the focus had been on "basic soldiering skills," combined with "some very sparse training on what you could expect in theater." The trainers, he said, were more familiar with Iraq than Afghanistan. "We didn't go over anything that we used in Iraq. Our training was just completely a waste of time."[65] He and others believed that the on-the-job learning during actual deployment far exceeded the value of any orientation provided in advance.

Some troops had the benefit of prior experience, whether in civil society or the military, that helped prepare them for the assault on their sense of humanity experienced in the two theaters. Sgt. Gregory Mayfield, whose earlier work as a policeman had "somewhat inoculated" him to the carnage of Iraq, was nevertheless taken aback by the scale and intensity of what he witnessed. In his thirteen years as a policeman in the States, he had seen two people die "in front of my face."[66] In Iraq, he recalled, "we sat and watched three people die in an hour." Damian Budziszewski, a Nebraska Guardsman who saw duty in Iraq, believed that he was adequately prepared to kill an enemy in self-defense. Doing so, in his judgment, would not "mess me up psychologically or any other way." Nevertheless, he expressed relief that he never actually had to do so. "I'm glad I didn't have to deal with that."[67]

Lt. Col. Rick Mayes, an Army reservist who had enlisted in 1977 and served during Operation Iraqi Freedom in an MP unit, had been exposed to violence as a police officer in Arkansas. "I never really remember terrible things," he said, or, if he does, they have "no impact on me whatsoever. God blessed me where I don't have recurring nightmares." However, he was alert to the emotional backlash experienced by members of his unit from a "friendly fire" incident and from having to guard mass gravesites. In the latter instance, he was particularly concerned about female soldiers who "have never had to deal with anything like that, and they're out there trying to pull pieces of people away from dogs and keeping the dogs from dragging off different parts. They remember that stuff." He called in a post-traumatic stress team to help.[68]

■ ■ ■

In sum, most of those interviewed found soldiering in Afghanistan and Iraq to one degree or another unnerving and disorienting. The scene seemed vastly different from what they were accustomed to in terms of geography and climate, language and customs, culture and politics. Many soldiers remained isolated from local people and institutions, interacting primarily in carefully structured situations and with heavy reliance on local interpreters. Some reached out to bridge the isolation, forging friendships with interpreters and local people. However, there were also undercurrents of animosity toward the locals in both theaters. While pre-deployment orientation sought to prepare troops for what they would encounter, most found the shock of the realities well beyond what they were prepared for. Their reactions to the volatile circumstances they confronted are the subject of the following chapter.

— FIVE —

Wrestling with Ethical Issues

U.S. troops operating on the front lines of the global war on terror in Afghanistan and Iraq experienced major problems in conducting military operations within traditionally accepted normative frameworks. First, the violent and dangerous situation on the ground led them to put a premium on their own survival at whatever cost. Second, efforts to observe the established rules of war seemed to put them at a disadvantage vis-à-vis a ruthless enemy. Third, enforcement of the rules of war by U.S. authorities, military and civilian, was uneven. The troops came to behave—and to be seen by others as behaving—in ways that robbed them of their humanity and undermined the stature of the U.S. and its military. In interviews and writings, veterans recount the ongoing struggle to survive and to function within accepted parameters.

SURVIVAL

U.S. troops found the situation on the ground in Afghanistan and Iraq maddeningly fluid and confusing. Multiple actors and agendas made it difficult to identify "terrorists," the target of U.S. and coalition military action, and to differentiate them from non-combatants, who, according to the rules of war, were to be shielded from attack. "Civilians and insurgents looked the same, and insurgents often fired at convoys from crowds," reported one observer. "Sometimes children waved, and the soldiers threw candy. Other times, children threw rocks."[1] With even children not beyond suspicion, how would soldiers recognize the enemy and make the requisite discrimination between combatants and civilians?

"That was the really hard part about it," observed Army Sgt. James R. Welch of Toledo, Ohio. "A lot of what we did as infantry is, we'd go into cities and towns, but we didn't know who the enemy was. Civilians and the enemy looked exactly alike. As far as what our soldiers on the ground knew, if they were a bad guy, they were a bad guy."[2] Yet the political and human geography of the landscape was complex and the categories "good" and "bad" murky. In both Afghanistan and Iraq, U.S. and coalition troops were killed and wounded not only by uniformed soldiers, but also by insurgents disguised as such.

Tyler Mueller, a tank driver in an armored cavalry unit in Iraq, told his interviewer in a matter of fact way of his twenty-six kills during his time in Iraq. "Six of them," he said without apparent emotion, were "under the age of ten." It wasn't that he was devoid of sympathy for children, he was quick to point out. "I've got sisters and brothers, and it's not pretty. But what are you supposed to do when you've got somebody walking at you with a hand

---

War is a phenomenon of organized violence that affects either the relations between two or more societies or the power relations within a society. War is governed by the law of armed conflict, also called "international humanitarian law." Throughout the ages, rules have been written and accepted by states to limit the use of force to protect societies from the long-term effects of war, by attempting to prevent conflicts from reaching a point of no return. International law does this by regulating war and prohibiting specific acts and behavior. . . . It also stresses the importance of distinguishing between civilians and combatants.

—*Francoise Bouchet-Saulnier**

---

* Francois Bouchet-Saulnier, The Practical Guide to International Humanitarian Law (Lanham, MD: Rowman & Littlefield, 2002), Definition of "War," 411.

grenade and it's either you or him? It doesn't matter how old they are. I've got a family to come home to. It's me or that kid. I'm sorry, but that kid is catching one [gunshot] between the eyes. I'll take care of business."[3]

In such a dog-eat-dog environment, the survival imperative trumps all else. "You see people out there walking around on the road and automatically you assume that they may have something to do with an IED going off," said Sgt. Steve Pink of New Hampshire. "It's unfortunate for Iraqi civilians, but any guy will tell you that it's gonna be our safety before theirs."[4] "On a practical level," added his cohort Sgt. Zack Bazzi, "when I'm on the road, it's my guys versus them. To hell with the immorality of it."[5] "When you go to war," said Derek Sutton, a first lieutenant in an Army engineering battalion, "nothing matters but coming home. You do what you have to do."[6]

As the wars continued and deployment time on the front lines was extended, the urge to survive grew stronger while the ground rules eroded. As noted earlier, some who had misgivings initially about the appropriateness of the U.S. mission became more persuaded over time. As the Iraq war wore on and the violence intensified, however, others became more conflicted. For some, violations of international law—for example, in the treatment of detainees—undermined the case for staying the course. "You know, I supported the mission," said Sgt. Mike Moriarty of the New Hampshire National Guard, "but I'm starting to say to myself, 'What the fuck?' If the problem isn't going away, then kick it up a notch! And I don't give a fuck if that means nuking this fucking country! Meanwhile there are fucking innocent fucking U.S. soldiers getting killed."[7]

"We were there when the prison abuse took place," recounted Sgt. Dave Bischel, a member of the California National Guard of his presence at Abu Ghraib, "but we didn't see any of it. We worked twelve-hour days with no days off for four months. . . . There was a point at Abu Ghraib—I didn't realize it [at the time] but I just started deteriorating mentally. I was like, 'Fuck Iraq. I want to kill these mother fuckers and go home.' You get to the point you lose it. It's like, 'Fuck it, fuck them. They don't want us here.' It drove me crazy."[8]

Specialists in military ethics confirm that such attitudes are neither uncommon nor without a certain apparent logic. "Research has shown that individual servicemen and women are not driven by high-flying ideals when under tension in the areas of operation," notes Cees van der Knaap, Netherlands state secretary for defense. "In that situation, they operate within the context of a small combat unit. Moral choices under those circumstances reflect loyalty to comrades [and] solidarity with the combat group. On the battlefield, the combat group operates as a kind of surrogate family. Threats to one are seen as being a threat to all of the members of the group."[9]

U.S. troops operating under duress in Afghanistan and Iraq came to place a premium on survival at virtually any cost. "When you're over there and people are trying to kill you," commented New Hampshire National Guardsman Sgt. Benjamin Flanders, "your survival trumps everything else: kill them before they kill you." In Pink's view, the assumption that the troops' behavior should be exemplary belies the nature of the war and the weapons at the soldier's disposal. "Why the fuck are we there?" he asked heatedly. "The U.S. Army is not the fucking Peace Corps. The Marines are not the Peace Corps."[10] The point is not that the troops were unsympathetic to the plight of civilians, whether Afghan or Iraqi. Indeed, some would agree with Marine Sgt. Travis Fisher that "seeing civilian casualties and deaths" was their worst experience of all.[11] The dynamics of desperation, however, placed a higher premium on troop survival than on avoiding civilian casualties.

Given the perceived vulnerability of U.S. soldiers to the no-holds-barred tactics of the enemy, a number of soldiers expressed the view that the U.S. rules of engagement, particularly in Iraq, were too restrictive. In the case of one of the New Hampshire units escorting convoys, "Insurgents fired bullets and rockets at their trucks, shelled their camp and left bombs along the roads they traveled. But the soldiers weren't allowed to chase down and kill those who fired on them. Their mission was to deliver supplies; if they were shot at, they fired back but didn't stop."[12] A number of those interviewed expressed frustration that, effectively, their hands were tied.

Moreover, the rules of engagement themselves evolved over time and were subject to varied interpretation. Reflecting a lesson learned from Vietnam, for example, mosques, which were occasionally used as launching pads by insurgents, were not to be attacked. Yet, as Army Sgt. James Maddix explained, his own commander defended those who fired on the enemy in such circumstances. "If you feel you need to shoot, shoot," he instructed his troops. "Do whatever you need to do to get yourself home alive."[13] Other commanders were less supportive, as one soldier who was disciplined for shooting in those very circumstances discovered.

Many soldiers, it appears from the interviews, simply did not comprehend or accept the rationale for the rules of engagement. "We're thinking: we're at war. We're away from our families. We all have jobs on the outside and you're worried about whether or not we should have shot?"[14] Sgt. James Welch disagreed with the court-martialing of a soldier for having shot and killed an Iraqi civilian who refused to stop his vehicle at a checkpoint. "I have to shoot to protect myself," he reasoned, as did the person on trial. "He was a guy who wanted to go home to his family."[15]

Second Class Petty Officer Eric Heath, an Arkansas native, served in a Navy unit managing a prison in Kuwait in which U.S. service personnel were confined. Some were accused of violations of the rules of engagement, others of breaches of military discipline. Heath had a running dialogue with his father back home about some of the detentions of Americans. "Dad, I'm having a hard time adjusting to the fact that some kid is in my prison for beating up an insurgent for trying to ascertain information about an individual who killed one of his buddies. I'm not so sure I wouldn't have done the same thing. I probably would slap someone around, too, if I knew that was going to get the information."

Heath believes that the proposition that some who "had put so much into serving their country and truly believed in what they were doing" would be sent home and be dishonorably discharged "was hard to get past." He was particularly uncomfortable accompanying his charges back to the States in handcuffs. Rather than meting out severe punishment, he reasoned, the authorities should have said, "These are our front line soldiers. These are the guys that protect your liberties back home" rather than "Maybe they made a mistake. Let's give them discharges."[16]

To make things murkier still, the political situation in both countries, never simple, became increasingly confused over time. At the outset, the U.S. focus was on terrorism and terrorists. Responding to a direct attack by

Al Qaeda on 9/11, U.S. military action in Afghanistan gave troops a sense of occupying the moral high ground. Targeting Al Qaeda and its Taliban hosts energized U.S. engagement in the early months. The sentiment was widespread that Afghanistan was the right war to fight.

Yet the Afghan conflict soon broadened to include rogue and criminal elements—sometimes allied to Al Qaeda and the Taliban, sometimes not—as well as other threats to the government of Hamid Karzai. Complicating the situation further, some local elders who supported the Karzai government were anything but friendly to the occupying troops stationed in their areas. There were also tensions involving newly uncooperative warlords whom the United States, during the Soviet occupation in the 1980s, had armed and bankrolled. Over time, the Taliban reemerged as a shadowy force to be reckoned with militarily even as ineptness and corruption increasingly permeated government structures.

Similarly in Iraq, U.S. troops experienced a worsening security situation along with heightened difficulties in identifying and targeting terrorists. Ongoing debate about the extent to which the Saddam Hussein regime had been involved in the 9/11 attacks and confusion about the objectives of the U.S. invasion muddied the picture further still. Was the purpose of the war to preempt weapons of mass destruction, to bring about regime change, to deny sanctuary to Al Qaeda, or some combination of these? By 2006, experts were concluding that much of the violence in the cities and countryside was not the result of terrorism but of civil war.

By mid-2007, the situation had grown even murkier. "Iraqi society has continued to fracture and is so incoherent that it can't even have a proper civil war any more," noted David Brooks of the *New York Times*. "What's happening in Iraq is not one civil war or one insurgency. Instead, Iraq is home to many little civil wars and many little insurgencies that are fighting for local power. Even groups like the Mahdi Army are splitting."[17] As in Afghanistan, the ranks of the "bad guys" had come to include a grab bag of people with weapons—criminals as well as insurgents and terrorists. By 2008, loss of life among U.S. and associated troops had declined, although targeted and random violence continued. Meanwhile 2008 in Afghanistan witnessed an uptick in violence and casualties.

The murkiness of the situation on the ground in each theater made it difficult for soldiers, struggling on a daily basis to survive in a hostile environment and being confronted with volatile situations necessitating quick responses, to maintain distinctions between civilians and combatants.

RULES

In neither Afghanistan nor Iraq, U.S. troops learned, did the enemy seem to spend much time worrying about international military ethics or world public opinion. New Hampshire's Sgt. Brian Shelton said of his adversaries along the Pakistan border, "They don't have rules. They're not afraid to die for whatever they believe in."[18] "If you're captured, you're dead anyway," explained the Navy's James N. Nappier, Jr., who served in the Ramadi area, "because they're just going to torture you."[19]

Others, too, questioned why U.S. troops should abide by the rules of war when there seemed no particular incentive or reward for doing so. Maryland National Guardsman Capt. William Jones, seriously wounded in the battle for Fallujah, was asked by an interviewer, "Don't you think you were endangering Iraqi civilians?" "No," he replied. "The enemy chose the area in which they would fight."[20] The responsibility for the carnage, he suspected, lay with the adversary, who set the terms of the encounter, rather than with U.S. forces, who simply responded in kind.

Indeed, with the amorphous "enemy" not playing by the book, observance of international rules of warfare seemed to place American troops at a distinct disadvantage. "The enemy don't have no rules—why should we?" asked Army Sgt. E-5 Bobby Lee Lisek, reflecting on his time in Iraq. The enemy, in his experience, would declare a cease-fire during Ramadan, and then violate it. "They're a conniving people. I don't like them. I won't trust a Muslim. I won't even go near one. I won't even let a Muslim doctor work on me." As for Lisek's superiors, "They kept giving us one set of rules of engagement," he said. "Then the next day they'd say, 'No, it's totally different. You do it this way.' And finally, you're there for so long, you've been blown up and ambushed and it's like, who cares?"[21]

A survey conducted by the Army in Iraq in 2006 found that more than one-third of the troops interviewed believed that torture should be allowed if it helped gather important information about insurgents. Some four in ten troops would approve of torture if it saved the life of a fellow soldier. About two-thirds of the Marines and half the Army troops surveyed said that they would not report a team member for mistreating a civilian or for destroying civilian property unnecessarily. "Less than half of soldiers and Marines believed that non-combatants should be treated with dignity and respect," the Army reported. About 10 percent of the 1,767 troops surveyed reported that they had mistreated civilians in Iraq, such as kicking them or needlessly damaging their possessions.[22]

Commenting on the study, Ward Casscells, assistant secretary of defense for health affairs, noted that Army researchers "looked under every rock, and what they found was not always easy to look at." The report observed that the troops' statements are at odds with the "soldier's rules" promulgated by the Army, which forbid the torture of captured enemy prisoners and direct that civilians be treated humanely.[23]

Confirming evidence is contained in an independent report based on discussions with veterans of combat in Iraq. The study, which suggests that "the killing of Iraqi civilians by occupation forces is more common than has been acknowledged by military authorities," found that twenty-four of the fifty soldiers interviewed "said they had witnessed or heard stories from those in their unit of unarmed civilians being shot or run over by the convoys. These incidents, they said, were so numerous that many were never reported."[24] The study quotes Sgt. Camilo Mejía, the Nicaragua-born soldier mentioned earlier, describing an incident in Ramadi in which he and his squad riddled with gunfire the body of a youth holding a grenade. "The frustration that resulted from our inability to get back at those who were attacking us," Mejía was quoted as saying, "led to tactics that seemed designed simply to punish the local population that was supporting them."[25]

The case for observing the international rules of war is based not on the premise that one should deny or ignore the brutality of war or the perfidy of the enemy, but rather that all parties have an interest in respecting established limits on violence. The animating force behind military ethics over the years has been not naiveté but hard-nosed self-interest. On the front lines of the global war on terror, however, few American soldiers looked beyond the restrictions that such canons imposed to the benefits that were to accrue to those who respected them. Viewing survival as their primary and overriding objective, those interviewed articulated a greater sense of the difficulties of functioning within established parameters than of the possible benefits of doing so.

Yet there were exceptions. Beyond the troops' restiveness under the rules of war emerged on occasion a sense of the importance of international standards. Disclosure in the spring of 2004 of abusive treatment of Iraqi prisoners by U.S. troops, intelligence operatives, and contractors at the Abu Ghraib prison near Baghdad—with interrogation practices including waterboarding, extended solitary confinement, and sleep deprivation—provoked extended and impassioned public debate about the use of torture as an instrument of war and, more broadly, about whether accepted definitions of torture, civilians, and combatants were applicable in the global war against terrorism. Judging from the interviews, this debate was more muted among U.S. military personnel. Those who do comment focus on operational impacts rather than broad policy issues.

While many of the soldiers interviewed sympathized with attempts to extract information from prisoners, some expressed revulsion at the practices that came to light. They objected not on grounds of moral squeamishness but because of the likely negative consequences for their own security and ability to accomplish their missions. "What they did was obviously wrong," said Michigan Guardsman Maddix, objecting to the humiliating treatment by U.S. personnel of the prisoners in their care. But there were practical as well as moral reasons for objecting to such behavior. "We actually started getting attacked more" as a result of the angry backlash triggered by the abuses, he said.[26] Capt. Michael Fortenberry read the events as a setback in terms of local perceptions of American troops and their cause. In his view, they confirmed the stereotype that Americans soldiers "do dumb things."[27]

Some soldiers were particularly irate because such behavior, carried out by U.S. personnel in the protected confines of detention centers, increased the vulnerability of other U.S. units that were considerably more exposed. Sgt. John McCary, an intelligence officer who served with an infantry division in Iraq's Anbar Province in early 2004, affirmed the importance of playing by agreed international rules in spite of the apparent short-term disadvantages of doing so. "What do you say to your men," he asked in an e-mail to his family in North Carolina, "after you've scraped up the scalps of an entire Iraqi family off the road, right next to the shattered bodies of your soldiers, held together only by their shoelaces, body armor or helmets? 'We're fighting the good fight?' I don't think so. We're just fighting. And now we're dying." Despite the brutality of the struggle, McCary was committed to fight fairly. "With all, we will be harsh, and strict, but not unjust, not indiscriminate. And we will not give up. We cannot. Our lives are tied to those lost, and we cannot leave them now, as we might have were they still living."[28]

The inhumanity of the conflicts led others beyond McCary to appreciate the value of rules designed to circumscribe the brutality of warfare on civilians. Sergeant Bazzi described a small but illustrative incident in which his platoon was ordered to keep Iraqi civilians off a road separating a residential area from a hospital. He was approached by a father with a sick baby who wanted to cross the road to get to the hospital for emergency treatment. "We're a disciplined army," recalled Bazzi, "so I had to say 'No.' But it didn't make any tactical sense." He then refused to translate the order into Arabic, holding that if his commanding officer wanted to convey the message, he would have to do so himself. Denying access to a hospital, he said in retrospect, "goes against why we're there. It goes against a lot of our beliefs and our value system we operate under as American soldiers."[29]

Jonathan Miller, a Massachusetts native who served two tours of duty in Afghanistan, came to a sudden and sobering realization that some of the enemy that he was seeking to kill may not have been fighting of their own volition. "Immediately" upon realizing this, he said, "you begin to lose the myth of war. These people might just be fighting for their families. What would I do if I was just trying to keep my brothers alive, my mom and dad? It starts to get real complex at that point. These are actually people that I'm going to be killing," he said with evident dismay.[30]

Numerous examples demonstrate an instinctive revulsion on the part of some soldiers for the deprivations and indignities that civilians suffer. Marine L. Cpl. William Schelhouse's comment in his journal regarding the death of a young Iraqi girl is one.[31] Her death takes some of the rejoicing out of significant military advances in the early days of the invasion that he recorded. Marine Sgt. Blake Cole recounts an incident in which he and his partner, discovered hiding in a building, opted against shooting their way out to avoid civilian casualties. As it turned out, they were welcomed by the community when they emerged.[32] Army Lt. Col. Maria Cochran was restrained by a colleague from intervening to halt a beating by a Taliban official of a veiled woman.[33] The satisfaction derived by so many soldiers from activities undertaken to benefit local populations (the subject of the following chapter) confirms a widespread concern for civilians among the troops.

Thus while some soldiers, reflecting their own perceived vulnerability, may have been cavalier in their approach to the rules of war, others seemed at a genuine loss about how to meet their legal obligations in the fast-moving situations that confronted them.

ACCOUNTABILITY

Most veterans interviewed do not seem particularly conversant with internationally accepted principles of military ethics or seized with the need to abide by them. In interviews and writings, they mention only rarely the Geneva Conventions and Protocols, which specify allowable military tactics and stipulate the obligation to prevent harm to civilian populations. The United States has ratified the Conventions, drawn up in 1949 following World War II, but not the Additional Protocols of 1977, which, reflecting the experiences of the Vietnam war, address in greater detail the ground rules for behavior in conflicts ostensibly such as those in Afghanistan and Iraq. Few veterans systematically applied to these conflicts the criteria normally used to determine the justness of a particular war (*jus ad bellum*) or the proper conduct of military action (*jus in bello*).

One exception was Army 1st Lt. Ehren K. Watada, a Hawaiian who in June 2006 became the first commissioned officer to refuse to deploy with his unit to Iraq. After considering the views of international law experts, Watada concluded that the Bush administration "had falsely used the 9/11 attacks to justify the war." Watada requested to be sent to Afghanistan, a war he believed met the requisite international standards. His court-martial

Journal Entry

March 23, 03
An Nasariah taken by Army. Encountered stiff resistance
lastnight until now. Bridges crossing Euphrates river secure.
SAD grade/Bt
Area to be secure in next 24 hours. Dest 4 Scud Launchers.
CO of Recon Unit surrenders. AF Director & other generals
considering conditions for surrender. Um Qasar secured. Al Basrah
secured. No resistance. Inhabitants friendly & anxious to see us.
unfortunate 5year old Iraqi girl shot in head MEDEVAC. 1 Scud
Launch

William Schelhouse (AFC2001/001/47506), Diaries and Journals (MS02) Journal Entry for March 23, 2003, VHP, AFC, LOC.

Lance Cpl. William J. Schelhouse was a member of a Marine Air Support Squadron that deployed to Kuwait in February 2003 and crossed into Iraq in early April. Following President Bush's declaration of war, he watched the initial missile attack launched from aircraft carriers, on the radar of the British unit to which he was attached. He spent his tour in the area south of Al Basrah, providing backup support for jet fighter aircraft, which cleared the way for advancing ground troops.

Before being deployed, he hadn't thought about keeping a journal. Once there, he decided that it would be a good idea so he "could reminisce about the experience in years to come and share it with children and grandchildren." The workday was organized into twelve-hour shifts, and "you could sleep, write, read, call, whatever you wanted" during time off. "I'd recommend keeping a diary," he says.

He views his overall experience in very positive terms. "Going over there—I was only twenty at the time—and seeing the living conditions of most of the people made me really, really, really appreciate what we have over here." He was "absolutely disgusted" at the media portrayal of the war. "Even if Saddam Hussein didn't have weapons of mass destruction, I know that what we did for the people of Iraq—including the ten year-old kids who were begging for food—makes this war 100 percent totally worth it." As for the injury sustained by the young Iraqi girl he writes about in his journal, he remembers thinking that, a child being hurt "affected us all."

The abbreviations used in his journal entry are dest (destroyed), CO (commanding officer), Recon (reconnaissance), AF (armed forces), and MEDEVAC (medical evacuation). His collection in the Veterans History Project contains a number of handwritten and typed documents.

ended in a mistrial in February 2007: in 2008 the military brought additional charges against him.[34] Discomfort with the conduct of U.S. military operations in Iraq led Camilo Mejía, a Nicaraguan national mentioned earlier, to refuse to serve, resulting in his court-martial. During the proceedings, the particulars emerged. Mejía's unit was to ensure that prisoners at a detention facility were deprived of sleep for periods of forty-eight hours. "I was a squad leader, so I didn't have to do it myself," he recalled, "but my men were doing it. I remember my platoon sergeant saying this doesn't meet Red Cross or Geneva Conventions standards. There were no medical people around except the platoon's medic, and God knows how many other violations were found. He was thinking of calling the Red Cross, but he was told that if he did that, he would piss off the commander and mess up his career, and conditions for these people would not improve. So he didn't do anything, and neither did I."[35]

"By Geneva Convention standards," Mejía recalled, "you were not supposed to conduct missions near hospitals, mosques, schools, or residential areas. We broke every rule there was." On one occasion, he was criticized by his superiors for "sending the wrong message to the enemy" by not having his unit stand its ground and fight following an ambush, even when doing so would have risked the lives of Iraqi civilians as well as American troops. Back in the United States to sort out issues related to the expiration of his green card, Mejía decided not to return to Iraq. He eventually served time for dereliction of duty and attracted public attention for his stand. "Maybe God put war in my path so I could see its ugly face and tell its story," he concluded.[36]

Watada and Mejía represent two of a larger number of soldiers, estimated by the Pentagon in early 2006 at 8,000, who deserted during the course of the Iraq war. The Pentagon number includes military personnel who deserted on grounds other than ethical reservations about the justness or the conduct of the wars.[37]

Judging from the accounts of veterans who served in Afghanistan or Iraq—and in this respect Mejía's experience is not exceptional—military officials brought the international law of war to bear on day-to-day combat operations unevenly and hesitantly. National Guardsman Patrick Resta of

Philadelphia recalled an exchange in Jalula where his infantry platoon was tasked with running a small prison camp. "The Geneva Conventions don't exist at all in Iraq," he remembered being told by his commanding officer, "and that's in writing if you want to see it."[38] That said, the interview data suggest that international canons of behavior were less often specifically rebuffed, as in this instance, than ignored.

While rank-and-file soldiers often acknowledge pre-deployment training in military strategy and tactics, few mention briefings in matters of international law and custom. Sgt. Gregory Mayfield's deployment to Iraq was preceded by stints at Fort Hood and Fort Polk. There he participated in "vignette training" exercises in which soldiers are presented with situations—for example, whether to use deadly force in this or that circumstance—which he says have "no real good answer." The emphasis is accordingly on problem solving. "They give you the structure: OK, here is your right limit and here is your left limit. We want you to do things professionally, but we don't care how much you deviate as long as you are within the guidelines. The rules of engagement are really clear-cut on paper," said Mayfield, "but when it comes down to execution, there is a lot of gray area in there."[39]

From interview comments, it seems that military leaders may have stepped up such training as the two wars proceeded. In the wake of the Abu Ghraib abuses in particular, some soldiers were given a crash course in the Geneva Conventions—reportedly conducted by trainers sent over from the States without much experience in the region. "The best training," concluded a soldier in the New Hampshire Guard who attended the hurry-up sessions, turned out to be "just going down [to the detention facilities] and doing it."[40]

"I had never heard the word 'detainee' until I got to Iraq, but I soon found myself in charge of a compound filled with nearly six hundred of them," observed Ryan T. McCarthy. "The only effective training we ever received was the news coverage of how real MPs treated detainees up at Abu Ghraib." McCarthy acknowledged, "the Military Police did provide us with some training, but a PowerPoint slideshow about prison cells in Fort Leavenworth [Kansas] is useless in a sprawling prison camp. The most effective training they provided," he said sardonically, "was their smug reminders that if an incident occurred with the detainees and we were to fall back on our training and experience as soldiers, we would go to jail."[41] Other interviewees noted that military police, without any specific training in the rights of detainees or the management of detention facilities, were sometimes pressed into the breach until regulars arrived, assuming interim responsibilities for which they had not been specifically prepared.

In the wake of public outrage at the disclosure of the Abu Ghraib events and following a number of high-profile incidents, mostly in Afghanistan, involving major civilian loss of life, the military began to pay greater attention to defending itself against allegations of misconduct. "We would document things—everything," recalled Mayfield, "Almost every incident where someone is killed or there is a gunfight, there is an investigation done to see if you were justified and following the rules of engagement. I don't think some of the previous soldiers in previous wars had to worry about that, but that was the environment we were in. You wanted to document things real well because there are real people, real soldiers over here charged with murder."[42]

The fact that those court-martialed for the incidents at Abu Ghraib were for the most part junior military personnel rather than higher-ups fueled the perception among the rank-and-file that accountability was selectively applied. Eric Heath, whose duties included guarding American service personnel imprisoned in a U.S. facility in Kuwait, suspected gross unfairness in the treatment meted out. "It's easier to hang them out to dry as an E-2 private," he remarked, "than it is for someone in a higher capacity to take the fall."[43]

The confusion in the two theaters regarding military ethics and the rules of engagement mirrored a lack of assertiveness and consistency in the exercise of authority by senior U.S. military leaders. Investigative journalist Seymour Hersh wrote in the *New Yorker* that Richard Armitage, then-deputy secretary of state, was quoted as observing that over the course of his several visits to Iraq, increasingly "the commanders would say one thing and the guys in the field would say, 'I don't care what he says. I'm going to do what I want.'" Armitage concluded, "we've sacrificed the chain of command to the notion of Special Operations and the Global War on Terror. You're painting on a canvas so big that it's hard to comprehend."[44]

Lax enforcement of international ethical canons by military officials reflected the sentiment in the political arena as well. In recent years, evidence has emerged that the commander in chief, the vice president, the secretary of defense, and senior Pentagon officials had sought during the early years of the two conflicts to redefine and relax the country's established international obligations. With respect to the Abu Ghraib abuses in particular, President Bush, Hersh concluded, "made no known effort to forcefully address the treatment of prisoners before the scandal became public, or to reevaluate the training of military police or interrogators, or the practices of the task forces that he authorized. Instead, Bush acquiesced in the prosecution of a few lower-level soldiers."[45]

When the administration issued an executive order in July 2007 to provide the CIA with ground rules for interrogating detainees in facilities such as Abu Ghraib and Guantanamo, some—but not all—of the methods that had been criticized as humiliating and degrading were proscribed. The list of specific interrogation practices thenceforth to be banned, however, remained classified in an avowed effort to deny Al Qaeda the opportunity to prepare its members for those techniques that might still be used.[46] It was not until January 2009, a week before the Obama administration took office, that Susan J. Crawford became "the first senior Bush administration official responsible for reviewing practices at Guantanamo to publicly state that a detainee was tortured."[47]

There would seem to be a connection between the views of senior administration officials who regarded the Geneva Conventions and Protocols as "quaint" and the actions of soldiers who felt no particular obligation to function within internationally agreed parameters. Yet it is also evident that some soldiers in both theaters were anxious to avoid harming civilian populations, even in circumstances in which doing so may have constrained the pursuit of military objectives. Moreover, the situations confronting U.S. military personnel were so complex that commanding officers could understandably disagree among themselves about how best to proceed. In both theaters, there were those who discarded the established laws of war as inapplicable as well as those who struggled to apply them.

CONSEQUENCES

While the rules of warfare have traditionally sought to humanize the conduct of hostilities, widespread and sometimes indiscriminate violence in Afghanistan and Iraq seemed to many of those involved to be beyond the civilizing potential of those canons. "War is war, and it is not pretty," said a chaplain in the Veterans Administration hospital system. "But this war seems especially nasty." That inhumanity was underscored by the special difficulties confronted by U.S. soldiers in dealing with Iraqi children. The conundrum touched on all of the major ethical challenges identified here, including the difficulties in distinguishing civilians from combatants, the perceived risks of treating them according to international law, and the wrenching impact of indiscriminate violence on Iraqis and American soldiers alike.

Capt. Ed Hrivnak, a veteran of Rwanda, Somalia, Bosnia, and Operation Desert Storm, recalled a conversation with a soldier whom he was treating during a medical evacuation. The soldier confided "that he had witnessed some Iraqi children get run over by a convoy. He was in the convoy and they had strict orders not to stop. If a vehicle stops, it is isolated and an inviting target for a rocket-propelled grenade. He tells me that some women and children have been forced out onto the road to break up the convoys so that the Iraqi irregulars can get a clear shot. But the convoys do not stop. He tells me that dealing with that image is worse than the pain of his injury."[48] The recollection was similar to one by New Hampshire Guardsman Kevin Shangraw, who recalled seeing the remains of a woman struck by a convoy being zipped into a body bag. "I'll remember that for the rest of my life. . . . The Iraqi people are who we are there to help and we just killed one of them."[49]

The traumatic nature of the scale and intensity of the carnage emerged in stark terms in depositions taken following the suicide of Tech. Sgt. David Guindon, a New Hampshire Air National Guardsman who took his own life on August 18, 2004, one day after returning from six months in Iraq. In a deposition following his death, the operations officer for his unit, Maj. Chris Hurley, said that "the Iraqis would actually send children out to blow up truck convoys, so when the children were seen in the road, the soldiers were told to actually keep going and run right over them . . . because if they stopped for the children, as would be the norm, there was a possibility that these children could be armed or wired with explosives." In his judgment, the state's Guard members, including Guindon, although they had received a certain amount of training, "weren't prepared for what they saw."[50] Several soldiers and their spouses confirmed that upon returning to their families after service in Afghanistan and Iraq, veterans had particular difficulties in reconnecting with their own children.

Yet children were not beyond suspicion as instruments of the insurgency. In an area where IEDs were frequently planted, a gunner told his partner about regularly seeing two young boys. "I told my gunner not to worry about them," recalled Mark LaChance, who served in Iraq with an Army unit in 2004–2005. "They were kids and there was nothing to fear from them." Several days later, however, in the investigation of a roadside bomb incident, a notebook was found on the boys, "filled with information on all the U.S. convoys that had traveled the highway in the past month. They had recorded the time of day, number of trucks, whether they were gun trucks or logistical trucks, and even had identifying features for each convoy. As it turned out, the two boys were selling the information to men from Baghdad for food for their families. I learned that day that there are no innocent people in war."[51]

"I trusted no Iraqi. I barely trusted the children," wrote National Guard Spec. Mark Mitchell from Pennsylvania, who served in Iraq for the last nine months of 2003. "You can't trust any of them. They smile in your face in the day, then shoot at you at night. In the daytime, they are all out there. They want to sell you this or that, all smiling, but when night falls, all you hear is a bunch of shooting."[52] Army Spec. E-4 Charles White recalled that he had been trained to "treat the children with utmost respect but at the same time to maintain situational awareness." This youngster or that, he mused, might turn up as your battlefield adversary ten years hence, even as Desert Storm youngsters were said to be resurfacing in Operation Iraqi Freedom.[53]

■ ■ ■

In sum, the ethical and legal issues associated with the declaration and conduct of the wars in Afghanistan and Iraq proved problematic for many of the troops, wrenching for some. The soldiers' concern for their own survival in the face of a ruthless enemy made the established ground rules of customary international law chafe. The uneven commitment to and application of the rules of war by U.S. authorities was also a source of confusion, as was the uneven application of the rules to all parties and ranks, civilian and military. Yet U.S. soldiers were also angered when flagrant violations of expected behavior by their own colleagues undermined their cause. They were pained when civilians were killed or wounded and they recoiled at the violence, particularly its effects on civilians, most notably on children. The relatively minor role played by the laws of war seems to have reflected and reinforced a perceived absence at higher military and political levels of accountability for their observance.

— SIX —

Winning Hearts and Minds

Many soldiers who deployed to Afghanistan and Iraq prided themselves on the help they provided to local communities. They viewed such "hearts-and-minds" aid as making direct and immediate improvement in the quality of the lives of local Afghans and Iraqis while strengthening their resistance to insurgent forces. For most veterans, the downsides of such efforts were generally dwarfed by their positive aspects.

REACHING OUT

The experience of Jeremy Krug, a Marine lance corporal in Iraq in 2003, provides a point of entry into the issues. Stationed at an airfield between Fallujah and Ramadi, he was tasked with providing security for helicopter squadrons and with keeping the Marine supply lines open. In the course of patrolling the area, he interacted regularly with the local population and took part in projects that included rebuilding bridges and installing water and electric supplies. In addition to connecting individual homes with clean water, his unit distributed school supplies collected back in the United States.

Krug found that the villages varied in their reaction to such activities. One was "extremely receptive," another more hostile, while a third took the assistance offered but "didn't want anybody to see us giving it to them." He concluded that the attitudes of local religious leaders played a key role in the different reactions. One constant throughout, he said, was that people were proud and wanted to solve their own problems, whether this led them to accept or reject assistance.[1]

While some aid activities were spontaneous, most were part of an organized program. In both Afghanistan and Iraq, U.S. forces took advantage of the Commander's Emergency Response Program (CERP) to mobilize funds for projects to benefit local populations. The program, in the words of Capt. Andrew Wells, an anthropology major and ROTC graduate from Iowa State, was a "humanitarian slush fund" that enabled the troops to respond promptly to local needs.[2]

An officer in the New Hampshire National Guard gave high marks to the thirty-five CERP undertakings he participated in during his tour in Afghanistan. They were a way of showing goodwill to local people, particularly those near military bases. "We wanted to make sure that the surrounding communities saw that we supported them," he explained. In choosing particular villages, special consideration was given to areas "friendly to us—if they actually provided information and helped us pursue different people who weren't so friendly to the United States."[3] Deploying medical and dental personnel to several secured villages, added Col. Benjamin Braden, who served in both Afghanistan and Iraq as part of a Marine Expeditionary Unit's Special Operations Command, was an effort at "doing the good-will things to show that we were not there to beat them up."[4]

Stationed in Afghanistan, Army Spec. Dennis Harvey had a close-up view of civic activities. He was familiar with the Provincial Reconstruction Teams (PRTs), an organized effort, piloted first in Afghanistan and later extended to Iraq, which dispatched civil affairs officers to discuss needs with leaders of Afghan villages situated near Joint Task Force military bases. As he saw it, local people wanted to cooperate with the U.S. military—their unmet needs provided them reason enough to do so—but were intimidated by the Taliban.[5] In Iraq, said Army Sgt. E-7 Rex Hendrix, hearts-and-minds activities "helped overcome popular resistance to the occupation."[6]

Civic action work served another important purpose: "to get people off post and actually expose them to the local economy and people and locals and so on. Quite a few people took advantage of that."[7] More specifically,

Mission: Civic Action

Metz Duites (AFC2001/001/58571), Photographs (PH 08), VHP, AFC, LOC. The photo was taken on October 18, 2005, by Metz Duites.

This Preventive Medicine Team, based in Iraq at Camp Bucca, provided medical services to about three thousand coalition forces and some nine thousand detainees. The team's vehicle, a Humvee, is "up-armored" to protect against occasional mortar and rocket attacks when traveling "outside the wire."

Capt. Metz Duites, shown on the far right, served with the 785th Military Police Battalion, based in Fraser, Michigan. As a preventive medicine officer attached to an army unit from Alabama, he was deployed to Iraq from August 2005 to August 2006.

"This is my favorite photo out of hundreds that I took during my deployment," explains Duites, who was born in the Philippines and is a naturalized U.S. citizen. "It gives me great pride every time I look at it because of the tremendous missions that we accomplished. We were a small team with a big mission. We stayed so busy that I thought about having a picture that would provide my team a lasting memory—a reminder of our year of hard work in a very harsh environment."

hearts-and-minds activities offered a way "to get females that were in uniform out on each mission so that they can interact with local females, who are pretty severely oppressed." [8] In Iraq as well as Afghanistan, female U.S. soldiers played important roles, interacting with local communities and monitoring the work of contractors reconstructing schools, roads, and other infrastructure. Given the circumscribed roles that local women played and the sensitivities of their interaction with male U.S. soldiers, the contacts provided by women in the military seemed particularly important. Hearts-and-minds work "modeled" roles for women otherwise unknown to people locally.

One female sergeant with the New Hampshire National Guard was intimately involved in civic action work. Serving as a truck driver and convoy gunner in Iraq for fifteen months beginning in late 2003, she observed "huge" changes. "We did a ton of humanitarian aid. Before we left, there were seventeen schools built. Thousands of school books given out, thousands of school bags. More people were thanking us for being there than were trying to shoot us."[9]

In April 2007, a well-publicized distribution, of school equipment and supplies as well as cookies by a U.S. Cavalry regiment, accompanied by Iraqi troops, won praise from those involved. In a U.S. Armed Forces news release, the first lieutenant in the U.S. contingent commented on the win-win situation: "It makes me feel all warm and fuzzy inside, helping the children," he said. At the same time, by giving them "the ability to learn and get an education, they're less vulnerable to other influences—like extremist views." A platoon leader involved in the operation was also impressed. "Seeing the kids respond to us handing out toys and book bags is always great—they are so happy. It's like we're Santa Claus." Doing such missions jointly with Iraqi soldiers in his view strengthened the Iraqis' hand as their government began to assume greater responsibility for social welfare programs.[10]

At the individual level, too, hearts-and-minds work was viewed as overwhelmingly positive. "Combat is only one facet of the military," remarked Warrant Officer Jared S. Jones, a twenty-three-year-old who served in Afghanistan with the Aviation Attack Helicopter Battalion of the Utah Army National Guard, "a necessary evil we must sometimes wage against evil people." The highlight of his year-long deployment was a series of civic action activities in the village of Jegdalek. In Operation Shoe Fly, Chinook helicopters dropped shoes, blankets, clothing, and toys on selected villages.[11] Army Sgt. Shawn Molloy recalled throwing stuffed animals out of Blackhawk helicopters to children waiting excitedly below.[12]

Schools were a particular priority. Since "Saddam Hussein had done away with a lot of the schools in southern Iraq," explained James Machen, a major in an Army chemical battalion, the reopening after twenty years of the school in the village of Atsu Schuwaih was great cause for rejoicing.[13] A U.S. engineering battalion and civil affairs unit from the nearby Tallil Air Base had helped with the construction. Navy Lt. Daniel Neville also found the military's role in reopening a village school "uplifting," given the grinding poverty of the area. Operating a clinic that was open during regular hours also offered the troops "a way to invite Iraqi women to bring children for medical treatment."[14]

For many soldiers, civic action activities provided an all-important link with people in their areas. "I dealt a lot with the Iraqi people," recalled one medic from the New Hampshire Guard. "They got dehydrated quite a bit, and we had to do a lot of IVs." While treating locals was not part of his unit's original mission, it became so over time. For Afghans who depended for their livelihoods on agriculture, services provided to their livestock by military veterinarians were much appreciated. Sometimes health and immunization activities were linked with voter registration efforts. "They would get people there to get medicine and then they would register them there for the vote so they could get a census for the country's population." The broader national reconstruction agenda was thus advanced.[15]

"Like most folks," says Army veterinarian, Maj. Jessica McCoy, "I never even knew the Army hired veterinarians." But since arriving in Iraq in May 2007—she had been similarly involved in Egypt and Afghanistan—she has been working with a State Department-led team of bilingual, bicultural advisers to help rebuild the Iraqi poultry industry, severely disrupted by the fall of Saddam Hussein and the war. In an area south of Baghdad, Operation Chicken Run has helped 300 poultry farms form a cooperative association across tribal and religious lines. The business model employed, in her judgment, will not only spur rural development but also serve as "a good tool for reconciliation."[16]

Civic action activities also connected American soldiers to communities in the United States. Army Sgt. August C. Hohl from Wisconsin distributed school supplies received from home to rural schools he visited regularly. "The kids sit there and learn with old bullet holes and bomb-scarred walls around them. They are usually lucky if they even have wooden benches to sit on. Most of the time there's just the bare floor or a plastic tarp. But the children there are so proud to open up their book bags and show you their math, writing, or art books and what they can do."[17] In 2004, a nongovernmental organization, Operation Iraqi Children, was founded, which seeks to keep U.S. troops well supplied with the ingredients for such programs.[18]

In a world of carnage, providing assistance gave soldiers something to feel good about. The experience of two medics who served in 2005 with an Alabama National Guard unit in Afghanistan offers a case in point. In civilian life a salesman and a volunteer fire fighter/emergency medical technician, the pair were responsible for what they called a "hugs and drugs" program in Paktia Province. "The medics traveled to villages to treat ill Afghans and opened their clinic for several days to treat sick villagers who came to the base." They insisted on treating women at a time when only men sought help. Over time they gained the trust of villagers, who were enormously grateful for their services, even though a clinic that was constructed did not outlive their departure.[19]

"We'd be riding through the streets" of towns in Iraq, recalled Spec. Eric James March of a similar initiative by the California National Guard, and "hundreds of kids would just flood our vehicles. Every person in our unit had families and friends just send tons of candies and toys and books and literature for the kids to read . . . we'd always stop in the community. . . . We'd show them that we care about you guys. We're not just here to occupy you guys' land. We're here to help you, we want to help you, so we would always take time out of our days to help the kids and give them toys and candy and put smiles on their faces."[20]

Lt. Jr. Grade Susan Diekman, deployed with a Coast Guard unit offshore Kuwait from February to June 2003, had a similar experience. The group's mission was to ensure that the Iraqi government did not detonate gas and oil platforms in the waterway leading to the port of Um Kasar, a primary destination for Iraq-bound ships carrying troops and cargo. During the latter part of her stay, she functioned as a project officer for a program to distribute school and sports supplies to a girls' school in the area. Materials were available through a Navy-wide "clasped hands" program. Enormously well received by the youngsters, aged seven to twelve, the undertaking offered "a sliver of hope" for their future. Diekman's involvement, she says looking back, represented "one of the most profound moments in her life."[21]

Such efforts seemed unquestionably constructive, given the extent of unmet basic human needs. "I get goose-bumps every time I think of it," recalled Metz Duites, an Army sergeant who arranged for the distribution of toys, school supplies, and snacks near Camp Bucha, the world's largest detainee camp.[22] A photograph of Duites unit can be found in this chapter. For Air Force Col. Linda McHale, who helped the Ministry of Health rebuild the health sector, her enduring impression of Operation Iraqi Freedom was of a young Marine, M-16 slung over his back, carrying an Iraqi child with cerebral palsy to a military facility for treatment.[23]

The Global War on Terror section of the Pentagon's website frames the military's civic action activities worldwide as "a force for good. . . . Every day the men and women of the U.S. military help others in humanitarian missions across the globe." Full-page advertisements in major newspapers encouraging enlistment in the National Guard emphasize the benefits of such activities to civilians under duress. "Whether it's rescuing local families from floodwaters, securing our borders, rushing humanitarian aid to the other side of the world or defending our homeland, that's where you will find the National Guard." Photos intersperse human-interest scenes (such as medics treating young children) with defense and security activities (helicopters and ground patrols). The Guard is presented as "the nation's greatest counterterrorism asset."[24]

As a video produced by the New Hampshire National Guard puts it, "In the wars, it is not enough to be a warrior. In the battle for the hearts and minds of Iraqi and Afghan citizens, kindness and generosity can be a Guardsman's most powerful weapon."[25] The state Guard's publications are replete with references to civic action activities. In 2007, C Company of the 172nd Infantry Regiment reported, "Our operations supporting the local children are in full swing. We regularly distribute shoes, clothing and school supplies to the kids in our area. It is truly a double benefit, as they receive much-needed items, and we receive the smiles, waves and hugs of grateful kids." The items distributed "were sent by our soldiers' families, friends, as well as organizations and schools in southern New Hampshire."[26] Hearts-and-minds activities by active-duty forces are also given top billing by military publicists and recruiters.

CROSS-CURRENTS

Most soldiers interviewed were enormously positive about civic action work on behalf of local populations. In settings characterized by deprivation and carnage, such work represented an affirmation of the humanity of Afghan and Iraqi civilians, of the troops themselves, and of Americans back home. A few soldiers, however, raised questions about the strategy and tactics underlying such efforts, their durability and sustainability, and the extent to which their positive potential is undercut by the violence with which the troops are also associated.

With respect to the underlying strategy and tactics of hearts-and-minds work, some boots on the ground sensed an implicit contradiction in having an offensive fighting force also provide succor. Spec. Gregory James Schulte saw a Catch-22. "You want to look scary on the roads so that you don't get attacked," he said. "At the same time you want to have a friendly face so that people understand that you're there to help them."[27] Some wondered if it is possible for an army of occupation to play both roles. However broadly compatible the roles may seem, will they at some point prove contradictory?

Aware of the problem that his dual roles might create, New Hampshire's SSgt. Brian Shelton made it a practice to take off his gloves when walking through local villages. His point was to show Iraqis "that he wasn't a monster or a machine; they might trust soldiers more if they recognized that they're human." Shelton's work, which combined civic action activities with combat duties, was, in the words of one observer, "part open hand, part closed fist."[28] Another New Hampshire Guardsman believed that in conducting work with local populations, a show of force would serve as a necessary deterrent, giving pause to "anybody that was driving by that wanted to do something."[29] While no incidents were reported, the fact that civic action work required armed military protection underscored the tensions involved and the politicized nature of the assistance.

Army Sgt. Gregory Mayfield described as "surreal" the twin agendas of "fighting a war and rebuilding simultaneously. We would rebuild a school or a road or something and it would get blown up the next day. I never did understand that aspect of it." On one occasion, a U.S. civil affairs group challenged local leaders for having countenanced an ambush of the reconstruction work. If "you don't want to play," the U.S. soldiers said, "we won't spend our funds fixing up your neighborhood. We'll go somewhere else." But suddenly the troops were surrounded by children and began passing out chocolate. "We just went through this God-awful ambush," a baffled Mayfield said, and "now we're being nice to people!"[30] Shelton himself observed, "You could be in a town all day long handing out food and blankets and water and pens and pencils and notebooks. And you'd leave the town and head back to the camp and they'd ambush you. Why are we doing all this stuff if they're not appreciative of it?" he asked.

Other soldiers identified a related difficulty. In selecting villages for assistance by asking, "Where do they stand on the insurgency?" the troops were in essence drawing local populations more deeply into the conflict.

Counterinsurgency operations can be characterized as armed social work. It includes attempts to redress basic social and political problems while being shot at. This makes civil-military operations a central counterinsurgency operations activity, not an afterthought. Civil-military operations are one means of restructuring the environment to displace the enemy from it.

—*U.S. Army Counterinsurgency Field Manual**

---

* David H. Petraeus and James F. Amos, Counterinsurgency Field Manual (Washington, DC: U.S. Army, December 15, 2006), A–45.

In the case of the clinic set up by the two medics in Afghanistan's Paktia Province, relations between the troops and village elders deteriorated after their base came under fire in circumstances that ostensibly implicated the elders. Rather than leaving medical and other supplies behind for use by the community as planned, the departing troops "blew up the remnants of their camp before leaving Afghanistan."[31]

The tensions identified lie at the core of the conduct of hearts-and-minds activities. The Army's counterinsurgency field manual situates assistance of the kind provided by the troops to civilians in both Afghanistan and Iraq as an element in U.S. counterinsurgency operations. Civilian aid agencies seek to conduct humanitarian activities without political objectives, assisting people because they are in need, rather than as part of a political agenda. With respect to the activities of the troops, however, the *Army Field Manual* specifies that there is no such thing as neutral humanitarian assistance. "Whenever someone is helped, someone else is hurt, not least the insurgents. So civil and humanitarian assistance personnel often become targets. Protecting them is a matter not only of providing a close-in defense, but also of creating a secure environment by co-opting local beneficiaries of aid and their leaders."[32]

Soldiers in both theaters also raised questions about the balance between offensive military operations directed at the enemy and assistance programs to address civilian needs. They sensed a contradiction between their counterterrorist strategies and local priorities. Several articulated the view with respect to Afghanistan in particular that the terrorist attacks of 9/11, which provided the rationale for international military presence there, seemed remote from the experience of most Afghans. "It didn't affect them, it didn't bother them, and it wasn't an issue with them," noted one soldier. "They just live their lives day to day, just plant their seeds, dig their crops, and eat and support the family. They don't have a preference for what type of government is in effect. They just want to know that things are good for them and their kids. They don't believe in the cause of the Taliban or the Al Qaeda."[33]

Sergeant Dougherty commented on the extent to which hearts-and-minds work in Iraq was dwarfed by "the destruction and unnecessary violence" of the war itself. She recalled an incident in which a water tanker for which she was providing convoy support lost a pallet of plastic water bottles. The soldiers ran over the bottles to destroy them rather than letting them fall into the hands of Iraqis, whose water is often contaminated but who "can't afford bottled water." She noted, "The same guys who ran over the water were the same ones you'd see go into an orphanage and give out care packages. Then they'd feel really good because they were helping. One day they do something great; the next day it's totally different. The most I can say is we gave candy to their kids. 'Sorry we blew up your neighborhood and killed your father, but here is some candy.'"[34]

But some soldiers felt that there should have been more hearts-and-minds projects. In this view, addressing the human needs targeted by "hug-and-drugs" activities was more essential to the future of Afghanistan and Iraq than were U.S.-led military efforts to defeat insurgents. What local people really needed, in their view, was a sense of visible progress in meeting immediate and longer-term needs. U.S. objectives would be advanced more decisively by employing the instruments of "soft power" rather than the sharp-edged sword.

Interviews with soldiers in the Veterans History Project collections and elsewhere are noteworthy for their relative absence of mention of the work of humanitarian and human rights organizations, international or local. This is to a certain extent understandable in Iraq, where UN agencies and other aid groups maintained a low profile in the years following the bombing of the UN's Baghdad headquarters in 2003. The soldiers' lack of comment on assistance efforts is more telling in Afghanistan, however, where countless agencies engaged in emergency and reconstruction activities during the time when U.S. and other coalition forces were present.[35] In both countries, the troops are more familiar with private DOD contractors such as Kellogg, Brown, and Root than with UN or private aid groups.

In Iraq and Afghanistan alike, the work of humanitarian and human rights agencies is critically important, despite their difficulties functioning in situations of great insecurity. Indeed, their work is often complicated by the presence of U.S. and other international military forces. In Afghanistan, such groups initially fiercely opposed aid work conducted under military aegis by Provincial Reconstruction Teams, although some later softened their opposition. In Iraq, some UN agencies and nongovernmental aid organizations found that the U.S.-imposed political-military framework compromised their independence and security and questioned the competence and the longer-term effectiveness of military activities in the human needs sphere.[36] Some groups challenge the military's description of its work as "humanitarian," as it lacks the essential elements in classical humanitarian action of neutrality and impartiality.

Striking the right balance in community development activities between military and civilian actors is an issue that vexes officials in Washington and other capitals as well as those on the ground. As policymakers commit more troops in their effort to keep perilous situations from unraveling—whether the surge decision in Iraq in 2007–2008 or the commitment of an additional 21,000 troops to Afghanistan in 2009—the fears expressed by some veterans that more inputs of a nonmilitary nature may be needed may be confirmed.[37]

■ ■ ■

In sum, most of the military personnel interviewed see hearts-and-minds activities as a positive contribution by the military in both Afghanistan and Iraq. Such activities provide soldiers with a rare opportunity to interact with local people and to offer needed supplies and services. They also affirm the humanity not only of local populations, but also of the troops themselves and their communities back home. Yet some raise questions about framing such activities as elements in a broader U.S. political-military and counterinsurgency strategy, about the appropriate balance between combat operations and assistance work, and about the competence of the troops to address humanitarian and reconstruction challenges of a nonmilitary nature.

— SEVEN —

Working with Private Contractors

Many soldiers stationed in Afghanistan and Iraq are struck by the sheer number of civilians involved in day-to-day activities on and around military bases. U.S. troops no longer carry out such traditional wartime functions as preparing meals, transporting supplies, running communications switchboards, and escorting diplomats. These functions have been largely outsourced by the Defense and State departments to the private sector. Contract personnel drive convoys, provide security for senior political and military officials, operate rendition flights, and sometimes even engage in combat. While veterans appreciate the services provided, they also raise questions about issues of cost effectiveness, comparative advantage, security, legal status, and accountability of contracted activities.

NEW ACTORS, NEW ROLES

In an unfamiliar and dangerous part of the world, soldiers were grateful for the creature comforts and services that private contractors and their extensive network of employees provide. In communications from abroad and interviews upon returning, veterans often speak of the panoply of contract personnel and functions that give military bases the feel of small U.S. towns, complete with businesses thriving and the local economy humming.

"I know there's a lot of complaints about Kellogg, Brown, and Root," noted Army Lt. Col. Rick Mayes, who served in Operation Iraqi Freedom.

"But when you ain't got nothing else and can go through and grab a hoagie sandwich or a piece of pizza and a piece of chicken, it makes you feel good."[1] Applebee's, Subway, Pizza Hut, and Kentucky Fried Chicken provided Army Sgt. Rex Hendrix and his colleagues in Iraq with "a taste of home."[2] The Pentagon also contracted out much of the food preparation, making "KP"—kitchen police—duty a relic of the past. Areas in Kuwait with fast-food and other vendors, patronized by U.S. troops moving into and out of Iraq, reminded Sergeant Mayfield of "huge truck stops" on interstate highways back in the States.[3] Soldiers express particular appreciation for telecommunications hook-ups operated by private companies that kept them in touch with people back home.

Private contractors are also entrusted with a multitude of brick-and-mortar tasks. Christopher Gamblin, a specialist in the Army Reserves who was in Iraq in the early days of 2003, witnessed the construction of military facilities from the ground up. "The place was like a landfill when we first got there," he recalls. His own engineering unit "built new roads onto the base and cleaned up a lot of the trash." But construction and maintenance of some of the military facilities themselves were then outsourced to the private sector. In addition, thanks to the efforts of "the KBR people, we got a new PX. We got two new dining facilities. We ended up having a Subway and Burger King and Pizza Hut by the time we left. That wasn't bad at all, but when we first got there it was a little rough."[4] The changes over time were particularly apparent to Army Sgt. Brian Coles, whose photos (which appear on the following page) and associated commentary contrast his first deployment to Tikrit in 2003, which felt "more like war," with a later posting in 2006, which seemed more like home.

The creature comforts that private contractors provide are welcomed by most of the soldiers. In a joint interview, Marine corporals John C. Little and Lucas Bollinger comment on the array of "comfort foods" available in their PX during Operation Iraqi Freedom. Many soldiers mention returning from combat missions outside the wire to enjoy down time in clean and comfortable mess hall, dormitory, recreational, and communications facilities. There was only an occasional dissenting voice. Marine LCpl. Jeremy Krug, a veteran of the fierce fighting in the Ramadi-Fallujah area, felt that

First Deployment/Second Deployment

Brian Coles (AFC2001/001/41574), Photographs (PH01), VHP, AFC, LOC.

Of the 1.8 million U.S. troops who served in Afghanistan and/or Iraq through November 2008, approximately 40 percent have been deployed more than once. One of the few who redeployed to his initial posting is Brian Coles.

Coles enlisted in the National Guard in February 1991. His father said it was either the military or college, and Brian chose the military. After a decade of training one weekend a

First Deployment/Second Deployment continued

month and two weeks each summer with the Iowa National Guard, he shipped out to Kuwait in March 2003, as part of the Army's 234 Signal Battalion. Stationed at the largest Iraqi airbase in Tikrit, he traveled widely in Iraq, receiving the Global War on Terror Expeditionary Medal and an army commendation for his contributions.

Returning to Tikrit in October 2006 with the 1461st Transportation Company of the Michigan National Guard, Coles noted that the differences were "like night and day." At the onset of the war in March 2003, he had shared a tent with five others. "We had the feeling of being out in the desert. It was more like war." The first photo, taken in July 2005 during his first deployment, shows a spray-painted Iraqi vehicle on the Tikrit runway. It is his favorite photo, he says, a reminder of how harsh the conditions were.

Three years later, the encampment at Tallil was more permanent and the troops had more amenities, including better living and eating conditions and improved communications with home. His second photo shows people picking up food at Pizza Hut and Burger King. Beyond them is the PX, which had "a little bit of everything," including small electronics items, clothing, food, and even motorcycles. While daily life was more enjoyable and secure, the war remained a harsh reality. IEDs were claiming more casualties—including one fatality in his unit—and even when picking up fast food, the soldiers carried weapons and ammunition with them.

---

the availability of amenities might have undercut the sprit of sharing and sacrifice so important to troop morale.[5]

And there was grousing about the mess hall offerings. "Everything was contracted out," said Army Sgt. E-5 Terrell Spencer. "All the jobs were hired to KBR and they in turn hired Pakistani or Indian people to come cook for a fraction of what they themselves made. They were trying to 'cook American' and it just didn't work out. I guess the food was all right, but half the time I just preferred to eat my Meals Ready to Eat. It was doubly hard for me, too," Spencer added, "because I had apprenticed as a chef."[6]

In addition to the services for the troops, most of the reconstruction of Afghan and Iraqi energy, health, and transport infrastructure was spun off to the private sector. The Pentagon contracted out much of the transport of personnel and heavy equipment from the United States and Europe into the two theaters. From DOD's vantage point, outsourcing to an "army" of private contactors had another attractive feature: keeping the numbers of uniformed U.S. troops to a minimum, a major priority given congressional wariness of additional troop call-ups or extensions of deployments.

The scale of reconstruction efforts undertaken by DOD through civilian contractors is mind-boggling. At a press conference in early 2009 reviewing accomplishments in Iraq, military officials cited "more than forty-four hundred projects completed since January 2004, valued at nearly seven billion dollars." Efforts were managed by the Pentagon's Gulf Region Division, with a staff of some 600 federal civilian and military officials who worked in turn with thousands of U.S. contractors and Iraqi associates. Employing 25,000 to 30,000 Iraqis per day, the overall effort had built or renovated 1,100 schools, 132 private health clinics and 41 hospitals, and improved water supply and energy infrastructure. The government of Iraq and other coalition partners joined the United States in providing funds.[7]

UNRESOLVED ISSUES

Fast food in military mess halls, activity rooms replete with exercise equipment and video games, and all manner of conveniences available for purchase at PXs did not still criticism of private sector contractors among the troops. The experience in the two theaters raises a number of questions concerning cost and comparative advantage, security, and accountability. The troops' expressed misgivings about the contributions of contractors are borne out by various studies. One review of "the unprecedented use of private contractors" by the military in Iraq found that "the most basic questions" regarding contractors still cannot be answered.[8] One leading analyst confirms "a growing tension between private contractors and American military units and how they coordinate their activities (or not)."[9]

With respect to cost and cost-effectiveness, hefty remuneration of KBR employees and other private sector suppliers—exceeding some soldiers' own levels of pay—particularly rankles. "One hundred and twenty grand to do the same job" that soldiers might do, muttered one member of the New Hampshire National Guard contingent, and at far lower cost.[10] The fact that the military itself needed to provide security for many DOD contractors added possible injury to perceived insult.

The impression was widespread not only that the profits received by commercial firms were unreasonable, but also that such firms were operating under contracts that had not been subjected to normal competitive bidding procedures. The role of Richard Cheney as head of Halliburton, KBR's parent, between stints as secretary of defense under President George H. W.

Bush and vice president under President George W. Bush, contributed to such suspicions, despite his resignation from the firm in order to serve as vice president. The belief that KBR, the largest private-sector operator in Afghanistan and Iraq, is "owned by Halliburton and run by Vice President Cheney" led one soldier to conclude, "everybody at KBR stands to make money the longer we're there."[11]

A second set of concerns involved the risks to the military of using contract personnel. The view that protection of commercial contractors jeopardizes the troops' own safety was particularly prevalent among units assigned to provide security for commercial convoys. As one member of the New Hampshire National Guard put it, the military was tasked with escorting "trucks filled with things like big screen televisions, plastic plants and pet goods, which were trucked onto military bases and sold to soldiers at the post-exchange or PX. 'I'm risking my life for kitty litter,'" said SSgt. Patrick Clarke with exasperation. "I could see the need for food, water, and fuel. I realize the PX was for our comfort. It's just kind of out of hand."[12]

"Almost all of the trucks that we guarded were operated by the private contractor, Kellogg, Brown, and Root," explains Sergeant Flanders. "Some of what we protected, including food and laundry, was essential, but a lot of what was in the trucks was not. When you were the one escorting the damn stuff, it was crazy. We were risking our lives for that. We guarded ice, which is frozen water. You just didn't know what you were escorting. We got ambushed. We had amputees. Some of the civilian drivers got shot in the head and died transporting Lord knows what."[13] The fact that KBR vehicles were often poorly maintained and driven by Third Country Nationals (TCNs) who did not speak English was perceived as creating added security risks beyond those that already existed when convoys contained only military vehicles. "I feel like the priority of KBR making money outweighs the priority of safety," said New Hampshire's Moriarty in a sentiment shared by others.[14]

"KBR kept scheduling us on the same routes, same days, same times," explains Navy Sgt. Cristina Frisby, a tow-truck driver and repair mechanic who dealt with the contractor on an everyday basis. "That is completely backwards to what the Army teaches you because the insurgents or whoever was blowing us up would know when and where we would be. The 40-mile highway to Kirkuk was completely demolished because of so many IEDs. We probably got hit fifteen times on that route." But the passionate critique doesn't end there. Frisby continued: "KBR also told us we could be personally 'responsible' if we broke a civilian truck trying to recover it. I thought that was ridiculous. We hated KBR."[15] Frisby's comment evidences some doubt as to who was working for whom. There's no way to fire contractors that don't perform or care, adds Sgt. Spencer. "They're not bound by any rules."[16]

Navy Petty Officer Samuel J. Main, member of a combat security element that provided convoy protection in Iraq, was himself familiar with day-to-day interactions with third country nationals (TCNs). During his months in Iraq, he traveled more than 12,000 miles on 109 missions and escorted more than 2,400 TCN vehicles. "Convoy security teams move everything in the country. We had to search every one of them," he recalls, a process that took about two hours per vehicle. "You have to make sure their passports are valid and that there are no guns or bombs or anything, even cell phones." The conditions of the trucks themselves left a great deal to be desired. "They're driving stuff that you wouldn't pick up from a junk yard and so breakdowns were common, especially in areas where you didn't want to break down. If their tires weren't aired up or roadworthy, we left them behind, because a breakdown puts everybody in jeopardy. We were pretty thorough."[17]

Several soldiers voiced the opinion that responsibility for accompanying and protecting private commercial vehicles had compromised the military's own security and mission. It was not simply that KBR trucks would occasionally stray from the convoy and, being unarmored, draw enemy fire and require military rescue. Private vehicles would also proceed unbeknownst to the troops or would press the military to provide protection against its better judgment. Confirming the problem, Secretary of Defense Robert Gates was reported to have said in October 2007, "30 percent of the calls for help from security contracts had come from convoys that the military did not know were on the road."[18]

While the troops were not averse to providing protection for private sector convoys, soldiers express the view that the military should keep contractors on a shorter leash, both in terms of items transported and go/no-go decisions. They believe that whatever functions are outsourced—and more examination of issues of comparative advantage is needed—the military's authority to monitor contractor performance should be strengthened. A group of sixteen Indiana National Guard personnel who had guarded KBR personnel at an Iraqi power plant are pressing to sue the contractor for having "knowingly exposing them to a cancer-causing chemical."[19] Evidence apparently implicating mid-level U.S. military officials in receiving kickbacks from local contractors underscores the accountability problem.[20]

There are also wider and more intensely political risks to the United States from reliance on contractors. In addition to firms on DOD contract for whom the military provides protection, the State Department hires armed security guards to protect U.S. diplomats, in earlier wars undoubtedly an exclusively military function. In one high-profile incident in September 2007, security guards employed by Blackwater USA killed seventeen Iraqi civilians in a Baghdad square. The Iraqi government ordered the contractor to leave the country, describing the incident as "the murder of its citizens in cold blood [and] a terrorist action against civilians just like any other terrorist operation."[21] The incident drew attention to the extent of privatization of the American presence in Iraq. At the time of the Blackwater incident, with U.S. troop strength at 160,000, there were an estimated 180,000 U.S.-funded contractors in Iraq (about 21,000 of them Americans).[22]

Early in the occupation, the United States granted immunity to "American military and civilian personnel from prosecution for crimes in Iraqi courts."[23] Over time, Congress tightened accountability to U.S. authorities and U.S. law. The 2008 Status of Forces Agreement (SOFA) between the U.S. and Iraqi governments included a provision, effective January 1, 2009, making private contractors, as well as U.S. troops, subject to Iraqi law.[24]

The concerns voiced by veterans are borne out by independent and government analysts. "Four years into the occupation," wrote analyst Jeremy Scahill with reference to Iraq, "there is absolutely no effective system of oversight or accountability governing contractors and their operations."[25] A 2007 report by the Congressional Research Service noted "a substantial shift in the types of contracts for troop support services, the size of the contracts and the lack of effective management control over the administration of the contracts and the oversight of the contractors."[26]

A 2008 CRS report noted that with fully 20 percent of expenditures for the war in Iraq paid to contractors, "the Pentagon's reliance on outside contractors in Iraq is proportionately far larger than in any previous conflict, and it has fueled charges that this outsourcing has led to over billing, fraud and shoddy and unsafe work that has endangered and even killed American troops. The role of armed security contractors has also raised new legal and political questions about whether the United States has become too dependent on private armed forces on the twenty-first century battlefield."[27]

■ ■ ■

In sum, the experience of U.S. troops with private sector actors in the Afghanistan and Iraq theaters has both positive and negative elements. Contractors ease the hardships of life under duress and reduce the numbers of U.S. troops needed. At the same time, their presence and activities raise still-unanswered questions of cost, cost effectiveness, comparative advantage, and accountability. Based on the experience of the troops themselves, whose very lives are at stake, the balance sheet to many seems more negative than positive.

— EIGHT —

Dealing with the Media and Public Opinion

Reflecting on their experiences in Afghanistan and Iraq, many soldiers express strong views about the roles played by the media. Most level sharp criticism at its perceived lack of accuracy. Many also hold the media accountable for what they see as a widespread lack of awareness among Americans about the conflicts and the U.S. stake in them. Individual soldiers offer their own correctives in the form of e-mail dispatches and blogs designed to keep families and friends in the picture. Yet those cyberspace connections, a major development in American military history and a significant complement to traditional media coverage, have their own limitations and liabilities.

MEDIA AS MIRROR

Many veterans express disenchantment in the strongest possible terms with the accuracy of the media's portrayal of what is taking place on the ground. "Reporters are a bunch of bullshit," exclaimed Army Sgt. E-5 Bobby Lee Lisek, who served seven months in Iraq. "Oh, God. Do they lie!"[1] From his vantage point on the frontlines, the Air Force's Amn. Mark Kaplan expressed the view that "the media gave a twisted picture that has nothing to do with reality."[2] Many of the boots on the ground believed that the media has a negative agenda that exaggerates the difficulties experienced by the troops while downplaying their accomplishments. Soldiers commented regularly on the media's perceived fixation on the carnage and its lack of attention to constructive developments, including hearts-and-minds activities. Soldiers frequently "lash out at the media for only reporting when a bomb is detonated and not when a school or water treatment plant has been rebuilt."[3]

One who sensed a strongly negative media bias was Spec. Brian P. Clousen of the Indiana National Guard. If you rely on the media, he said, "You don't see the soldiers going out and building schools and setting up hospitals for the Iraqi people. . . . They don't show the people just trying to actually live their lives and get through another day. They're not all over there trying to kill us or plotting our destruction. They don't all hate America. That's all you see on TV. . . . It seems that the news people there want you to think that this is the worst thing that happened in the world: that we went over there. A lot of the people there hate Saddam and tell you that and are glad to see us over there."[4]

Media bias is confirmed for some by the attention lavished on the abuses committed by U.S. personnel at Abu Ghraib. "Of the hundreds of thousands of soldiers who have rotated into and out of Iraq," observes Army Capt. James R. Sosnicky, "a handful has embarrassed us" through their despicable conduct at Abu Ghraib. Yet it is they who capture the media's attention. Forgotten in the hubbub are "the faces of countless Americans rebuilding hospitals, delivering text books to schools, or providing Iraqis with clean water to drink."[5]

Coverage of the "sick pranks" in which Iraqis were abused and humiliated went on month after month, complained Army Sgt. James J. Maddix Jr., while after only a few days the media moved on quickly from the beheadings of U.S. soldiers to other issues. "Which is more important," he asked, "a person being humiliated or an American soldier getting his head lopped off?"[6] "I just know the media will only let you know how bad something is, not how good it is," added Mississippi Guardsman Justin C. Thompson following his time in Iraq. "I quit watching anything on the news about the war because it was mostly out of context or misinterpreted."[7]

Disenchantment with the media is deepened by its perceived lack of resonance with the soldier's direct experience. Army First Lt. Derek Sutton commented on how all the news he saw is from Baghdad, with very little from Mosul, Iraq's second city, where he was stationed. "The true story is not being told," he concluded.[8] Contrary to the media's view, said Sgt. Nathan Fegan, a driver in an Army transportation battalion who traveled widely in Iraq, "most Iraqis welcomed us."[9] Navy Lt. Daniel Neville believed that the media was denying the American public information about positive developments in order to sell stories. "A school that reopened after a couple of years isn't quite as big a headline as a U.S. soldier killed in the line of duty."[10]

On numerous occasions, troops returned from dangerous activities outside the wire to watch televised news that seemed unreal or unimportant. "Only the sensational gets reported," fumes Sgt. Matthew Miller, a paramedic with the Maryland National Guard in Iraq. "You hear thirty Iraqis killed by a suicide bomber, but the one private that got killed in the Humvee, you don't hear about. That happens a lot."[11] "I have lost all faith in the media," remarked New Hampshire Guardsman Steve Pink, "a hapless joke I would much rather laugh at than become a part of."[12] The fact that media coverage was virtually continuous—"this war has been fought in our living rooms more than any other in our history," an Army chaplain observes—increases both the media's opportunity to present a balanced view and the troops' disenchantment with its perceived failure to do so.[13]

As the attention of the media—and the nation—shifted from Afghanistan to Iraq following the U.S. invasion in March 2003, some troops deployed to Afghanistan criticized the media strongly. "Everything's Iraq, Iraq, Iraq, Iraq, Iraq," observed a sergeant.[14] "You don't really hear anything about Afghanistan." Yet there is "more progress" to report in Afghanistan, he believed, and Afghanistan, after all, is "the foundation" for the war against terror. But coverage of Iraq also came in for criticism. In the Global War on Terror study conducted by the New Hampshire National Guard, many returning troops expressed a sense of the "failure of the media to report on the progress made in Iraq."[15] The shift in late 2008 and early 2009 from Iraq back to Afghanistan had taken place too recently to be reflected in interviews with veterans.

Air Force M. Sgt. Mark Kaplan, a fighter pilot who deployed to Germany when the Vietnam War was winding down, faults the media for its

Soldiers and Civilians

Gregory Marinich (AFC2001/001/54920), Photographs (PH01), VHP, AFC, LOC.

In this photo Lt. Col. Gregory V. Marinich offers candy to a child in Mazar-e-Sharif, northern Afghanistan. The encounter took place in March 2005 on the city's main airfield. On that day, a steady stream of civilians passed along the dirt road en route to an area hospital that had been built by U.S. and Jordanian troops. The area was heavily mined with unexploded ordnance.

The photo was taken by U.S. Navy Commander Tom Cawley, who, like Marinich, was among the American troops attached to the International Security Assistance Force (ISAF). The United States and some forty other countries joined the effort to promote security and reconstruction around Afghanistan. Marinch's duties included medical evacuation of wounded troops and civilians, while Cawley served as the chief of operations for the ISAF Tactical Air Operations Center.

Looking back, Marinich, now a professor of military science and leadership of the Army ROTC program at the University of Memphis, says that "the photo reminds me of all the good that is going on in that country that never gets reported and the generosity [of NATO and U.S. forces] toward the people of Afghanistan that I consistently witnessed."

coverage of events in Iraq. The perceived negative slant does not surprise him, however. The media's unrelenting hammering away at abuses by U.S. troops at Abu Ghraib reminds him of its witch-hunting during the Indochina conflict. Stationed in San Francisco in the late 1960s, he had mixed and mingled with antiwar demonstrators and now implicates the same leftist and communist elements for fomenting public disapproval of U.S. involvement in Iraq. Those elements, he believes, had planned demonstrations against U.S. policy even before the U.S. invasion in 2003. "'You supply the war and we'll supply the protests,'" he heard them saying. Kaplan also saw parallels between Iraq and Vietnam in the overly restrictive rules of engagement; policymakers and the media alike place the troops, also branded as "baby killers," in a no-win situation.[16]

A more nuanced view is offered by Bryan Groves, captain of a Special Forces team in Iraq for eight months beginning in November 2004. He presented his perspective during a panel discussion among veterans who, upon returning to the United States, had resumed their studies:

> From what I have seen, the press does not provide adequate coverage of the positive actions taken by our military, the Iraqi military, or the Iraqi government. Most of the airtime allotted to the war focuses on the violence that occurred that day, not on the bad characters that were removed from the streets, the infrastructure projects that were completed, or the political negotiations conducted. The broadcast media could do a better job of highlighting the political sticking points the Iraqi government needs to navigate in order to achieve national reconciliation: oil-revenue sharing, revision of de-Baathification, demobilizing militias, and amending key points of their constitution. Those are the issues of utmost importance for Iraq and America alike.[17]

In short, the media did not meet its responsibility to help educate the American people about the issues and the progress of the war.

Lt. Col. Jude Ferran, an Army operations research officer stationed in Kabul, had a less critical take on the media's coverage of events in Afghanistan. The day-to-day priorities of his unit—including monitoring poppy cultivation and eradication, strengthening the Afghan national army, and finding sites for reconstruction projects—did not "rise to the level" of issues attracting media attention, even though his unit had a public relations officer who informed journalists of such developments. "I realized that different things were going in Afghanistan than Iraq," where the media at the time was focusing its attention, "but I didn't feel disrespected." Having been on the scene, he feels now able to "read between the lines" and sense the importance of what does get covered.[18]

If one of the major criticisms of the media concerns its accuracy and balance, a second involves its perceived failure to convey a sense of the wider importance of what was taking place. The stakes of the global war on terror for the United States and Europe—to say nothing of the Middle East—are perceived by veterans as far exceeding what the media conveys. "Is this war in the present tense, here in America?" asked Brian Turner, an award-winning poet who served as a captain in an Army combat brigade in Mosul in 2004. "Iraq is on the other side of the globe and the events there are mostly reported in the past tense."[19] While some soldiers hold the media accountable for the limited engagement of the American public with the issues of the wars, others fault politicians for prevailing on the media to limit coverage of certain aspects of the war, thus avoiding fuller ownership of the conflicts by the general population.

Many soldiers in both theaters are frustrated that Americans seem so minimally engaged. Marine Col. Benjamin Braden, who served in the Special Operations Command in Operation Desert Storm and then in ground operations in Afghanistan and Iraq, believes that the media has failed to capture the essence of nation-building, a more rigorous challenge for the military to meet and for the media to convey than that of expelling Iraqi forces from Kuwait during Operation Desert Storm.[20] Tyler Benson, a specialist E-4 in an Army signal battalion who is pictured on the cover of this volume and in this chapter, is critical of his fellow citizens, particularly in the American South, for provincialism and prejudice against Islam—and implicitly of the media for not widening their perspective.

Criticisms notwithstanding, many veterans credit the media with playing a significant role in promoting popular appreciation of the contributions of the military in Afghanistan and Iraq. Amn. First Class Quincy A. Boggan, an Air Force transport logistician stationed at Bagram Air Base in Afghanistan, appreciates the thank you's received from strangers and friends for his work, although, he sensed, nobody really comprehends the extent of the sacrifice and inconvenience involved.[21] Navy Petty Officer Samuel Main is guarded in his judgment about the media. "Are we getting the right news?" he was asked by an interviewer. "I don't know," he replied, "because we only saw what we saw. It's hard to say what is really going on," in part because most people keep things to themselves. Sometimes, he said, "your best information is through the media," even though the news often seemed "light compared to what was really happening."[22]

In Afghanistan and Iraq, as in earlier wars, the media have functioned as a point of entry for the American public into the issues of the conflict. That role is noted in an editorial in the *Rutland Herald*, written upon the return in 2006 of 170 Vermont National Guard troops from eighteen months in Iraq. "From a safe distance," the paper wrote, "Vermonters have been trying to comprehend the full complexity and tragic cost of the war—the competing values, the clashing goals, the frustration and sacrifice."[23] In this context, the question asked by so many of the troops is an important one: How well has the media conveyed to the American public as a whole the progress and the longer-term importance of what is taking place?

The interview data are largely silent on a number of issues involving the media that sparked discussion among policymakers and the general public during the decade. Apart from one mention of a Reuters' photographer, there were few comments by soldiers on the embedding of journalists within the ranks, a development heatedly debated among journalists themselves. Similarly, the Bush administration's ban on photographing the offloading of caskets at Ramstein Air Base in Germany or at Dover Air Force Base in Delaware, an item decried in some quarters as an example of "managing the news," does not draw comment in the interviews selected.

An Obama administration review of the no-photography policy, initiated during the Persian Gulf War in 1991 during the George H. W. Bush presidency, found people divided. According to the *New York Times*, "Supporters of the ban say it protects family's privacy and keeps the deaths from becoming politicized; critics say the government is trying to sanitize the wars and reduce public awareness of their human cost."[24] On February 26, 2009, Obama's secretary of defense, Robert Gates, announced that news media would henceforth be permitted to cover the repatriation of remains, subject to the agreement of the families involved.[25]

Similarly conspicuous by its relative absence in the interviews is reference to soldiers from other countries, whether as part of NATO forces in Afghanistan or of the multinational force in Iraq. By and large, the wars seem to be regarded by veterans as largely an American project. The troops do not picture themselves participating in a wider war on terror which, Bush administration rhetoric to the contrary notwithstanding, strikes them as global neither in the nature of the threats nor in the ownership of the response.

BEYOND THE MEDIA

One corrective to the perceived limitations of the media has been information conveyed by the troops themselves. Veterans' communications from the field represent an important—and alternative—source of information and opinion. "More than any generation of troops before them," observes the editor of a compendium of dispatches from the front, "servicemen and women today have the ability to see and hear what the media are reporting back home and how the conflicts in which they are fighting are being portrayed."[26] If newspapers offer the proverbial "first draft of history," dispatches from soldiers may provide significant corrections for the historical record. Some have even suggested that by virtue of the photos they take and transmit, cell phones have replaced newspapers—which are experiencing problems of their own—as history's first draft.

Although American troops stationed in the Balkans a decade earlier made use of the Internet, the conflicts in Afghanistan and Iraq are the first wars in which most soldiers in theater have been in instant and regular communication with friends and family. Thanks to developments in satellite technology and to the efforts of several private foundations and the military itself, cyberspace has given those deployed overseas a virtual seat at their own kitchen tables. "A person can now keep his commitment to his family and keep his commitment to his country," noted an official from Freedom Calls, an organization facilitating such contacts.[27] The group has "enabled 30,000 service members in four camps to reach relatives [for] free in the past two years, setting up live teleconferencing to broadcast the births of babies, birthday parties, weddings and graduations."[28] In no earlier war had a soldier stationed overseas been able to engage in a real-time game of Canasta with his wife in the States, a pastime that Marine Sgt. E-5 Terry Bruns looked forward to following completion of his daily shift of guard duty at the Abu Ghraib prison.[29] Nor were earlier generations of fathers able, as was Marine Lt. Col. Robert C. D'Amico, to help his daughter nightly with her homework.[30]

The blogging phenomenon began in 1999. In those early days, Web logs (better known as blogs) were mostly online diaries and homepages, but they've evolved into portals about current events, politics and economics, law and medicine . . . and more, including the military. Like everything else, blogging changed after September 11, 2001. The United States and its allies were officially declaring a war against terrorists worldwide. Soldiers were being deployed in massive numbers to the Middle East. The world was rapidly changing. People were nervous and curious about what was going on with the government and the military—curious beyond their nightly or cable news. In Afghanistan and Iraq, technologically adept young soldiers were making sure they didn't lose contact with family and friends back home. Blogging was the perfect way to maintain contact, to tell their stories. And those blogs—soon known as milblogs (military blogs) were ideal for filling in the gaps that both the media and the military left out of the war. Now anyone with an Internet connection had the ability to find out what was happening overseas from the soldiers themselves.

—*Maj. Matthew Currier Burden**

---

* Matthew Currier Burden, Introduction, The Blog of War: Front-line Dispatches from Soldiers in Afghanistan and Iraq (New York and London: Simon and Shuster 2006), 3–4.

"We always had access to phones and the Internet where people could e-mail home," confirms one New Hampshire guardsman. "I could e-mail home multiple times a day. A lot of people had digital cameras. This is probably the most photographed conflict and the most communicated conflict there has ever been. I know if something happened to me, people already knew about it quickly, which is good and bad. It's good to stay in contact because you see the news on TV and it's negative, negative, and negative. All you see is just the bad stuff happening." In an example of the potential of communications from the field to correct information otherwise available, he shared with his e-mail network his personal elation that, despite threats, 70 percent of the Iraqi electorate had turned out to vote. "To me that made it all worthwhile and told the world, 'Guess what? The Iraqis do want us here.'"[31] For Army Capt. Ryan P. Aument, the use of a Kevlar helmet as a ballot box for a 2003 election for the council in a town near Kirkuk is a symbol of constructive change—and the military's role in it—that he took pleasure in sharing with his Listserv.[32]

Communications such as these had overwhelmingly salutary results among those on the receiving end. Internet-based telephone calls kept families in touch with the day-to-day lives of loved ones, even though soldiers often sanitized what they shared. Regular contact is particularly important for children, psychologists report, who are bearing the burden of having one or, in some instances, both parents absent and in harm's way. Cyberspace also gives soldiers an up-to-date sense of what is happening at home, although sometimes the news is unsettling. "The constant communication makes for fewer unpleasant surprises after couples reunite, though there can be a downside," observed one reporter. "It brings the anxieties of the living room into the war."[33]

Sgt. Todd B. Walton of the Nebraska National Guard found it stressful to learn from his wife, at home in Kearney with his thirteen-year-old daughter and fifteen-month-old son, that "there was moisture on the bathroom floor." He maintained that the stress he experienced as a medic accompanying convoys around Fallujah was minimal compared with his home-related stress.[34] Soldiers worry a lot about their families, Army Lt. Col. Rick E. Mayes points out. "I was able to call home almost every day. If all of a sudden your son or daughter gets in trouble, gets involved in a fight at school, or gets hurt, you want to know it as soon as possible. You feel helpless over there because there's nothing you can do."[35]

Instant communication links between soldiers and their families offer a coping mechanism of enormous potential. "We went over there," recalls Navy Petty Officer 2nd Class Samuel Main of his deployment to Iraq, "thinking I was going to be able to call home once a month." Two months after arrival in Iraq on September 11, 2003, however, and aware for the first time of how dangerous his posting was, "I didn't think I was going to come back home. So I told my wife, 'This is worse than we had planned for.' So I promised I'd call her every chance I get. 'If I have an hour of sleep and I can make it to a phone, I'll call you.' Once I came to terms with that, everything got easier for me. Once I realized that I'm a goner and may not make it back and I would call home more often, my attitude changed. I was sleeping better and I was eating better because I had come to terms with, 'My, we're going to die.'"[36]

From the standpoint of military officialdom, direct communications between the war theater and the home "theater" were a mixed blessing. While e-mail access 24/7 represents a tremendous boost to morale, notes one officer in the New Hampshire National Guard, it posed "a huge challenge" for him as commander. There were occasions when word of injuries or deaths spread among families back home before the authorities were prepared to release it, leading officials to close down Internet access until affected family members could be notified. Such interruptions in information flow themselves created anxiety. "If we'd had a tough few days," recalls Main, "I might not call home," alarming his family with his silence.

On one occasion, the authorities, concerned lest news of a unit's departure for the United States leak through cyberspace to the enemy, kept the particulars from the soldiers themselves. Officials were also concerned that domestic issues—the health of a parent, the moodiness of a spouse, the latest temper tantrum of a child—might interfere with demanding task of soldiering. Liabilities notwithstanding, concluded a National Guard official, the communications potential of the Internet was "excellent and allowed people to communicate back and forth and stay in touch."[37] Tyler Mueller, an Army tank driver whose unit served as a leading element in military maneuvers in Iraq, noted the unusual difficulties of keeping in touch precisely because their forward position prevented them from calling home.[38]

Sgt. Tina M. Beller, a U.S. Army reservist stationed in Baghdad with a civil affairs unit, lived through a mortar attack on the Green Zone in September 2004 that killed a number of her cohorts. In the evening, she e-mailed her parents in Pennsylvania, anticipating that they would have seen pictures of the attack and be alarmed. They received her communiqué on September 11. "I am just writing to let you know that physically I remain unharmed. Emotionally and mentally, is a different story." Her superiors, she explains, "told me not to write home about it. 'We don't want it all over the Internet.' But even talking to all the right people isn't helping the heavy weight I am carrying on my tightened chest. And somehow, writing usually does."[39]

In 2005, the military tightened operational security regulations to limit veterans' access to the Internet and avoid transmittal of sensitive information. Unrestrained blogging and the posting of photos and other material on websites, the Pentagon said, "needlessly place lives at risk and degrade the effectiveness of our operations."[40] In May 2007, further restrictions prohibited access by the troops to thirteen communal websites, including YouTube, "to protect operations from the drain on computer capacity."[41] Even so, information flow remained far more regular and rapid than in earlier conflicts.

Improvements in technology have not only accelerated awareness of developments in Afghanistan and Iraq, but have also helped knit together networks of engaged family members and citizens in the United States. The websites of groups such as Veterans for America, Iraq and Afghanistan Veterans of America, Military Families Speak Out, and the Servicemembers Legal Defense Network contain a rich array of regularly updated information about pending legislation and changes in regulations, recent reports on items of interest such as protective gear, announcements of workshops and conferences being held around the country, and news about the progress of the wars themselves.

Interview

Tyler Benson (AFC2001/001/52131), Photographs (PH 07), VHP, AFC, LOC. Photograph © Linda Cullen, used with permission.

Spec. Tyler Benson of the Minnesota National Guard's 134th Signal Battalion, Bravo Company, answers questions from John Hines, a radio talk-show host on K102 (Clear Channel) radio in the Minneapolis-St. Paul area.

The interview took place in January 2005 at Camp Liberty, Baghdad, one of the largest military bases in Iraq and home to the Blackhawk helicopters that are used for combat operations and for evacuating the wounded. Seated on the roof of the brigade headquarters, Benson and Hines look out over the sheet metal that served as a barrier against incoming mortars. In the background, a U.S. military communications tower tops Signal Hill.

Hines, along with Clear Channel executive and photographer Linda Cullen, were embedded in the Minnesota National Guard unit—the first instance, to Hines' knowledge, in which non-broadcast personnel were permitted such access. While in Iraq, they interviewed approximately 150 soldiers. As part of Clear Channel's "Operation Northern Lights," a promotion intended to provide phone cards to Iraqi troops from Minnesota, interview excerpts and selected photos were broadcast back home and some were transmitted live to large screens in the Mall of America in Minneapolis.

Looking back on the interview in December 2008, Benson says, "I appreciated that these civilians from our area showed their support by coming over to Iraq and experiencing first-hand what we were going through."

COMMUNICATION AND THE ARTS

If the pace of communication between veterans and their families has accelerated, so too has the speed with which developments in the global war on terror are being processed by society as a whole. Arts critics have commented on the "cornucopia of works being done in the United States and Great Britain that approach Iraq from perspectives both political and personal." One such stage play, *The Rhode Island Project*, is an amalgam of the stories of soldiers, families, and others touched by the Iraq war, drawn from a state in which the National Guard is the fourth-largest employer and has deployed some 4,000 troops to Iraq.[42]

Another play, *The War Anthology,* premiered by Denver's Curious Theater, is an amalgam of pieces written by eight authors, each keyed to photographic images of combat over the years. "We're not interested in making an anti-war movie," explains dramaturge Bonnie Metzger. "This project is about using war photography to frame the question, "What does it mean to be a citizen in this country at this moment in time?"[43]

A third play, David Hare's *Stuff Happens,* stars President George W. Bush ("I don't feel like I owe anybody an explanation") and Colin Powell ("Politicians start wars; soldiers fight and die in them"). The title is a quotation by Donald Rumsfeld, whose other lines include, "A war on terror. That's good. That's vague."[44] *The Guardians*, a play by Peter Morris with adumbrations of Abu Ghraib, opened in London and then again in New York City. Tony Kushner's *Homebody/Kabul* opened in New York in December 2001. "I didn't imagine when I was working on the play," Kushner said, "that by the time we produced it, the United States would be at war with Afghanistan."[45]

Meanwhile, the movie-going public has visited and savored the conflicts through a variety of films. These include *No End in Sight, Generation Kill, Redacted, Gunner Palace, In the Valley of Elah*, and the aforementioned *Fahrenheit 9/11. In the Valley of Elah* "features real-life veterans of the Iraq war playing fictional characters who give voice to reasons for supporting the effort."[46] The reading public, too, has had choices. There has been an abundance of first-person accounts of the conflict, some of them listed in this book's bibliography and enriching the book's narrative. One veteran credits

One Bullet Away with helping his girlfriend understand his war experience. Columnist Nicholas Kristof of the *New York Times*, who has sponsored Iraq poetry contests for several successive years, reminds his readers, "throughout history, the most memorable accounts of war—from Homer to Wilfred Owen—haven't been journalistic or historical, but poetic."[47] DOD has contributed to the production costs of reenacting Greek tragedies for the benefit of veterans struggling with issues of pain and loss.[48]

Over the years, photography as well as cinematography has been an essential means for connecting the American public with its wars. But here, too, there may be some special elements. Art critic Holland Cotter has described the war in Iraq as perhaps "the most intensively photographed war in history."[49] In Afghanistan as well as Iraq, the lens has been a powerful instrument, often wielded by the troops themselves. A number of low-budget documentaries which open up key issues for viewers include, in addition to *Combat Diary: The Marines of Lima Company,* two that have provided provocative materials for this book: *The War Tapes,* filmed by three members of the New Hampshire National Guard, and *The Fog of War*, featuring veterans from World War II and since.

What strikes knowledgeable observers of this flourishing of the arts is not simply the cornucopia of treatments of the conflicts, but the rapidity with which the artistic renditions are coming. "It takes about three years for events to shift from basic journalism to a deeper reflection on what they mean to the state of our nation and politics," said Oskar Eustis, artistic director of New York City's Public Theater, in April 2006. "We've watched in the last six months as America has awakened, not just about the war but about the administration's attitude toward the war. There's a greater urgency for people to grapple with, in cultural form, not just the events but what they mean." While the Vietnam War was the subject of numerous plays, the difference, says Eustis, is that this new generation of plays is "coming faster," appearing while the conflicts are still in progress.[50]

■ ■ ■

Is the media playing a more active—and perhaps a more negative—role in the Afghanistan and Iraq conflicts than in previous American wars? Has it been pursuing its own agenda? What effects has coverage had on the actions of the military and on public attitudes toward the Global War on Terror? More time and reflection is needed before such questions can be answered.

The unprecedented access enjoyed by the troops to Internet and phone links has given Americans an added source of information–perhaps even some alternative narratives—about what is taking place, a more up-close-and-personal sense of day-to-day developments, and, potentially, a greater awareness of the importance of the outcome. But here, too, questions remain. Why does increased information flow not result in greater public engagement in the conflicts, wider concern for their impacts on Americans—and, for that matter, on Iraqi civilians—and more assertive public demands for accountability on the part of political and military decision makers?

PART III
Reentry

Serving in Iraq, observed one veteran, represented "a fundamental transformation" of his life. Judging from the interview material, most of those on the front lines of the global war on terror in Iraq and Afghanistan would whole-heartedly agree, although individuals would differ in what they identify as the positive and negative aspects of the experience and the overall balance between them. Chapter 9 examines the efforts of returning veterans as individuals to reestablish normalcy. Chapter 10 reviews the institutional resources available to them in negotiating that transition. Chapter 11 reviews comparisons veterans draw between the Global War on Terror and other American wars. Chapter 12 offers some of their thoughts on the meaning of their experience and the importance of seeing these events through veterans' eyes.

— NINE —

Reestablishing Normalcy

In transitioning from Afghanistan and Iraq back to life in the United States, veterans have taken many different paths. Members of the active-duty forces have returned to military bases and surrounding communities, while those in the National Guard and Reserves have more typically repaired to their home areas. For some, the global war on terror represents the final chapter in military careers; for others, additional time will now be spent in the Guard or Reserves. For many with active-duty or reserve status, the possibility of another tour in Afghanistan or Iraq looms.

Yet however different the individual reentry trajectories and outcomes, certain elements are common to all. Virtually every veteran has found himself or herself making initial adjustments needed upon returning, reestablishing some sense of normalcy for the future, and reclaiming a sense of humanity after the in-theater experience.

FROM HELL TO HOME

The event was front-page news. "Nebraska National Guard troops returned from the Middle East this week to hometown welcomes that saw hundreds and thousands of their fellow Americans line the streets to cheer their return and thank them for their service. In Kearney and in Kimball, in Scottsbluff and Gering and Chadron, the troops were hailed by folks who wanted to shake their hands, to express their thanks and to say they were happy that most returned safely home." The 1057th Light/Medium Truck Company of the Nebraska National Guard had been gone fifteen months and seven days, first for training at Fort Carson and then on to Kuwait and Iraq.[1]

Homecomings typically involved a tangle of emotions. The most common feeling was probably that of relief. Sgt. Michael A. Thomas of the Colorado National Guard, who served with a military police unit in Tallil, Iraq, described touching down in Bangor, Maine, early one morning en route home. "We were tired, hungry, and as desperate as we were to get to Colorado, our excitement was tainted with bitterness. While we were originally told our National Guard deployment would be mere months, here we were—369 days later—frustrated and angry." Bitterness was transformed into gratitude by a contingent of veterans, including some who had served in Vietnam, from the Bangor VFW post, who had waited out a thirty-six-hour delay to embrace the returnees and thank them for their service and sacrifice.[2]

Many soldiers returned with a new or renewed sense of values, a deeper appreciation of family, community, and country, and new purpose and direction to their lives. Maj. Tracey Ringo, an African American medical doctor with the Ohio National Guard, was enormously positive about her experience in Iraq in 2004. "It's the best work I have ever done." Back in the United States, she finds, "The flag means so much more to me than it ever did before. I've always been patriotic, but even more so now."[3]

For some, returning home was the mirror image of the process of deployment, which had involved progressing from the familiar to the unfamiliar almost overnight. For others, the process was more extenuated, reflecting the official view that decompression and reacclimatization should be approached gradually.

On his way back from Iraq, Petty Officer Samuel Main and his unit spent four or five days in "warrior transition" In Kuwait. "It's so you can get used to a normal life again," he explains. While the idea may have been a good one, he considers the actual arrangements "a total crock." Even with the stopover in the region and an intermediate touchdown at his base in Mississippi, less than a week would elapse between leaving Anbar Province in Iraq and "sitting on my own bed in Oregon," "It's too fast!" he exclaims.

"Dad and Me—It's Good To Be Home!"

Antonio Ruiz De La Torres (AFC2001/001/31834), Photographs (PH 58), VHP, AFC, LOC.
Photograph by Reina Prado.

Marine Lance Cpl. Antonio Ruiz De La Torre served with a Marine aircraft group, first in Kuwait during February 2003 and then in Iraq from March to October 2003. His unit, in charge of setting up forward operating bases and supply lines for Huey and Cobra attack helicopters, was later redeployed back to Iraq. Ruiz would have gone had he been required to, but he received an honorable discharge. He now works for a NASA contractor and is studying for an MBA. "I had always wanted an MBA," he says, and "the Marine Corps provided the organizational skills, the discipline, and the foundation for achieving it."

The photograph was taken upon his return from Iraq to Camp Pendleton, California. In addition to his father and mother, the welcome committee included his brother, two cousins, and two aunts. "It was kind of surreal," says Ruiz, recalling the homecoming scene. "It didn't really settle in until I was on the way home with my family." The transition back to the States and eventually to life as a civilian was "really tough," even though he did not suffer from PTSD or other health issues. His overseas posting had exposed him to some danger, but he was not involved in active combat.

As anxious as everyone else to get home, he would have been better off, he thinks, decompressing elsewhere and sparing his family the process.[4]

For some soldiers and families, the initial days back home were the most difficult. "When I got home from Iraq," recalled Sgt. Nathan Fegan, who had worked in an Army transportation battalion, "I was kind of 'weirded out.' I didn't want to talk to anybody." Over time, he came to realize that "my main goal in life was to get an education" and plunged into his studies, assisted by the GI Bill. He found that what he wanted most was "to be nice to everyone and to live a peaceful and happy life."[5]

"I was home for like half an hour," says Army Sgt. Todd B. Walton of his post-Iraq reunion with his wife, "and finally she said, 'Do they speak in full sentences where you come from?' And I had to stop and think about that and said, 'I don't know.'"[6] During a cross-country drive with his wife shortly after returning from a year in Iraq, the normally outgoing Gen. Carter Ham, Commanding General, U.S. Army Europe, recalled, "I probably said three words."[7] Sgt. Shane Slager, returning with the Nebraska National Guard, told a local newspaper reporter, "I want to go home and not be seen. I've been living with 150-some people for over a year and I'm looking forward to some time alone."[8]

"I had expected the man I met at the door to be somehow different from the one who had walked out of it all those months ago," mused Dana Canedy as she awaited the return of Army 1st Sgt. Charles M. King from Iraq. While he was gone, she had given birth to the couple's first child, Jordan. Her husband, who had hoped to be present for his son's birth, had chosen instead to lead his 100-person contingent, hard-pressed by insurgents. "But I had not expected his suffering to show so soon. What he had seen and done over there I could not imagine. But clearly there was no way to emerge from a world in which you are routinely involved in taking and saving lives and not be transformed."[9]

"I was a little different when I got home," recalls Army Spec. Christopher Gamblin. "A little more on edge, a little testier, a little quick to get angry, until I settled down and unwound. I've seen it in a lot of guys. You just get really tightly wound. Somebody will be talking about something stupid that has no significance really—just ordinary talk for most people. When you first get home, it's just, 'Why are you talking about that? Shut up. Leave me alone.' But it got better, probably. It took a few months to settle down to where I wasn't just abrasive to everybody I talked to, but it's just a transition thing. It's kind of hard to relax at first."[10] Recalls Army Capt. Ryan Aument, "The most difficult thing for me was learning to relax again."[11]

In retrospect, Gamblin believes he hurried the psychological reentry process too much. Starting back at work only a week or two after returning, he found himself "getting really pissed off at people and being a huge asshole to all of my friends." Was there anything he could have done to ease the adjustment? "There's not really anything to do. It's not something where you can go talk to a therapist and get a hug and be all better. It's the transition of life."[12]

Army Spec. Gonzalo ("JD") Gonzalez had a similar experience. Despite no real down-time during his first ten weeks as a gunner escorting convoys to Fallujah and other hotspots in Iraq, he hadn't been aware of problems developing. These surfaced as soon as he returned home. In the headlong rush of waiting family members into the arms of returning vets, his niece put on the brakes. "You're not JD," she said, and "started crying, turned around, and walked off." The reception from his nephews was hardly more reassuring. "What's wrong with you? You look different," they said. "It was just the impact of everything that had gone on, everything that we'd seen," Gonzalez recalls. "I guess it just all hit" at that moment.[13] While the older members of his family proved more understanding, the transition remained rocky. Marine Corps Lt. Col. Robert C. D'Amico received a similar reception. One of his youngsters didn't recognize him at first and then didn't speak to him for a week.[14]

Army Sgt. Gregory Mayfield, who had experienced withering violence in Sadr City and Fallujah, encountered major difficulties upon reentry. He slept poorly, a sign, he believes, that he had reached his limit. "You can only live with that adrenaline high for so long, and then you crash. When you crash, it is a bad crash." Returning home for his mother's funeral midway through his tour, he had found himself "just so numbed out from the shock of all the combat we'd seen that I couldn't even cry. That is an emotional hit right there." At the end of his tour, he realized that the return to normalcy would be a long time coming and warned his wife that he would be hard to live with. "You know, I will never be the same. It feels like I left a little bit of my soul over there."[15]

"The toughest part of fighting a war is coming home," said Army Capt. Andrew Michael Wells. "People want to know everything you experienced, but they don't really want to understand—and can't possibly understand. So it's kind of an interesting dichotomy to put yourself into that kind of environment." As "patriotic fervor" wanes and people become less interested in the troops that have returned, Wells has found himself more appreciative of simple thank-you's than of the occasional probing question.[16]

Ceremonies such as the Nebraska one have been replicated across the country. A chaplain in Vermont described his unit as "ecstatically happy to be back." The welcome received, he pointed out, was significantly different from that accorded U.S. soldiers returning from Vietnam. "Some Vietnam vets made a personal commitment to ensure that our reception was what theirs should have been," noted Captain Aument. "Folks will disagree with the public policy of the war but have always treated me with respect as a soldier."[17]

I told my wife a couple of times since I've been back that I will never be the same man you knew before I went over there. And she says, "Why not?" "I can't explain it to you, but I just won't be. I have seen things that I will never be able to share with her. If I do share them with her, she will not be able to understand them. Because you can't explain what fresh blood smells like. You can't explain to someone that constant 24/7 fear. I told a buddy of mine from high school who asked if I was scared, "Yeah, I was scared twenty-four hours a day." He said, "You weren't." "Yeah, I was." You develop an underlying fear that goes with that underlying alert level and that is the survival mechanism. War is an abnormal environment and you just can't switch it off. When you get back you expect everything to be normal. I am still not normal.

—*Gregory Mayfield**

---

* Paul Gregory Mayfield Collection (AFC2001/001/60193) video recording (MV01), VHP, AFC, LOC.

The nation has indeed learned a lesson from Vietnam, observed Dr. Matthew J. Friedman, executive director of the DVA's National Center for PTSD: to separate the warriors from the war. Unlike Vietnam, "Americans no longer confuse the war and the warrior; those returning from Afghanistan and Iraq enjoy national support, despite sharp political disagreement about the war itself."[18] Numerous veterans mention being thanked in airports by total strangers for their service. Yet there were uneasy undercurrents too. "I returned home to the dichotomy of being universally welcomed with open, respectful, grateful arms," wrote Air Force SSgt. Parker Gyokeres, "by a country that is increasingly against why I was ever in Iraq."[19]

The strains that long absences or deferred returns place on marriages became quickly apparent. Although the troops had been alerted to anticipate reentry problems, many were still unprepared. One Vermont Guardsman described his anguish at the discovery that his wife had taken up with his best friend. Many soldiers experienced difficulties not only reconnecting with spouses, but also in relating to their own children. Karen Cox, wife of New Hampshire Guardsman Lt. Ken Cox, found her husband "changed. His temper is shorter and he sometimes yells at his sons when he doesn't mean to."[20]

Problems of communication between spouses were commonplace, but often not for lack of effort by both parties. "After War, Love Can Be a Battlefield," read one newspaper headline in April 2008. "Wives want to talk about what happened in Iraq. Their husbands don't."[21] Randi Moriarty, the wife of the New Hampshire Guardsman, took a dim view of how much could be shared. "He so badly wants me to understand what he went through," she acknowledged. "I will never understand, just as he will never understand what I went through."[22] Explained Samuel Main, "There's stuff I still don't want to talk about. I'm not going to talk about it. I'm going to keep it to myself, probably forever, if I can. Other stuff is kind of neat for people to know."[23]

"I don't really tell a whole lot of people about my experience because they don't understand," explains a female National Guard soldier. "Until you actually smell and feel the environment, you don't understand what it is like."[24] On returning from her year in Iraq, Colorado's Dougherty found that "you stop talking to people"—even to friends who might be expected to want to know what the war was like. "It was hard to relate to people that I'd been through such a huge experience, and it had a huge effect on thousands of lives instantly and so many more through the association. I didn't understand why everyone didn't care about this war."[25]

At a time when communication was as difficult as it was necessary, some veterans found it easier to speak with fellow veterans than with next of kin. Sgt. E-5 Dax Carpenter, a Marine who returned from duty in Afghanistan and Iraq with serious physical and psychological wounds, found that "the biggest gratification is being able to talk to other people who have lived the same style, not necessarily the same combat situation. That's something you're not going to get with a spouse. That's something you're not gonna get with some shrink or doctor. It's only something that can be produced healing-wise through talking with other veterans."[26] Carpenter, like many other veterans, believes that people who haven't lived through such an intense experience will never have a sense of what it was like.

Yet not everyone struggled upon returning. "After exchanging the required hugs and kisses" with his wife, recalls Jeffrey D. Barnett, who returned from Fallujah to a storybook welcome at Camp Pendleton, California, "I thought, 'What do I do now?' I thought for a moment and offered the suggestion, 'Let's go home.' And that's what we did. At T plus four [hours] from setting foot in the continental United States, it was as if I was just coming home from another day of work."[27] Judging from their comments, few veterans managed this kind of nonchalance.

A "NEW NORMAL"

In returning to the States—whether to home towns in the case of National Guard personnel and reservists or to military bases in the case of active-duty soldiers—veterans sought to reestablish familiar ways of functioning. In the wake of their overseas experience, what they put in place over time was, in effect, a set of post-deployment routines, a "new normal." Making the transition from abroad to home, they were confronted with the need to unlearn skills that had been essential in Afghanistan and Iraq and to relearn skills necessary to function back in the States. The skill sets, it turned out, were quite different, sometimes even diametrically opposed.

Army Sgt. Abbie Pickett, whose first encounter with the carnage of battle had been so traumatic, had difficulty reorienting herself to day-to-day life in Wisconsin. "Things that make me abnormal here," she found, "make me a better soldier there. Over there, the whole heightened sense of alert: hearing a really big bang and throwing somebody on the ground is O.K. Hearing a big bang and throwing your roommate on the ground—it's not so socially accepted here."[28] Replacing the heightened sense of suspicion and distrust, the greater watchfulness and defensiveness that had been so essential in-theater with the qualities needed for the home scene did not come easily for many.

"Combat has taught them to make life-or-death decisions within seconds," noted one observer, "and some have trouble changing that behavior when they come home. Their tempers are shorter; they drive faster and make decisions without consulting spouses. Sometimes they spend money impulsively."[29] When soldiers are in the line of battle, New Hampshire's Sgt. Shelton said, "you can't let your emotions make decisions for you. You have to deal with your emotions later."[30] When soldiers returned to their states and communities, "later" had become "now."

Indeed, many veterans describe returning with a residue of unprocessed experiences and emotions. Army Spec. Tina Garnanez, the medical technician with outspokenly critical views about the military's mission in Iraq, found her life upon returning to the States totally consumed with the transition. "There's so much inside, so much pain and anger and suffering," she told an interviewer. "It never goes away. Most of my day is spent just dealing with myself."[31]

Veterans who had managed their fears and insecurities in Afghanistan and Iraq by ignoring or denying them had a backlog of sorting out to do. Responding to a standard interview question about coping with stress, Army Sgt. E-5 Nicole Ferretti said, "I just blocked it off, tried to forget it. We had long days and we didn't really get to stop and discuss our emotional issues, so I went into a state of denial."[32] Demond Mullins reflected, "I wouldn't think about what I was doing while I was doing it or else I wouldn't be able to do it."[33] Army Lt. Col. Rick Mayes's approach in Iraq had been "to minimize down-time." Sometimes he even refused to take "down-time" because "you want to keep your mind occupied."[34] The strategy for dealing with stress employed by Sgt. Cindy Clemence of the Vermont National Guard was straightforward. "Suck it up and move on," she said. "If you stew too much, it might eat you up."[35]

Dax Carpenter, a Marine diagnosed with PTSD and TBI from tours in Afghanistan and Iraq, held himself to "Marine standards" of toughness. "How do you deal with difficult emotions such as anger and sadness?" an interviewer asked. "I 'locked and loaded.'" he replied. "You shouldn't need to talk to somebody while you're in a combat situation. You suck it up, you deal with it. However, coming out of such a situation, coming out of the military, you should have that chance. You don't go up to a football player five minutes before the game and say, 'Where do you hurt?' Their job is to feel invincible; so is ours, but in a whole 'nother degree."[36]

Some sought to relieve the day-to-day tensions of deployment by calling or writing family and friends. "Being able to communicate with people back home," says Marine Sgt. E-5 Travis Fisher, was "a big stress reliever."[37] Christopher Gamblin "read a lot of books while I was over there." Sometimes, he recalled, "we'd sit around and play poker. Video games, watch movies. I had my laptop and a pretty extensive DVD collection from shopping at the PX. Pretty much anything to waste time. Anything that was available to just go numb for a while and let time slip by."[38] Sergeant Mayfield puzzled over the popularity of a video shooting game called Halo. "You were in a live firefight today and now you're down here playing Halo," he said to one of his cohorts. "But that's how they relaxed. We each had our different ways."[39]

For many soldiers, much that had been swept under the rug would now need revisiting. "You can't store anything inside you," said Specialist Gonzalez, he of the painful airport encounter with his niece, "because sooner or later the jar is going to burst. And if it bursts, there's pretty much one emotion that comes out, and that's anger."[40] Army Capt. Andrew M. Wells grew concerned about one of the gunners in his unit who was troubled by nightmares and arranged stress counseling for him. In one of the dreams that was holding him hostage, the gunner would be sleeping in bed at home with his wife. However, when he turned his mate over, it turned out to be a dead Iraqi.[41]

Teresa Little, the young Army specialist who described her effort to "hold inside" the emotions generated by having seen a dead body hanging out of an incinerated vehicle in Iraq, described how important it was for her—but also how difficult—to get everything out of her system. "If they don't talk about it," she said, "they're just bottling everything up, like I did. I think it's good to get it all out," even the "really harsh things I wouldn't talk about, because you feel relieved." The psychologist she consulted upon returning provided some help, although she remained haunted by nightmares.[42]

For some, the "new normal" involves ready access to good food and drink and clean surroundings. Veterans speak of their great pleasure in pulling a beer out of the fridge, wandering through well-stocked supermarkets, patronizing fast food restaurants, and simply bathing and shaving whenever they feel the urge. Dax Carpenter, who had had only eight showers during his eight months in Iraq, recalls, "When I came home from Iraq, I flushed the toilet twenty times just to watch the little water swirl. I was so proud. It beat sand coming up my ass while trying to use the restroom in the middle of the desert during a sandstorm."[43]

Veterans returned to families that, with varying degrees of success, had functioned while they were gone. Spouses had taken over the management of household finances, children had assumed greater responsibilities, and new divisions of labor had been put in place. Spec. 5 Jack C. Van Zanten, who served two rotations with the Army in Iraq, observed on returning that "the dynamics of the family change." He saw his own reentry confirming the need to "reunite slowly and work through things carefully."[44]

Families soon begin to realize that their soldiers may have difficulty unpacking the experiences and resist pressure, even from loved ones, to get the necessary help. Returning from a year in Iraq, California Guardsman Sgt. Michael Durand wrote about his encounter with a mental health worker whose help he had sought out after a month of languishing at home. "What I didn't want was this to be another bullshit-feel-good-I-have-problems-please-feel-sorry-for-me headshrinker deal. I have had enough of those. Look," Durand said, "I have shot more goddamn people than you ever have. So don't bullshit me about 'Duty, Honor, and Country.' Been there, done that. . . . And you know what? It ain't there, man. It's just War, and War don't give a good Goddamn what the fuck."[45] Soldiers reported with great remorse their often unsuccessful attempts to persuade others to seek professional help, especially when suicide resulted.

Participants in a Vermont focus group described a range of reentry reactions. One woman reported that her husband, mild-mannered when he left, had returned hating the world and "angry at everybody." Another's spouse, once mellow and easy going, had turned into someone with "an attitude." One wife who had struggled to reestablish communication following her husband's return was pleased when he had agreed to attend a "marriage enrichment weekend" sponsored by the military, only to have the retreat cancelled at the last minute. She doubted their marriage would survive a then-rumored second deployment, which she suspected he would not discuss.[46] A woman who had found her spouse maddeningly uncommunicative since his return described herself as "ready to walk out" of their marriage. "God bless the wives," says Dax Carpenter, "because it takes a real woman to be able to deal with someone that can get angrier faster than you can ever imagine."

When Specialist Ferretti returned from Iraq, "it seemed like the only stable thing I had was my family, so I chose to move back home with my dad and my stepmom, and still it was a little different." While she was away, her two sisters had moved out. "It seemed like everyone's lives had continued to progress and mine had come to a halt. It seemed like I was in a totally different world. It's like I wasn't in my own life anymore." Now twenty-six (she had enlisted at twenty-one), she said, "I'm trying to get back in the rhythm of my life as I used to know it and it's just never happened. My life is so different now."[47] Many veterans found themselves estranged from their spouses. War and absence, said Army Spec. Nicholas Fosholdt, contributed to his divorce six months after returning home. "We just grew apart, being away for so long."[48]

For the mother of a young person who had deployed to Iraq just after high school graduation, the change had been more positive. Directionless before his military service, he now took greater interest in family and community events, reflecting the upswing in community involvement among veterans noted earlier. Deployment, observed another participant of the

Vermont focus group, represented "a new experience for Vermont and the Vermont National Guard and everyone here." The fact that the focus group met regularly while family members were away had provided a source of strength and solidarity. Their comments, however, seemed to confirm the view expressed by a military chaplain that "the whole shape of the family has changed as a result of deployment."[49]

In reconnecting with family and friends, veterans often found it hard to convey the intensity and of what they had experienced. "My frustration coming back is, I go to work and I talk to guys and they don't care," said Sergeant Moriarty, recalling an explosive scene during a ceremony in which his company president and coworkers had gathered to welcome him back. "Somebody will even ask me a question: 'Jeez, do you have any pictures?'" Moriarty continued. "And I will say 'Sure' and I'll take out some pictures and start to show them and they're like, 'Yeah, yeah, yeah,' and I want to grab them by the throat and say, 'You look at my f-ing pictures. You asked me to look at 'em. Okay, I'm not going around showing 'em off to everybody. You asked to look at them. Give me the goddamned respect of looking at my pictures. Do you have any idea of what I've done?"[50]

Even before New Hampshire Guardsman Pink returned to the Granite State, he had been aware that a new normal would be hard to establish. "Every once in a while as we're driving down the road or creeping along in a patrol, I have a recurring epiphany: this is happening and will have a lasting impact on me for the rest of my life."[51] But the full extent of the change foreshadowed would become apparent only as veterans sought to reconnect with families and friends, jobs and pastimes. For some, the reconnecting process would take years, if it happened at all. In fact, mental health professionals themselves comment on the widely varying timing and triggers of the process from one veteran to the next.

A SENSE OF HUMANITY

The challenge of the reentry process, as veterans present it, is to reverse the toll taken by their steady diet of danger and violence in Afghanistan and Iraq on their sense of humanity and well-being. Judging from the interviews, the process of reconnecting has different dynamics, contours, and timing depending on the person involved and their experiences of war. Coming to terms with it all seems to involve finding effective ways of moving past the violence and affirming some sort of new future for themselves.

For most veterans, the process of transitioning back into American society requires relearning basic instincts. "You take a tiger and you put him in the wild, and he's happy," Dax Carpenter observes. "He knows how to hunt. He knows how to do his job to survive. You take him and put him in a cage and part of him dies. Put a military member back into the civilian populace, it kills him, 'cause civilians don't have that high intensity that they're used to." Reflecting on his own attempt to come to terms with both PTSD and TBI following three deployments, Carpenter describes being cycled through a detox center, "almost like a detox center for drug addicts, where you can get re-civilized, where you are around people again, not in a combat situation."[52]

A number of veterans comment on the general dehumanization of the enemy that had taken place over time in both theaters. A case in point is the observation of MP Stephanie Corcoran, noted earlier, about the hate toward the people of Iraq expressed around her. She voiced her revulsion at "racist and ignorant views heard by people expected to promote great things like the rights of life, liberty, and property. I've learned that it's very easy to hate everything about Iraqis if you let yourself."[53] Even Colorado's Sgt. Kelly Dougherty, who criticized the racist elements she perceived in the treatment of Iraqis, particularly women, caught herself expressing hateful sentiments when at heart she believed otherwise.

"You take 150,000 U.S. soldiers out of America and transport them to Iraq for a year," said Sergeant Moriarty, "with absolutely zero training whatsoever about the culture. It doesn't take a shrink to tell you ignorance is one of the first steps toward prejudice."[54] Others suspected something less circumstantial and more inherent in the nature of war. "Every war has got its own little term to dehumanize the other side. And we had 'Gooks' in Vietnam and this war has 'Hajjis,'" observed New Hampshire Guardsman Zach Bazzi, himself an Arabic-speaking American of Lebanese extraction. "The bad guys, or the insurgents, I'm sure they have their own derogatory term towards us. Maybe it's just part of human affairs in war."[55]

The theme that dehumanizing the enemy not only stokes the conflict but also undermines the self-respect of soldiers is elaborated by Stan Goff, an Army paratrooper who served in Vietnam. Drawing a parallel between the contemporary characterization of Iraqis as "ragheads" or "hajjis" and the descriptions in his own day of Vietnamese as "dinks and gooks," he wrote, "When you take away the humanity of another, you kill your own humanity. Do whatever you have to do to survive, however you define survival," he wrote in a November 2003 letter to GIs (including his own son) in Iraq. "But don't surrender your humanity. Not to fit in. Not to prove yourself. Not for an adrenaline rush. Not to lash out when you are angry and frustrated. Not for some ticket-punching fucking military careerist to make his bones on. Especially not for the Bush-Cheney Gas & Oil Consortium."[56]

In Afghanistan and Iraq, many veterans had particular difficulty coming to terms with the violence against children. Upon returning to the United States, some experienced serious difficulties in reconnecting with their own youngsters. Army Specialist Gonzalez, who as a gunner providing escort protection during Operation Iraqi Freedom had been exposed to violence on a daily basis, credits the "critical incident debriefings" held by the Army with having played a positive role. "It's always good to talk to people," he says with reference to the officers, chaplains, and psychologists who were available to him. Upon returning to the States, however, he found that spending time with his family provided the essential key to getting past his anger and allowing love to resurface. "It really helped me out—just being around children." He even arranged employment at a school "where I'm around children all the time."[57]

Some veterans found the transition from toughness to tenderness particularly difficult to negotiate given the prevailing ethos of military culture. Training and discipline put a premium on toughness. "There's tough, and there's Army tough," proclaim the recruiting ads. Army Sgt. Bobby Lee Lisek speaks of the transformation "from green to mean in 120 days."[58] "The armed forces can train you to do things you wouldn't normally do," observed the father of Josh Barber, a thirty-one-year-old veteran of Iraq who haunted by the thought of "going to hell for killing an innocent Iraqi," took his own life. "But they've never been able to train people how to forget."[59]

Processing the soldiering experience is the goal of The Combat Paper Project based in Burlington, Vermont, where veterans use paper made from the pulp of their own uniforms to create cathartic works of art. "The goal," explains the group's website, "is to use art as a means to help veterans reconcile their personal experiences as well as challenge the traditional narrative surrounding service, honor, and the military culture."[60] The fact that the resulting paper also incorporates fragments from the uniforms of veterans from earlier wars underscores the universality of the combat experience and the reintegration challenge. One art critic writes that an exhibit of the group's work "assures that people cannot look the other way from the reality of war. The truths told in these art works," she concludes, "are not just military truths but human truths."[61] The initiative is credited with having assisted in the transition from uniform to pulp, from battlefield to workshop, from warrior to artist.

For many—family and friends as well as veterans—efforts to reclaim a sense of humanity have not had happy endings. "I got my husband back whole physically, and I think his heart is here too," said Stacy Bannerman, "but I'm not sure about his mind. He still checks to see where his weapon is every time we get into a vehicle. Although his body is back, there is a war that rages between us. I am left to deal with the lost years of time, the lost love of my life. I want to talk with my husband about what he's going through, but I don't have the words. Hell, I don't even have the questions. What's the conversational opener to this: 'So you inadvertently killed Iraqi children? How's that going for you?'"[62]

In fact, the struggle of individuals like Carpenter to undo the ravages of PTSD has led some soldiers and health care professionals to question the nomenclature given to the illness. The experience of alarming numbers of soldiers of being "weirded out" or feeling "numbed" upon returning to the States raises a question about the "D" for "disorder" in PTSD. Carpenter's observation that "PTSD comes from people that are in high-stress jobs within the military that have seen more than their fair share [of] combat"[63] seems to be borne out by a body of evidence from the field, as examined in Chapter 10. Perhaps, as some veterans and mental health professionals suggest, the pathology is in the violence rather than in the reactions of veterans to it.

RETURNING TO THE FRAY?

The question posed by some interviewers in the Veterans History Project—"Would you go back to Afghanistan or Iraq?"—elicits responses all over the psychological map. The answers convey a great deal about soldiering in the global war on terror.

A number of veterans, often quite irrespective of their personal experience on the ground, say they would go back "in a heartbeat." "I don't think war is fun or glorious or anything like that," said Army Sgt. Jeremy Lima, "but I am willing to do it again. In fact, I want to do it again. I think the military services are absolutely necessary, especially with the world as it is today." With everyone else taking freedom and leisure for granted, Lima is prepared to put his body again on the line.[64]

Other veterans share the reservations of Michigan Guardsman Spec. Jeffrey Bartling, who lives, he says, in perpetual fear of being redeployed. He describes his deployment to Iraq as "a good experience to do once, but it's not something I would like to do again."[65] A good experience, it seems, was no guarantee that a person would be willing to extend a tour or willingly return for another deployment. The comment of Mike Moriarty of the New Hampshire Guard mentioned earlier deserves recall. "I'm so glad I went. I hated it with a God-awful passion and I will not go back. I have done my part and I feel like it's someone else's turn."[66]

The decision to return to the fray, of course, is not entirely up to veterans themselves. Although they have enlisted in an all-volunteer military, they are subject to involuntary assignments. Their tours of duty in Afghanistan and Iraq could be, and often were, extended beyond their planned duration or contractual obligations through "stop-loss" arrangements or other unexpected events.[67] Those who completed active-duty service and transferred to the inactive Reserves also remained subject to being called up for another tour. As indicated in Chapter 1, an unusually high number of persons have been deployed more than once to Afghanistan or Iraq, some of them returning as many as three or four times.[68]

The reluctance that many soldiers express about returning to the front lines is understandable. More difficult to comprehend is the willingness of significant numbers to go back for another tour. Their readiness to do so reflects both "push" and "pull" factors. The continuing problems of reentry and of finding a new normal exerted something of a gravitational pull back to Afghanistan or Iraq. For some, the reality that "home" is a greater "hell" than the more obvious perils of those theaters lends an additional nudge. In addition, the more difficult the problems of reentry, the more attractive appears a return to the fray. At least on the front lines veterans had a sense of playing an essential and appreciated role on a well-functioning team.

Indeed, among the pull factors for many was the sense that for all of its dangers, deployment had been meaningful—for some, the most successful and rewarding chapter of their lives. Many had surprised themselves at what they were able to accomplish and how well they were able to function under duress. The experience for many was a "confidence builder," observed Specialist Gamblin, "Your boundaries for human tolerance are a lot higher" than you might think. "Some people are thinking, 'That looks really hard and disgusting and I don't think I could ever do that,' but if you have to, you have to. It's all possible."[69]

Many veterans took great satisfaction in how well they had performed in the most difficult of situations. Even battered Sergeant Lisek, whose multiple physical and psychological wounds are described in the following chapter, intimated that he would go back, were he able. "I loved being in the army. I put my men above everything else." He conceded, however, that in his condition, redeploying is a physical impossibility. "I know that my time is done."[70]

Awareness that fellow soldiers are still in harm's way also exerts a definite pull. Capt. Lynn Wagner, pictured in Chapter 10, who served in Iraq for ten months with the Army's 129th Transportation Company, was diagnosed with PTSD after returning from her first tour. Two years later, however, she asked to be redeployed to Iraq. She felt "incredibly guilty" that her brother, with a wife and two young children, was returning for a second tour while she herself, a single woman, was not. She was one of those who would go back "in a heartbeat," she told an interviewer.[71]

That sense of solidarity led many to express willingness to return to their duty stations. In fact, solidarity often overcame any and all lingering doubts. One reporter found that "No matter how the soldiers felt about

Barracks Scene

Jeffrey Lima (AFC2001/001/53039), Photographs (PH06), VHP, AFC, LOC.

Marine Corps Sgt. Jeremy Lima, a Hispanic American, was born in Los Angeles and later moved to Colorado. He served in the Third Marine Aircraft Wing Provisional Security Wing in Iraq, following training at Fort Bliss, Texas and Camp Pendleton, California, and a tour in Okinawa. This photograph from his Veterans History Project collection shows his unit enjoying some down-time.

In response to one interviewer's question, "How do your experiences contribute to your thinking about war and military service?" he answered. "I don't think war is fun or glorious or anything like that but I am willing to do it again. In fact, I want to do it again. I think the military services are absolutely necessary, especially with the world as it is today."

their reasons for being in Iraq, once they got there, they were there for each other."[72] As Specialist Pickett's experience suggests "it's easy to go back over there. There's always the army to fall back on." Easy? Perhaps. However, her earlier experience had included not only withering confrontation with carnage but also a personal incident of sexual harassment.

The extraordinary sense of solidarity that developed under duress in Afghanistan and Iraq was the product, in the words of Marine Lt. Col. Robert C. D'Amico, of "sharing bad times with good people. Sharing a difficult situation has a tendency to bond you for the rest of your life."[73] "Being away from home," explains Air Force Col. William Andrews, "you know you miss your family but you're with another family. The squadron that you're a part of kind of takes on a family atmosphere of its own."[74] "The troops are the only source of support and entertainment," adds Army 1st Lt. Trevor Bradna.[75]

A dramatic example of the strength of those ties is provided by a young sergeant who was injured by a mortar on the final day of her unit's deployment in Iraq. Returning home and enrolling in a federal program, the Wounded Warrior internships, to assist veterans back into the workplace, she told her new colleagues at the State Department—from her wheelchair—how grateful she was that her mishap hadn't occurred earlier in her tour, thereby forcing her to leave while her compatriots were still deployed.[76]

The solidarity that develops among persons exposed to the same risks often seems to override an individual's concern for his or her own safety. An e-mail home by an Air Force psychologist stationed with a medical unit in Qatar explained how solidarity affected individual decision making. "No one ever feels like they are doing enough," wrote Air Force captain Dr. Lisa R. Blackman. "If you are in a safe location, you feel guilty that your friends are getting shot at and you aren't. If you are getting shot at, you feel guilty if your buddy gets hit and you don't. If you get shot at but don't die, you feel guilty that you lived and more guilty if you get to go home and your friends have to stay behind."[77]

The same educational and economic factors that figured in people's original decisions to enlist may also encourage them to reenlist and redeploy. The U.S. Army Information website in January 2009 was advertising "enlistment bonuses of up to $40,000 and 100 percent college tuition reimbursement."[78] Moreover, the deepening economic crisis in the United States tipped the balance for some. In one instance, the manager of an American car dealership in Carmel, New York, a twenty-two-year veteran of the National Guard, extended his tour of duty in Afghanistan, his fourth deployment. "Guardsman would rather face Taliban than U.S. economy," read the headline.[79] In fact, DOD's projections for 2009 anticipated less difficulty than in recent years in meeting retention and recruitment targets.[80]

One reflection that captures the bittersweet elements of the reentry process for many veterans is an entry by 1st Lt. Lee Kelley of the Utah National Guard in his blog, "Wordsmith at War." Returning from a year in Ramadi, Kelley was both grateful and sardonic.

> We wouldn't expect you to alter your lives for us—you're not soldiers. You don't have to travel seven thousand miles to fight a violent and intelligent enemy. We'll take care of that. You just continue to prosper in the middle class, trade up on your economy-size car, install that new subwoofer in the trunk, and yes, the red blouse looks wonderful on you—buy it. . . . But please remain constant as well, because we have changed. . . . Just be Americans with all your ugliness and beauty, your spectacular heights, and your flooded cities, climbing the corporate ladder or standing in the welfare line. Live your lives and enjoy your freedoms. We're not all walking idealist clichés who think your ability to work where you want and vote and associate with whomever you want are hinged completely on our deployment to Iraq. But you know what? Our work here is part of that collective effort through the ages that have granted you those things. So don't forget about us, because we can't forget you."[81]

■ ■ ■

Soldiers in Afghanistan and Iraq experienced major changes, even transformations. Returning to families, friends, and communities has been an uneven and, for some, tortuous process, in part because those on the receiving end have moved on in their lives. Given the traumatic nature of the soldiering experience, veterans have struggled to discover a new normal and to reclaim their often-eroded sense of humanity. The in-theater challenges identified earlier—the foreignness and complexity of the terrain, the difficulty of identifying the enemy, the ruthlessness of the warfare, the tensions between survival and norm-sensitive deportment—have made the reentry process all the more difficult. For many, the struggle is ongoing. The following chapter examines the institutional resources available to them in the process.

—TEN—

Accessing Institutional Resources

The reentry paths for individuals described in the preceding chapter take place within the context of an array of institutions offering health, education, employment, and other services. Already struggling under existing caseloads, the capacity and competence of such institutions are monumentally challenged by the return to the United States of over two million soldiers from Afghanistan and Iraq. This chapter examines the scale of need, the institutions to which veterans turn for assistance, and the extent to which the system is proving able to expand to meet the heavy demand.

WELCOME TO THE BUREAUCRACY

Most veterans of the Global War on Terror return home intent on picking up where they left off and getting on with their lives. Whether retiring, continuing in active-duty status, or resuming post-deployment lives as members of the National Guard or Reserves, they seek out the institutional resources available to them. For treatment of health issues, many turned to their Tricare insurance. For those intent on pursuing educational goals—some in new areas spurred by their recent experience—the provisions of the GI Bill, with enhanced benefits after August 2009, beckon. Veterans returning to private sector employment count on employers to reinstate them in their jobs.

Some veterans express satisfaction at the benefits and services received. When Army 1st Sgt. Gregory Mayfield returned, he had already made use in theater of a combat stress hospital to help deal with sleeping and emotional problems. "You need to learn to relax," he was told. "Man, how do you expect anyone to relax?" he countered. "In a place where you get rocketed and mortared very frequently and you're so attuned to being switched on, you can't just flip the switch off. I think the first time I started relaxing is when we got back to Kuwait," and he continued the process back in the States. "I knew I was messed up. The things that I did and the things that I saw pushed me over the edge. But I was wise enough to know that I needed to go and talk to someone." He sought out and received help. With reference to his PTSD in particular, Mayfield said, "The fact that they have people dedicated to just focusing solely on it now is good testament to the concern at the command level of taking care of the troops' welfare." [1]

Frustration and anger, however, were more typical reactions among veterans upon reentry. The troops were particularly incensed by conditions such as those at the Walter Reed Army Medical Center in northwest Washington, D.C., disclosed in a series of articles by two *Washington Post* reporters in early 2007. Sgt. Terrell Spencer, injured in Iraq, sounded off about "guys at Walter Reed who lost half their brains being made to scrub toilets with toothbrushes and crap. They're living mold-infested in rats. Those guys can't even use the bathroom on their own and they're treating them like asses. What chance they're gonna take care of me? All I did was break my neck. That's nothing compared to these guys. These guys need help and they can't get it." Spencer was critical as well of the living conditions, both before deployment and after returning, at Fort Dix.[2]

Sgt. Bobby Lee Lisek, an infantry squad leader in Iraq, returned with major wounds from having "been blowed up about eighty times." He recalled "waking up at Walter Reed" a month after being medevaced from the frontlines. "I still thought I was in Iraq." His wife and (by telephone) his mother filled in some of the details for the interviewer. His condition included major wounds to his skull, shattered bones in his extremities, a prosthetic replacement for one arm, permanent damage to his sight and hearing, and PTSD and TBI (traumatic brain injury). He has gone through some two dozen operations in Iraq, Germany, and the United States.

Citing the quality of nursing care and his difficulties in dealing with the medical system, Lisek described Walter Reed as "a horrible place." His family agreed. Lisek's father, who had returned from Vietnam with major medical issues, had experienced similar problems with treatment and post-combat disability pay. When Lisek learned one day that President Bush was making the rounds at Walter Reed to bestow service awards, he said, "Fuck President Bush. He ain't pinning my Purple Heart on me. My company commander and battalion commander will." He considered it a victory of sorts that the president "never came in my room."[3]

Veterans express particular frustration that, despite the personal inconvenience and mortal risks they had assumed on behalf of their country, the institutional uptake on their needs was neither prompt nor seamless. "Don't join the army because you think you owe America" Lisek advised, "because America won't take care of you when you come back all jacked up."[4] Many veterans sense a bitter irony: In what seemed would eventually become a trillion-dollar war, the department charged with their welfare would nickel-and-dime their needs.

Based on personal experience, "I can honestly say without a doubt," lamented Sgt. Dax Carpenter, the Arkansas Marine who served in both Afghanistan and Iraq, "that mental health within the military units is extremely lacking. I fought for two years all the way to Washington, D.C., to get the 40 percent disability rating from the Marine Corps so they'd put me on a temporary retired list." What he felt should have happened was quite different. "It should've been, 'OK, you're hurting. We see that. You've done more than your fair share on it. Here's your benefits and your family's benefits. You have a nice day, sir, and if you need anything, don't hesitate to call.' But it took those two years, a push from Washington, D.C., and they still weren't gonna give me enough to medically retire me."[5]

The experience of veterans returning to Fort Drum in upstate New York suggests that the problems of individuals such as Lisek and Carpenter may not be exceptional. "Of all U.S. Army divisions," observes one study, "the 10th Mountain Division, based at Fort Drum, New York, has been the most affected by our country's crushing recent deployment cycle. Since September 11, 2001, the 2nd Brigade Combat team is the most deployed brigade in the Army, having recently completed its fourth tour." Deployed for a total of forty months since 9/11 with less than the prescribed time between deployments, the Brigade has had 52 members killed in action, 270 wounded, and 2 missing. Notwithstanding the unit's almost continuous immersion in active combat and thus its ostensible need for mental health services, however, recent returnees have had to wait "up to two months before a single appointment can be scheduled."[6]

The frustrations of returnees have not been solely in the health sector. Third Class Petty Officer Philip Thomas, who served from 2001 to 2005 in Iraq, had similar frustrations upon reentry. Shifting upon return from active duty to the Reserves, Thomas waited six months for his final paycheck. Anxious to become credentialed as an electrician, he enrolled in school at the first available moment. His zeal outran the bureaucratic machinery, however, and, his school wouldn't let him enter his second semester until it had received the Navy's delayed payment for the first. "Everything with the Navy is a hassle," he concluded.[7]

Some veterans linked such problems to the existence of two massive government bureaucracies, the Department of Defense and the Department of Veterans Affairs, and the difficulties of interagency coordination. Others suspected a certain political animus behind the bureaucratic runaround. "On several occasions," observed [Army] Capt. Marc A. Giammatteo, an Iraq veteran who served on the Dole-Shalala commission reviewing the response of the bureaucracy to health care needs, "I, and others I have spoken to, felt that we were being judged as if we chose our nation's foreign policy and, as a result, received little if any assistance."[8]

Struggling with emotional problems following her return from Iraq, Army Spec. Nicole Ferretti sought help from a DVA counselor. Eight sessions were originally planned. However, the counselor stopped after seven, having failed, Ferretti said, to get proper Tricare authorization. "I would have continued had she not made that error and tried to impose the fees on me, but it was too difficult for me to start over with someone new." She found the costs of continuing Tricare coverage prohibitive in relation to the benefits received and opted out, arranging for ongoing care at her own expense. In short, she said, "the Army hasn't covered much."

Ferretti, a Brazilian national, also raised the issue of expedited citizenship that figured in the hopes of a significant number of enlistees. She had lived in the United States since age six and placed her life in harm's way in Iraq on behalf of her adopted land. "But I would certainly hope," she said, "that I have my citizenship before I get sent off somewhere else." With the process often delayed, she regretted that she hadn't initiated it herself rather than leaving it to the military.[9]

SYSTEM UNDER DURESS

The institutional apparatus for responding to veterans returning from Afghanistan and Iraq has given every indication of being unprepared and overwhelmed by the scale of the need. The New Hampshire experience serves as something of a microcosm of the situation nationally.

In early 2005, New Hampshire received some 800 soldiers in its National Guard unit back from Iraq. The suicide of David Guindon, one of five earlier returnees, on his first day back had alerted Guard officials to the life-and-death issues involved. "We started to realize that there was more to this than we thought," recalled Col. Deborah Carter, the New Hampshire National Guard's human resources director.[10] The focus shifted overnight from ordering bunting for welcome home ceremonies to identifying needs among returning Guard personnel, facilitating immediate access to support networks, and coordinating and expanding available services. "The complexity of going from warrior to citizen in the course of just a few days," recalled Nancy Rollins, director of the New Hampshire Division of Community-based Services of the Department of Health and Human Services, called for an all-hands-on-deck approach.[11]

One crucial decision by Guard officials in New Hampshire proved to be their insistence that the standard debriefing for soldiers en masse be followed up by one-on-one counseling sessions for each returnee. Officials were stunned by the results. Of the roughly 800 returnees, 48 required immediate assistance, 398 requested a follow-up phone call during the first month, and 84 had sought help before the first year was out. In all, some 530 of the 800 soldiers availed themselves of mental health services at one point or another. Studying the data compiled, Colonel Carter identified a pattern. The greater an individual's exposure to combat, the more likely the need for mental health services and support.[12]

Full Battle Rattle

Gregory Marinich (AFC2001/001/54920), Photographs (PH01), VHP, AFC, LOC.

As a child, Lynn Wagner dreamed about being in the Army. When she enlisted in the Army Reserves in 1996 at age twenty-two, she was carrying on a family tradition of military service and also, thanks to an enlistment bonus, helping fund her college education. As a student with a strong interest in science, she considered herself a "soldier-scientist": someone who—armed with the Ph.D. she wishes to pursue—would someday help protect her fellow soldiers.

Her initial assignment was with the 129th Transportation Company, which specialized in transporting M1 Abrams tanks and other heavy tracked and wheeled vehicles using the Heavy Equipment Transporter System (HETS). In November 2003, slated to go to Iraq

Full Battle Rattle continued

with the 349th Chemical Company, she was deployed instead as a member of the 737th Transportation Company, which was short-staffed.

Following three months in Kuwait, she spent nine months in Iraq, where she drove large unarmored tanker trucks filled with highly flammable fuel to military bases throughout Iraq. She had to steer her tanker through IEDs and small arms fire attacks launched from the median strip. The experience took its toll. "I was traumatized by the things that I saw and had to do in Iraq," she says. Upon returning to the States, she was diagnosed with PTSD and underwent two years of counseling. She came to realize that she was "not as mentally healthy as [she] thought." She credits people in her unit in Iraq and at the VA for helping her through the process. "It's all about trying to feel safe," she tells an interviewer gamely.

"Out of the close to five thousand pictures I have [from] Iraq," she says, "this is my favorite. I think the reason is because I can look at it and it brings me right back. Hardly a minute goes by that I don't think about Iraq." Fellow soldier, Spec. Chris Slater took the photograph on Christmas Day 2004, en route to Baghdad International Airport. "The photo shows me in 'full battle rattle,' as we say. I'll always have a piece of Iraq in me," she comments. Even given her harrowing experiences and her PTSD, "The Army is one of the best things that has happened to me."

She received a number of medals, including the Army Commendation Medal, the Army Achievement Medal, the Global War on Terror Expeditionary Medal, the Global War on Terror Service Medal, and the Iraq Service Medal. She is currently employed in the office of the Army Surgeon General at the Pentagon.

In New Hampshire, the needs discovered in one-on-one debriefings were so extensive that the New Hampshire Guard's commanding officers, who (along with soldiers' families) had originally fiercely resisted delaying reunions with families by an extra day or two, ended by expressing gratitude for mandatory individualized screenings. Mandating individual sessions seemed particularly essential to National Guard officials inasmuch as Guard personnel, unlike active-duty forces, quickly disperse, many to communities lacking adequate mental health services. How many families would pick up the warning signs of serious emotional problems when they first appeared? How many rural health practitioners would be familiar with PTSD or knowledgeable about the experiences that had made the condition so prevalent among returning veterans? "My family doctor from childhood tried to help with meds and treatment, but [dealing with] veterans was a completely new thing for him," said Jennifer Pacanowski, an Iraq veteran whose PTSD waited two and a half years to be diagnosed and then waited another nine months for treatment charges to be reimbursed.[13] "The nature of the National Guard itself," observed one New Hampshire social service provider, "involves one person here, one person there."

The return of active-duty contingents confirmed the correlation established by the New Hampshire Guard authorities. The 4th Combat Brigade, stationed at Fort Carson, Colorado, offers a case in point. In fierce fighting in places such as Fallujah and Ramadi, Baghdad and Sadr City, the 3,500-strong brigade experienced 113 deaths, with hundreds more wounded. One therapist who treated soldiers upon their return to Fort Carson commented, "It got to the point I stopped asking if they have deployed, and started asking how many times they have deployed." Over a three-year period, nine current or former Brigade members were charged with killings. Families of returning veterans also experienced higher levels of domestic violence.[14] Disturbed by such incidents, an Army task force was established in 2008 to search for explanations.[15]

The intensive screening and follow-up approach implemented in New Hampshire served as a model for other state National Guard units and for the active-duty military. In late 2008, the director of health services at the Army's Fort Campbell in Kentucky noted that "for the first time, every soldier returning home will have an individual meeting with a behavioral health specialist and then go through a second such session ninety days to 120 days later."[16]

Annual reviews by a DOD Mental Health Advisory Team (MHAT) beginning in early 2003 serve as a barometer of the impacts of exposure in Afghanistan and Iraq on U.S. military personnel. The fourth MHAT report, based on Operation Iraqi Freedom surveys conducted in mid-2006 and released in November 2006, concluded, "the level of combat is the main determinant of a Soldier's or Marine's mental health status." Soldiers who had deployed more than once reported higher acute stress levels. "Only five percent of soldiers reported taking in-theater Rest and Relaxation, even though the average time deployed was nine months." MHAT-IV recommended more extended time between deployments, "Battlemind Warrior Resiliency Training" before deployment, and more intensive positioning of mental health resources.[17]

A report of the DOD Task Force on Mental Health in mid-2007, noted in Chapter 1, identified the nationwide universe of need. The report analyzed data from a Post-Deployment Health Reassessment, administered to veterans 90 to 120 days following their return from the Afghanistan and Iraq theaters. The survey found that "38 percent of Soldiers and 31 percent of Marines report psychological symptoms. Among members of the National Guard, the figure rises to 49 percent. . . . Further, psychological concerns are significantly higher among those with repeated deployments, a growing cohort."[18]

The fifth MHAT report, released in March 2008 and based on data collected in 2007, confirmed the findings of earlier studies—those who deployed three and four times demonstrated higher stress levels than those deployed once or twice—and provided comparisons between the two theaters. The levels of combat exposure in Afghanistan had increased while those in Iraq had decreased. Morale had improved among the troops in Iraq from 2006 to 2007; there was a higher incidence of mental health problems in Afghanistan in 2007 than in 2005. Yet the rates of stress in the two theaters were generally comparable. While some officials described the latest findings as "a 'good news' story," the data themselves remained sobering.[19]

New Hampshire authorities also found a link between reentry and homelessness, a major problem among veterans across the nation. "On any given night," Leslie Kaufman of the *New York Times* wrote about veterans from America's wars, "a virtual army of one hundred and fifty thousand veterans are homeless across the nation, including an estimated twelve hundred in New York City."[20] Veterans for America, which placed the total of homeless veterans at just under 200,000 in Fiscal Year 2006, has noted that "Vets from Afghanistan and Iraq appear to be seeking out mental health services at higher rates than vets from other conflicts." The director of a San Diego vet center remarked in late 2007, "We anticipate that it's going to be a tsunami."[21] The Veterans for America's *Survival Guide* for veterans counsels, "If you are moving around, ask to receive mail and phone calls for the short term at a local drop-in center, shelter, the VA regional office or clinic, local veterans' service organization, or your church."[22]

"No one keeps track of how many of the troops who have been deployed to Iraq or Afghanistan since 2001 are homeless," noted the *Boston Globe*'s Anna Badken in mid-2007. But there has been a significant change since the days of reentry following Vietnam. She continued: "The approximately seventy thousand veterans of the war in Vietnam who became homeless usually spent between five and ten years trying to re-adjust to civilian life before winding up in the streets. Veterans of today's wars who become homeless end up with no place to live within eighteen months after they return from war."[23] Iraq and Afghanistan Veterans of America urged the Obama administration in its first hundred days to give priority to the needs of homeless veterans from Afghanistan and Iraq, of whom it said there were already 2,000.[24] Veterans for Common Sense linked homelessness to delays in federal processing of veterans' disability benefit requests.[25]

Responding to massive need for health and social services has been complicated by a shortage of facilities and health care personnel. One DVA official noted that a nationwide shrinkage in medical infrastructure following the end of the Cold War—he himself had seen a reduction from 129 to 79 facilities during the years 1987–1995—meant that Guard personnel and others had fewer treatment options and had to travel greater distances to access them. In most rural states, he said, soldiers had access to only a single DVA facility. As the conflicts proceeded, however, the DVA's budget for mental health matters, including PTSD, was significantly increased and additional mental health clinicians were hired.[26]

The experience of Marine Sgt. Luis Almaguer (whose photograph appears in Chapter 4) illustrates the problems that some have faced. Returning from Iraq with eighty percent disabilities, he moved his family first from his home in the small town of Del Rio, Texas, along the Rio Grande River (population 36,000) to San Antonio, two and a half hours away, to be closer a major veterans facility. From San Antonio, he traveled for extended treatments to San Diego, where TBI treatments are administered at Camp Pendleton's Defense and Veterans Brain Injury Concussion Clinic and at the Navy Medical Center in San Diego.

A number of well-publicized false starts undermined veterans' confidence in the institutional reentry process. The suspicion that veterans were getting the run-around seemed confirmed by an e-mail to staff from a VA team leader in Temple, Texas, in May 2008. "Given that we are having more and more compensation-seeking veterans," wrote Norma J. Perez, a PTSD program coordinator in an internal memo, "I'd like to suggest that you refrain from giving a diagnosis of PTSD straight out" and consider instead "a diagnosis of Adjustment Disorder." The suggestion was immediately rejected by the national DVA head as representing the misguided view of "a single staff member, out of the VA's two hundred and thirty thousand employees, in a single medical facility."[27]

In January 2008, Army officials reportedly instructed the DVA employees not to help returning veterans, as they had in the past, with the preparation of paperwork necessary to process health care and disability payments. One veteran described his feeling of being "tossed aside like a worn-out pair of boots."[28] Delays in receiving prompt and quality medical and mental health treatment have been a recurring problem. In a number of highly publicized incidents, veterans seeking help have been rebuffed or put on a waiting list. "Told to Wait, a Marine Dies: VA Care in Spotlight after Iraq War Veteran's Suicide," read one *Boston Globe* headline in February 2007.[29]

A series of reports on National Public Radio beginning in December 2006 highlighted incidents in which veterans were returned to Iraq and Afghanistan before their medical and psychological problems had been fully addressed. Sgt. Metz Duites, who served in Iraq for a year and one of whose photos appear in Chapter 6, required surgery for a torn rotator cuff, which the DVA arranged. However, the Army, unaware of an injury that rendered him no longer able to throw a grenade, sent him back to Iraq.[30] Some veterans came to believe that the imperative to get them suited up and redeployed in the global war on terror was not matched by a commitment to see that their needs were met upon returning.[31]

Veterans were also outraged by a change in regulations, instituted by the Bush administration in March 2008, which narrowed the injuries qualifying for reimbursable treatment to only those sustained directly in combat. The Disabled American Veterans condemned the change as embodying a "shocking level of disrespect for those who stood in harm's way."[32] Some suspected DVA medical personnel of attributing wounds to preexisting conditions as a device for limiting the scope of insurance coverage.

The two needs among returning veterans that have caused greatest concern in terms of incidence, on the one hand, and the lack of institutional capacity, on the other, have been the "signature injuries" of the wars in Afghanistan and Iraq: PTSD and TBI. A 2008 study entitled "Invisible Wounds of War" by the RAND Corporation concluded that an estimated

300,000 service personnel from Iraq and Afghanistan were suffering from PTSD or major depression, an estimated 320,000 from TBI. The RAND report found that only about half of those affected had sought help, with about half receiving "minimally adequate treatment."[33] "We've come a long way," said one DOD official in commenting on the report, "but we still have a long way to go."[34]

Mental health professionals are bracing for a major upsurge in demand for PTSD services and in the overall costs of providing them. Although the DVA had treated more than 52,000 Iraq veterans for PTSD as of mid-2007, "the greatest effect of those mental health issues has yet to be experienced," according to *Medscape Medical News*. Estimates of the cost of treating the identified number of 300,000 PTSD cases over the lifetimes of those involved are placed at some $660 billion.[35] PTSD is also linked to a doubling in recent years in the suicide rate among active-duty personnel returning from Afghanistan and Iraq.[36]

The TBI outlook is also daunting. Reflecting in particular the status of roadside bombs as the weapon of choice of the insurgents, soldiers in Iraq and Afghanistan are in greater danger of sustaining TBI than their predecessors in other recent conflicts. "The IEDs have added a new dimension to battlefield injuries," observes Ronald Glasser of the *Washington Post*. "Wounds and even deaths among the troops who have no external signs of trauma but whose brain has been seriously damaged."[37] The Dole-Shalala commission reported 2,726 TBI cases among those who had served in Iraq.[38]

Experts are cautious in quantifying the TBI numbers of such injuries since some 70 percent are not identified as such through normal magnetic resonance imagery screening.[39] In addition, the late onset nature of TBI means that for some of those affected, symptoms do not manifest themselves until years after an injury was sustained. "The Department of Veterans Affairs is now planning for the large influx of veterans with TBIs from the current conflicts who will need continuing care during the coming years," writes one of the officials involved. "These patients because of the nature of their brain injuries can be the ones at highest risk of falling through the cracks."[40]

The gravity of the psychological impact of the wars in Afghanistan and Iraq on those involved has been flagged in alarming terms by DVA officials such as Dr. Matthew J. Friedman. He has concluded that "most people who have survived this experience will be changed by it, whether crossing some psychiatric threshold or not." In his judgment, "the wars in Afghanistan and Iraq are likely to produce a new generation of veterans with chronic mental health problems associated with participation in combat."[41]

In a strange twist, fresh wounds from the global war on terror have brought new attention to still-festering wounds from Vietnam. Dr. Gonzalo Vera, chief of mental health programs at the VA hospital in Northampton, Massachusetts, has noted that "of his caseload of 120 psychiatric patients who have fought predominantly in Vietnam but also in the Gulf War and elsewhere, 'virtually every single patient has been affected by the Iraq war and has experienced a retriggering of trauma.'"[42] Global War on Terror veterans express particular appreciation for the support of other veterans, whether from earlier conflicts or from Afghanistan and Iraq.

STEPS FORWARD

Dissatisfaction with the inadequacies of the institutional system for reentry spiked following the *Washington Post* exposé in early 2007 on conditions at the Walter Reed Army Medical Center. The uproar led to the firing of the commander of Walter Reed, resignation of the secretary of the Army, and creation by President Bush on March 8 of a Commission on Care for America's Returning Wounded Warriors. Following hearings and testimony from more than 1,700 veterans, the commission, headed by former Senator Bob Dole and former Health and Human Services Secretary Donna Shalala, issued a report entitled "Serve, Support, and Simplify."

In what it termed a "bold blueprint for action," the commission made six recommendations seeking "to ensure that those who have served in Iraq and Afghanistan are able to successfully transition back to civilian life or active duty service." The recommendations included a complete restructuring of disability determination and compensation systems, the development of individualized patient-centered recovery plans, and aggressive prevention and treatment of PTSD and TBI. Acknowledging the systemic shortcomings such as those flagged by individual veterans, Shalala commented on unveiling the report: "The system should work for the patient, instead of the patient working for the system."[43]

Once again, states played an innovative role. New Hampshire early on had formed an interagency task force that conducted a statewide survey of social services. It concluded that some 80 percent of the services needed already existed; the remaining 20 percent would have to be devised or adapted. The process also sought to anticipate future needs rather than waiting for them to materialize. Soldiers readying themselves for future deployment were encouraged, by New Hampshire social service guidelines, to think in terms of "your boots, your belt, your shirt—and your pre-deployment social worker." One DOD-funded New Hampshire initiative, the Joint Family Support Assistance Program, involves meeting with individual soldiers and families at every stage of the process, from predeployment to reentry. In 2008, the legislature created a commission, originally for three months but later extended to two years, to coordinate the statewide effort.[44]

> The Commission acknowledges the heroic services veterans from Iraq and Afghanistan have rendered to our country, and cannot state strongly enough the obligation our nation and New Hampshire owes to those men and women who have been injured as a result of their service. Through extensive meetings and presentations, the Commission has learned that the hidden injuries of combat, including post-traumatic stress disorder and traumatic brain injury, can be severe and lifelong, and require a comprehensive, coordinated, and funded system of services and supports. While there are promising new and existing programs to assist veterans with TBI and PTSD, and their families, in general resources are fragmented. Some veterans don't know about, and have trouble accessing, treatment and services, and some veterans fall through the cracks.
>
> —*Interim Report, Commission on PTSD and TBI**

---

* State of New Hampshire, Commission on PTSD and TBI, Interim Report, November 28, 2008

The state of Minnesota, which has also contributed large numbers of National Guard troops to the conflicts in Afghanistan and Iraq, has also played a lead institutional role with its Beyond the Yellow Ribbon program. This, too, is an interagency effort in which government at every level joins with private agencies to assist newly returned Guard members in the reentry process. Focusing on the period after yellow ribbons expressing solidarity with the troops have been taken down, the program reconvenes veterans at regular thirty-day intervals to check on such concerns as mental health, anger management, domestic relations, and employment. Having assisted several thousand veterans throughout the state since it was launched in 2005, the Minnesota program is poised to become a national undertaking.[45]

A similar effort has been initiated in New York State, home to unusually large numbers of veterans from Afghanistan and Iraq, to assess their needs and the capacity of existing institutions to meet them. Underwritten by the New York State Health Foundation, the undertaking seeks to provide a more detailed analysis of a situation in which "returning veterans who do not receive timely and appropriate care for mental health issues seem to be at risk for chronic illness, substance use issues, family life challenges, domestic violence, unemployment, homelessness, and even suicide."[46]

Comparable initiatives are also taking shape at the national level. A provision in the FY08 National Defense Authorization Act—one in which then-Senator Barack Obama played a lead role—mandates a nationwide assessment of the needs of soldiers who have served in Afghanistan and Iraq, and the needs of their families. The survey will be conducted by the Institute of Medicine of the National Academies, with the initial hearings conducted in February 2009. Also at the federal level, passage of the Dignity for Wounded Warriors Act of 2008 increases the amount of treatment provided for medical needs related to military service.

The reintegration challenge is not simply to coordinate and expand existing programs but also to sensitize people and institutions to the special situations of returning veterans and their families. Thus, teachers and administrators in public and private schools needed to be more sensitive to the special situations of children in military families. Classroom teachers needed to be alert to the potential damage to children of deployed parents from off-hand comments or casual discussions about the global war on terror or from insistence on homework when home situations conspired against its completion. State agency personnel also had some learning to do. A military chaplain in Vermont described an incident in which a newly returned veteran driving down an interstate highway was confronted by a state policeman who jumped out from behind an overpass, radar gun poised. The veteran's instinct was to take evasive action à la Iraq, where overpasses and bridges were a favorite hiding place for insurgents and explosives. The incident was incorporated into a statewide police training program.

Reemployment of returning veterans was also a major challenge. In New Hampshire, "35 percent or more of all the reserve military personnel are employed as civilians in local, state, and federal government agencies."[47] The group included public safety personnel such as state and local law enforcement officials, emergency medical technicians, firefighters, corrections personnel, educators from kindergarten through college, and a sitting judge. Some departments were more affected by the post-9/11 call-ups than others. The state corrections department had more than fifty-five of its employees deployed, forty-five of them at the same time.[48]

The remaining 65 percent of New Hampshire Guard troops and reservists were employed in private sector jobs. The most difficult reentries were often the self-employed, a numerous category given the structure of the state's rural economy. Private employers of a certain size as well as government agencies are legally obligated to release employees for military service and to reemploy them after their return. From the employer's vantage point, particularly in smaller offices and enterprises, the challenge was both to maintain productivity while employees were absent and to re-engage them once they reappeared. Younger enlistees were easier to accommodate than people further along in their careers. Some state agencies found it difficult to "back-fill" jobs while regular employees were deployed, even though their absences were only temporary.[49] Some veterans have taken employers to court in order win their jobs back.[50]

Throughout the nation, the preparedness of the penal system at various levels to deal with returning veterans is also being tested. Eric Heath, an Army 2nd Class Petty Officer who accompanied American soldiers accused of crimes and facing dishonorable discharges and jail time back to the

United States, had his doubts. "The prisons back in the United States have no concept of what's going on in Iraq and Kuwait and Afghanistan," he observed. When U.S. soldiers were detained in military facilities overseas, guards like himself realized that "they've been in combat stress" and thus avoided yelling and screaming at them. Many prison officials back in the United States, by contrast, will scream at them and make them stand at "parade rest." Add to this treatment the veteran's realization that "I'm no longer a soldier—I'm an embarrassment to the country," and the stage is set for major problems.[51]

With each contingent returning from Afghanistan or Iraq, the adequacy of the response of the system's institutions is tested anew. In late 2008, 15,000 soldiers in the Army's 101st Airborne Division returned to Fort Campbell, Kentucky, many from their third or fourth deployment. Uneasy about the anticipated demand for reentry services, the vice chief of staff of the Army, Gen. Peter Chiarelli conceded, "I don't know what to expect. I don't think anybody knows." Chiarelli issued an urgent call for additional counselors.[52]

"The government does not want to face the lifelong legacy of combat in its individual, community, financial, and other dimensions," said Jay Craven, whose documentary, *After The Fog,* provides compelling commentary by soldiers on their experiences from World War II through the global war on terror. "Military service confers on combat soldiers a lifelong sentence," Craven observed. In the case of veterans from Afghanistan and Iraq, the data suggest, that sentence is proving particularly harsh and resistant to commutation.[53]

I oftentimes say being commander in chief of the military is the thing I'll miss most. Coming here to Walter Reed is a reminder of why I'll miss it.

—President George W. Bush, on his final trip to Walter Reed Army Medical Center[*]

---

* Dan Eggan, "Bush Visits Injured Soldiers at Walter Reed," Washington Post, December 23, 2008, A 04.

The accession to power of the Obama administration in January 2009 offered an occasion for stocktaking on the institutional response to date. Veterans groups took the opportunity to present recommendations for the future. As an example, the agenda recommended by Iraq and Afghanistan Veterans of America for the first hundred days of the new administration identified four priority areas. Veterans should be given precedence in the economic stimulus package, including "shovel-ready projects like repairing veterans' hospitals and cemeteries." The DVA budget should be advance-funded to eliminate the hassle and indignity of fighting for hospital and clinic funding. Improvements in educational benefits slated to take effect in mid-2009 should be expedited by giving the bureaucracy a "kick in the pants." Finally, mental health needs should be aggressively addressed, in part by attracting more psychiatrists and psychologists into the Defense and Veterans departments.[54]

■ ■ ■

In sum, progress is being made in identifying veterans' needs and in expanding their access to institutional resources. However, a "tsunami of need," both current and future, is still far outrunning efforts of the system to respond, and by all projections will continue to do so.[55]

From time to time, gaps in the reentry process are illuminated by reminders of the continuing need of veterans of the Global War on Terror. Reminders come in very particularistic forms: a hometown son or daughter killed in action, a spouse's efforts to arrange for a veteran's rehabilitation, a suicide or other crime of violence by a returnee, graduation of a veteran made possible by the improved GI Bill, the latest incident at a local VA hospital or vet center of a soldier's rehabilitation or exclusion, action by a college president to open up undergraduate education to newly returned Afghan or Iraq veterans, the release of a new state or federal study, and so on.

Individual breakthroughs notwithstanding, few would maintain that the nation has fully succeeded in mobilizing the institutional resources—financial or professional, short or long term—to meet the complex, costly, and ongoing needs of the generation of veterans that loom on the horizon. This is one of the major concerns articulated by the voices of the veterans themselves, to which we now turn.

— ELEVEN —

The Global War on Terror and Earlier Wars

The question in the Veterans History Project protocol, "How did your experiences contribute to your thinking about war and military service?" encourages interviewees to reflect on their soldiering in the broader context of American history. Indeed, a fair number of them share their views about how the global war on terror compares and contrasts with earlier conflicts. Their views are shaped by family traditions of military service, by the histories of the individual services and units with which they are affiliated, and by their own earlier military experience. In a broad sense, their soldiering is of a piece with the military service of their predecessors.

Reflecting on their experience in Afghanistan and Iraq, veterans identify differences that set the current conflicts apart from earlier wars. Yet commonalities also emerge. This chapter draws together comments from interviews about soldiering then and now. The narrative offers not a tightly woven presentation of U.S. military history, but rather a compilation of observations that strike veterans as significant.

DISCONTINUITIES

Veterans of Afghanistan and Iraq highlight a variety of ways in which those wars were significantly different from earlier conflicts. These include the existence of an all-volunteer military, changes in communications, developments in military strategy and tactics, difficulties in identifying the enemy, and progress in battlefield medicine. Veterans also underscore specific contrasts such as the welcome home they received and the reception accorded their Vietnam War counterparts.

One item of recurring comment concerns the differences between the all-volunteer force deployed to Afghanistan and Iraq and the armed forces conscripted for earlier wars. Although the U.S. volunteer military still uses involuntary call-ups and stop-loss extensions of deployments, the fact that all of the men and women who have served in these conflicts have voluntarily chosen the armed forces is seen as making a huge difference, both symbolic and practical. This is the case even though some did not envision an assignment in a global war on terror at the point of enlisting. Like it or not, "We all signed up for this," Navy Cdr. Mark S. Kirk points out.[1]

Lt. Col. Jude Ferran, who served with the 11th Armored Cavalry Regiment, saw the building of an all-volunteer Army, begun in the aftermath of Vietnam and continuing through the Reagan years, as having produced a more highly skilled, motivated, and professional fighting force.[2] As members of an all-volunteer force, soldiers had the satisfaction of knowing that they were making a difference, said Marine Col. Benjamin Braden. That was, after all, why many had enlisted—and, in some cases, reenlisted.[3] Unlike Vietnam, where individuals were rotated in and out, Army Capt. Ralan Hill pointed out, the use of stop-loss arrangements made for greater unit cohesion (although few people were enthusiastic about having their tours extended).[4]

Yet the absence of conscription, in the view of some, had a downside as well. "I don't fuckin' believe for one moment," said Sgt. Jeremy Lima, "that the Marines or veterans of World War I or World War II ever said, 'We are going to go to Japan to kick Japanese ass or Germany to kick German ass in the name of freedom.' They did it because they were drafted. They wanted to come home to their families. They did what they had to do. Now that there is not a draft today, no one is willing to defend the things that they love. They just bad-mouth it. That's why I'm willing," he said, "to serve and then to extend my service."[5] Lima and others are personally committed to avoiding a situation in which "they gave a war and nobody came."

Indeed, some veterans fear that, in the absence of a draft, the armed forces would be hard-pressed to meet recruiting targets, whether for Afghanistan and Iraq or for the conflicts of the future. "After three decades, our national experiment with an all-volunteer force has foundered during its first encounter with combat operations that last for an extended period of time," wrote Maj. Gen. Walter L. Stewart Jr. (retired). The U.S. force, he continued, "relies on fewer and fewer to bear the blood burdens of defense, absolves the many of any fiscal, physical, or mental hardships, and, in a dawning age of asymmetric, non-state and ascendant-state warfare, denies human power in favor of a near mystical belief in technology." The prompt reinstatement of conscription, he believes, is indispensable in safeguarding the nation's future in a hostile world.[6]

A second difference between Afghanistan and Iraq and earlier American conflicts is the revolution in communications. As a result of greater availability of information, observed Army 1st Sgt. Paul Mayfield, "we are probably the most informed military that has ever fought in a war. The average soldier is probably a little more educated and little smarter. We live in the information age."[7] As for military communications specifically, said Col. Braden, the manual typewriters and typists of yesteryear have given way to laptop computers and communications specialists with more advanced and specialized skill sets.[8]

"The difference between me and a person who served in Vietnam," explained Navy Petty Officer 2nd Class Samuel Main, "is that he didn't have twenty-four-hour coverage. Twenty-four hours a day, I can watch it. I can know what's going on there. For me to get there and not know what to expect would be pure ignorance on my part. This is the information age. I can look online and find out how many guys died today; how they died; where the battle's at, what political scene is there. It's all online! Everything is available if you want to know it, and you should know it if you're going. That's part of being an adult."[9]

"We are completely connected by e-mail" with family and friends back home, observed Commander Kirk of his time in Iraq. "The distance and separation of the planet was dramatically contracted from the isolation that veterans of previous wars went through."[10] Army Sgt. Metz Duites describes the back-and-forth by telephone and text-messaging as his wife approached childbirth. He could hear the "commotion" in the delivery room, he recalls, as her doctors discussed and then performed a Caesarian.[11] The connectedness most veterans enjoyed with families and friends may have diverted their concentration and raised potential security issues. On balance, however, those liabilities were far outweighed by the advantages realized in terms of morale, staying in touch with family, and easier reentry.

Some veterans witnessed the communications revolutions in the course of their own deployments. Larry Bond, a veteran who had served as an Army sergeant during the Cold War from 1976 to 1983, returned to the National Guard ranks in 1995, deploying to Iraq in 2003–2004. Years ago, he recalls, it was hard for soldiers to stay in contact with their families. In Iraq, by contrast, everyone had cell phones and there were no long queues waiting to use the landlines.[12]

As recently as Desert Storm and Desert Shield, when he had been serving on board a ship, Marine Corps Lt. Col. Robert C. D'Amico felt he had been living in an "information vacuum." News and information about developments in-theater arrived only once every twenty-four hours, while letters to and from the States—"everything was letters"—usually took six weeks. By contrast, in Operation Enduring Freedom and Operation Iraqi Freedom—he did two tours in Afghanistan and seven in Iraq in his various several roles as Marine and FBI agent—news was available 24/7 on both television and the Internet. "Everything now is more instantaneous," he said, thanks to cell and satellite phones, video chats, and BlackBerries. "Technology has really helped the soldier stay in touch."[13]

A third item of recurring comment involved changes in military strategy and tactics. One of the most obvious differences between Afghanistan/Iraq and preceeding conflicts involves the blurring of traditional distinctions between front lines and rear lines. Army Lt. Col. Gregory V. Marinich draws contrasts with the days of the Cold War and its sharply etched enemy, the Soviet Union. "Today," he said, "the enemy is not very well-defined, there are no front lines, and the enemy is all over the place. This saddens me. I don't want this enemy to be around when my children are of age to go into the service."[14]

Capt. Michael Daake, who served with an engineering battalion in Operation Iraqi Freedom for nine months beginning in December 2004, signed up in 1988 during the Cold War, when the Soviet Union was the adversary and U.S. units were trained for land battles in Eastern Europe. His exposure in Iraq "changed not only my view of war but also of what war would be like."[15] Col. William F. Andrews, an F-16 pilot who flew missions from the United Arab Emirates during Desert Storm, noted that during the Cold War, his squadron, based in Germany and focused on Central Europe, had been "staring down the Soviet military threat, with large armored formations on wooded, hilly terrain. "We weren't trained for exactly the kind of mission we were going to face" in Iraq, he said, but they were able to adapt to it.[16]

"When I first got in the army, it was the end of the Cold War," muses Sgt. Todd Walton. "It was very simple: if they carried an AK, they were bad; if they carried an [M]16, they were good. You know, that's a great old cheat sheet. Well, with the way the world has changed, our former enemies are now our allies." His unit fraternized with the Ukrainians, Czechs, and Romanians with whom they shared their own base. "To see the Rising Sun driving around out there was just bizarre. I mean, we were just talking about World War II. That's the last time the U.S. and the Japanese were in a combat zone at the same time."[17]

The novelty of the political as well as the geographic terrain also struck Army Lt. Col. Gregory Marinich. What was it that had impressed him most, an interviewer asked, from his service in Desert Shield and Desert Storm and from his stint with the International Security Assistance Force (ISAF) in Afghanistan? "The drastic difference between cultures," he replied, "and the importance of our really being able to talk and dialogue between countries and peoples and religions." He was struck by "how differently they think about things in the Middle East and yet how important it is for us to be educated to these facts and to try to the best of our ability to understand the differences in order that we can have a peaceful future."[18]

Several soldiers expressed the view that the United States had been inadequately prepared for the changes in warfare encountered in Afghanistan and Iraq. A significant number lamented the absence of the necessary body armor and armored vehicles. One veteran confided that she had stolen fire extinguishers for Army vehicles from the Kellogg, Brown, and Root (KBR) warehouse, knowing that private sector stocks would be better provisioned than government stores. Unprepared American units were forced to improvise. "We were taking some equipment that was really built for the Soviet doctrine," observed one veteran, "and using it in a non-standard way and we were actually being quite productive."[19] Another felt, more ominously, that the United States was not learning rapidly enough. "A lot of what we do is still based on the whole World War II concept that there is a front line and then there is a rear echelon that is further back . . . and that it's safer. That's not the case right now."[20]

Some soldiers observed differences between the Soviet Union's conquest of Afghanistan during the Cold War and U.S. involvement in the current conflict. "Afghanistan historically is the number one most-invaded country in the history of all time," noted Marinich. "It's very tribal." As he saw U.S. involvement, however, "we are doing the most right thing that can be done. We are succeeding where just about every other sovereignty from the outside has failed. We have a different mindset. We are enabling. We are not taking anything."[21]

With the Cold War past, classical confrontations in which military formations face off against each other have given way to smaller scale conflicts, often needing a lithe fire brigade rather than a buxom heavy-artillery-centered army. As noted earlier, holding forward operating bases (FOBs) rather than large swathes of territory has often exposed supply troops to combat.

As a result, traditional distinctions between combat and support functions—and thus the traditional division of labor between active-duty and support soldiers—have been overtaken by events. The skill sets and training needed differ from what was required when logistics and administrative backup could be provided in relative safety away from the front. "Some units will go out and be the ones that kick down doors, do raids that go out looking for bad guys so they can kill them," a National Guard officer observed. "And there are some people whose jobs are to move equipment around to feed those troops and provide other support roles. But we're all right in the same area all the time. . . . We all have to train to be warriors."[22] Indeed, many soldiers—both active duty and National Guard—expressed their views, for the most part more positive than negative, on how well the citizen-soldiers who make up the Guard acquitted themselves under fire.[23]

Some soldiers perceived an evolution in warfare during the course of the Iraq conflict itself. At the outset, observed Col. Mark Warnecke of the New York National Guard, the enemy's tactics involved complex and co-ordinated military operations by substantial numbers of soldiers designed to take and hold territory. Over time, however, hit-and-run guerrilla op-erations designed to intimidate coalition forces came to predominate. With the defeat of the Iraqi army and the ascendancy of an insurgency that relied on ambush tactics and low-tech munitions such as IEDs, Warmecke ob-served, military strategy and tactics began to look more and more like those used in the Indochina war.[24]

A fourth major difference between the two current conflicts and earlier American wars drew constant comment: the difficulty of identifying the enemy, now no longer wearing uniforms or bearing weapons in the open. In this respect, the battlefields of the global war on terror were more like those of Indochina than the World Wars or Korea. There were evident parallels with Vietnam, where combatants were often difficult to distinguish from noncombatants and the proximity of combat to civilian populations and infrastructure created difficulties for the use of high-tech weaponry.

"We soldiers operating in Iraq, we can't tell who are insurgents and who are civilians," says Aric Arnold, an Army major who spent nine months there beginning in August 2003. "It makes it extremely difficult to pick the right from the wrong. It is difficult for soldiers trying to do the right thing. We have never been in this kind of environment. It is unlike anywhere ex-cept Vietnam, but even in Vietnam, there was a discernible enemy."[25]

A fifth difference involved major advances in battlefield medicine and in rescuing and treating soldiers wounded in combat. During the first year of the Iraq war, the Pentagon tallied 18,000 medical evacuations (with 11,700 individual soldiers transported). Thanks to "far-forward surgical and medical teams and technologies to care for casualties within minutes of injury, 98 percent of those wounded who reached medical treatment sur-vived their injuries."[26] "Never has military medicine been able to save so many as they can now," notes Maj. David Ball, Germany-based U.S. mede-vac flight coordinator.[27] Interviews with individual veterans provide first-hand accounts of various stages in the process, from treatment on the spot to more specialized care elsewhere in Afghanistan and Iraq, in Germany, and back in the United States.

Improvements in battlefield medicine resulted in a far higher survival rate among those wounded in action. Medics in particular noted the speed with which medical evacuations could be mounted and the effectiveness of the network of emergency treatment facilities arrayed near combat zones, in neighboring countries, in Germany and the United States. "We're saving a much higher percentage of wounded than we did in Vietnam," noted Army Lt. Col. Maria Teresa Cochran, who described an all-hands-on-deck scene at Camp Balad in Iraq following a mass-casualty incident. "But we must provide the quality of life afterwards. I think America has to get used to seeing guys on crutches, in wheelchairs, and without legs. We have to build the means to support these guys and get them self-sustaining and back into society. We're going to see a lot more of them."[28]

There were indications, too, especially in Iraq, of progress in addressing the in-theater psychological needs of veterans more seriously. First Sergeant Mayfield, after almost twenty years in the Army, tells an interviewer about seeing a big, hand-lettered sign that showed up overnight at his base near Baghdad: "It said, '785th Combat Stress Hospital,' with an arrow pointing down the road. We were, like, 'What's a combat stress hospital? I've never even heard of that before!'"[29] Critical-incidents debriefings were also instituted as a means of assisting soldiers exposed to extreme violence. In such debriefings, participants were sometimes told, in an effort to reassure, that PTSD involved normal reactions to abnormal situations.

The experience in Afghanistan and Iraq is already having major implications for the preparation of troops for future conflicts. "During the Cold War," observed one senior New Hampshire Guard official, "we were deploying to hardened bases in Europe and Asia. With the new global war on terror and our basing in Afghanistan and Iraq, we have sent people into areas that don't have a hardened facility." In her view, the "more austere environments" in which future conflicts may take place will require not only more careful screening of recruits, but also more thorough immunization of those deployed (for example, against anthrax and smallpox). Post-Gulf War innovations that deserved to be continued, in her view, include advance "blood banking" for all of those deployed and mandatory individual mental health screening upon reentry.[30]

Other differences noted between these and earlier wars were more individualistic. Air Force Special Agent John R. Cencich found the 9/11 attacks far more egregious than the bombing of Pearl Harbor. While the latter had a military target, the former was a crime against humanity that provided every justification for a U.S. reprisal against Afghanistan.[31] Based on his own experience, another soldier found conditions in East Africa even more rugged than those in Iraq. In Somalia, he said, the posture of U.S. troops had been defensive, the rules of engagement more unsatisfactory, and the UN involvement a seriously complicating factor.[32] He came away from postings in Somalia and Jordan with the same basic lesson: "Just do your job," however constraining the setting and rules of engagement and however formidable the geographical or political obstacles.

Compared to Iraq, commented Marine SSgt. David James Paxson, Kosovo was "a fairly easy deployment." There were no IEDs, no armed insurgents blending in with crowds of civilians, no suicide bombers. The troops in Iraq were tested in a major way when the Republican Guard removed their uniforms, "making it hard to tell who was friendly and who was the enemy." Attacks against U.S. convoys and civilians were part of a last-ditch effort, he felt, to intimidate American troops. While augmenting the number of troops would increase the risk, there was simply no substitute for putting more boots on the ground in an effort to flush out the insurgents. "Now that we're there," he concluded, "if we leave now, no matter if the war was wrong or right, we're going to look like the bad guys." In his view, U.S. troops need to remain until the Iraqi army can take over. If they can't assume responsibility, this will be considered "the Vietnam of our generation."[33]

Of all the points of discontinuity, veterans most frequently contrasted the appreciative receptions they received upon returning from Afghanistan and Iraq with the hostile welcomes accorded returning Vietnam veterans. A number took pains to point out that despite the growing unpopularity of the Iraq war, returning veterans were still receiving far better treatment than their Vietnam predecessors. In fact, several soldiers had experienced both receptions themselves. Ty Simmons, chief warrant officer with the Illinois National Guard, had enlisted in 1968 and served in Vietnam for a year. "After Vietnam, I was a nobody," he recalled. "I was spat upon, discarded. I was called a baby killer. I hope and pray that we never do that again, that the young soldiers will not have to go through that. The soldiers are just doing their job the best way that we can. Always support the soldier in the fight, even if you may not like what the government is doing. You may not like why they are there, but please support the soldiers. . . . These young soldiers are heroes. We need to support them no matter what."[34]

In the same airports where returnees from Vietnam had been hassled and mocked as baby killers, complete strangers now approach returnees to thank them for their service. "Some Vietnam vets have made a personal commitment to ensure that our reception was what theirs should have been," commented a thankful Army Capt. Ryan Aument. "Folks will disagree with the public policy of the war but have always treated me with respect as a soldier."[35]The difference has not only eased their immediate reentry but also facilitated their quest for a "new normal" once they are home. That difference notwithstanding, Amn. Mark Kaplan noted a parallel between the popular outrage in the United States at the Abu Ghraib abuses and public opposition to the Vietnam War. Similarities notwithstanding, he said, the Abu Ghraib reaction was focused and specific while the Vietnam backlash was broad and sustained.[36]

CONTINUITIES

In addition to discontinuities such as these, veterans also observe parallels with predecessor conflicts. The most frequent points of comparison are the military technology and firepower utilized, the impacts of warfare on military personnel, and the injustices experienced within the ranks by women, gay men and lesbians, and minority groups.

With respect to military technology, some veterans draw an ominous parallel with the Indochina chapter in U.S. military history. In that war, overwhelming U.S. firepower did not ensure an American victory, nor did it set the stage for a favorable political settlement. Similarly, in the face-off against an arsenal of low-tech but lethal weaponry in Afghanistan and Iraq,

Direct Hit

Cristina Frisby (AFC2001/001/53197), Photographs (PH40), VHP, AFC, LOC.

Sgt. Cristina Frisby served in Iraq with the Army's 113th Medical Company, Second Medical Brigade, driving a tow truck and rescuing and repairing disabled U.S. military vehicles. This picture was taken on July 21, 2005, on a highway between Tikrit and Forward Operating Base Speicher. "The IED was hidden on the bridge and blew [out] the Humvee's right side."

"We were getting hit by so many 'fire bombs,' as we called the IEDs, that everyone quit wearing seatbelts. When hit, the truck cabin would be immediately engulfed in searing flames and you only had a split second to grab the door and bail or be cooked." In the incident pictured, the two soldiers in the cab managed to escape unharmed.

In her VHP interview, Frisby describes the strenuous and stressful roles that she and other women in her unit played. She recalls the combat stress involved in simply going about her work, "every day knowing that it could be us who would be hit, but not knowing when it would happen." Being a woman in this type of exposed and hands-on job didn't seem to be problematic. "Nobody cared whether you were a woman," Frisby observes. "The only thing that mattered was whether you were a good recovery mechanic."

"My biggest fear," she remembers, was witnessing someone burn to death, "I did everything I could to prevent it from happening, and it never did." She faults substandard equipment—including vehicles without up-armoring—for unnecessary injuries to the troops. Frisby received a commendation for her efforts, which frequently exposed her to hostile fire. This photograph is one of more than three hundred in her VHP file; it was taken by Spec. Cory Hoerler, another driver on her recovery team.

the world's most advanced warriors are seen to have lost the advantage they enjoyed in more symmetrical warfare. "We're supposed to be the most technological army in the world, and we can't figure out where the hell these guys are shooting from," exclaimed Steven Rizza of the New Hampshire National Guard. "We've got more aircraft. We could probably line the Persian Gulf with aircraft and just walk across."[37] But the race is not necessarily won by the technologically superior.

The asymmetry of the conflicts in Afghanistan and Iraq—that is, the overwhelmingly disproportionate resources of foreign interveners yet the difficulties of achieving a decisive victory—seems comparable to the conflict in Indochina. Each placed a premium on understanding the dynamics of the local scene, obtaining accurate intelligence, mounting quick responses to attacks, and maintaining control over strategic areas once captured. Counterinsurgency operations are also seen to be important in both types of settings. An additional constant is the predicament of being caught in the crossfire of internal armed conflicts and for that matter, being vulnerable to "friendly fire." Civil wars increase the peril faced by outside interveners while delaying achievement of political solutions that could form the basis for durable peace and social reconstruction.

Another point of continuity for those who served in Afghanistan and Iraq involves the impacts of the war on those who waged it in theater. A number of soldiers pointed out that PTSD has been a feature of every major American war, although called by a variety of names. The working definition of PTSD, mental health professionals point out, is applicable to all wars and even to non-war situations: "exposure to a traumatic event in which the person experienced, witnessed, or was confronted by serious injury to others and responded with intense fear, helplessness, and horror."[38] The differences across the span of American wars are not in kind but only in degree.

Many veterans express alarm about the incidence of PTSD—and, for that matter, TBI—in the current conflicts. Their concern is not just that with the large numbers of persons affected, the high cost of treatment, and the difficulties of reentry into society. "It is also," explained one chaplain who has facilitated numerous discussion groups of PTSD sufferers and their families, "that those affected seem less able to buffer the shock, in part because they have a less well-developed framework of values and codes of conduct."[39] At the same time, some mental health experts question whether the concept of PTSD itself may have become overly broad and dysfunctional.[40]

Another point of continuity involves issues related to the treatment of certain identifiable minority groups within the ranks and its wider implications. The treatment of women, gay men and lesbians, and blacks drew particular comment from veterans.

The contributions made by women are widely acknowledged and applauded. "When the books are closed," says Mayfield, "people will see that the female soldier was more of a combatant in Iraq—I don't know about Afghanistan—than any other conflict I have been in." By all accounts, the roles played by women in these conflicts were in many ways new to the military. With respect to the National Guard, for example, women have been accepted only since 1956 and only since 1968 have they served in active-duty ranks and performed in "almost all military specialties except in direct combat roles."[41] Women now represent not only a larger proportion of total forces—ten percent of global forces—but also play a wider array of roles.

In both Afghanistan and Iraq, women in National Guard units have assumed leadership roles, including in combat situations. One female officer who commanded a unit that included six female soldiers observed, "My females saw combat. My females were in combat. My females did combat, and a lot more than some of these 'all-male focused' combat units."[42] While the experience in Afghanistan and Iraq helped lay to rest the stereotype that females could not handle combat, there was, she believes, room for improvement in the military's ability to harness the differential abilities of men and women. Women also played key decision-making roles in stateside Guard hierarchies and in hearts-and-minds activities.[43]

The conflicts have also taken their toll on women, not only with respect to casualties but also with respect to health. Asked about a differential in the rates of PTSD among women and men, one DVA mental health professional notes a general finding that "when they are exposed to the same trauma, women are twice as likely to get PTSD" as men.[44] According to DOD, in the Afghanistan conflict as of January 3, 2009, fourteen female soldiers had been killed, seventeen wounded, for a total of about 1 percent of U.S. casualties. In Iraq as of the same date, 101 female soldiers had lost their lives, with 598 wounded, representing about 2 percent of U.S. casualties.[45]

Female interviewees comment with some regularity on incidents involving sexism, including sexual abuse. New Hampshire's Schwab, who was otherwise highly positive about her experience in the military, filed a formal harassment complaint against one of her superiors. "I felt like I had to continually defend my honor for a year," she explained.[46] Spec. Abbie Pickett chose not to make an issue of an incident of attempted rape because she "just wanted to be one of the guys." Nor were such experiences isolated incidents. The majority of the women from the New Hampshire National Guard interviewed by Joelle Farrell of the *Concord Monitor* "had dealt with sexual harassment at some point in their careers."[47] Their experience confirmed the observation of Gregory Mayfield that "military culture is a pretty high-testosterone environment."[48] The "band of brothers" feeling which is credited with strengthening the sense of solidarity among those exposed to common dangers does not always, the data show, treat sisters as full partners.

Interviews also recount a number of incidents involving abusive attitudes toward homosexuals and racial minorities. As noted earlier, the military's "don't ask, don't tell" policy deprived it of the services of numerous American interpreters, already in short supply and by all accounts essential to the successful conduct of military operations. As with women, however, stereotypes were often altered as a result of performance under shared duress. Navy Photographer's Mate 3rd Class Maria Zambrana noted a significant difference in attitudes toward women between her two tours in Iraq. In the first, she felt, there was little sense of cohesion. In the second, women were "so much more integrated into the total operation."[49]

In the view of one acknowledged gay, Captain Hill, "the vast majority" of people in the Army "really didn't seem to care one way or the other. I'd run into people every now and then that would say something that would betray an animosity, but those people can be found anywhere and everywhere and are a not unique to the army." He found it mind-boggling that "an army which preaches so hard and so long and so forcefully on the importance of racial integration would completely ignore it when it comes to another characteristic that for some reason doesn't fit their idea of what diversity is."[50]

Navy Sgt. Cristina Frisby, an Army tow truck driver who took the photograph shown in this chapter, found people in her unit generally accepting of her sexual preference. But being a lesbian in the ranks was stressful. She felt lonely and isolated; only a few close friends were aware of her sexuality. "I didn't want to create problems or violate policy," she says. While she was deployed, her partner back in the States terminated their relationship and a close friend, who returned to Iraq for a second tour without having been screened for problems following her first, took her own life. The face-sheet on Frisby's VHP collection notes, "Veteran received discharge papers and was not recommended for future commission because of prior homosexual experience." For both Hill and Frisby, however, their high levels of commitment to the military and their professional approach to their tasks outweighed their distaste for the military's "don't ask, don't tell" policy.

Interviews of black veterans did not bring to light specific incidents of perceived discrimination on grounds of race. However, a number of interviews of white service members convey negative stereotypes. One veteran comments on how attending boot camp in the South involved first-time and unsettling contacts with non-whites; another referred to blacks as niggers. In broader compass, Pentagon officials acknowledged a general trend toward the "rejection of military service as an option of young blacks throughout the country" during the global war on terror years. However, this development may have had a variety of causes, including the existence of economic opportunities for blacks outside the military, rather than simply discomfort with the treatment of African Americans already in the ranks.[51] The lament of a Native American from Arizona about the insensitivity of the Texas Guard unit to which he was assigned has also been mentioned. More positive in terms of the diversity of the armed forces was the substantial presence within the ranks of non-U.S. citizens. One historian of the Vietnam War observed that the barracks photograph in Chapter 8 conveys a demography that contrasts sharply with the makeup of U.S. units in Vietnam.

In identifying such issues as sexism, homophobia, and racism, veterans are not simply flagging the shortcomings of the military as an institution.

They are also calling attention to unfinished business of society as a whole, reflected in the composition and practices of the armed forces. In this sense, the Global War on Terror may prove to be of a piece with other American wars. World War II offers perhaps the best example of how, in fighting for the country's ideals, soldiers turn the spotlight on American institutions, military and civilian alike, whose blemishes thus appear in more stark relief.

Comments by President Obama in his January 2010 State of the Union address, views that were reinforced in February by senior U.S. military leaders, committed the administration to reverse the prevailing "don't ask, don't tell" policy regarding gays and lesbians in the military.[53] While many commentators drew parallels between the impacts of World War II and the global war on terror on the treatment of minorities, some observed a significant difference. Unlike the Truman decision to integrate the military, which came at a time when U.S. public opinion nationwide did not support racial equality, public opinion today arguably leads military policy in attitudes toward homosexuality.

WIDER RIPPLES

Discussions among veterans on the links between these wars and earlier conflicts mirror a much wider debate involving policymakers and independent analysts. Bush administration officials and members of Congress have tended to emphasize the uniqueness of the global war and the resulting need to develop new approaches to combat a more devious and elusive enemy. Practices such as the abusive treatment of detainees in theater and at Guantanamo Bay, rendition, the perceived nonapplicability of traditionally accepted international laws of war, and the domestic wiretapping of U.S. citizens are presented and justified as new strategies and tactics necessary to counteract the unprecedented and insidious nature of post-9/11 threats to national security.

Some independent analysts have also underscored the novelty of the challenges to which the global war on terror responds. "September 11 left nearly five times as many Americans dead as all terrorist incidents of the previous three decades combined," wrote Strobe Talbott and Nayan Chanda in their edited volume, *The Age of Terror: America and the World after*

September 11. "The carnage was . . . about double what three hundred Japanese bombers left in their wake at Pearl Harbor. Commentators instantly evoked that other bolt-from-the-blue raid, sixty years before, as the closest thing to a precedent. But there was really none. This was something new under the sun." [53]

Other analysts have underscored the continuities between the current threats to U.S. national security and earlier challenges. Louise Richardson rejects the view that "we inhabit an entirely new world in which the experience of other countries has no relevance, our national security doctrine is irrelevant, and our protections of civil liberties are unaffordable." She concludes a lengthy review of the issues in *What Terrorists Want: Understanding the Enemy, Containing the Threat* with the observation, "It is not quite true . . . that, in the words of President Bush, 'September 11 changed our world.' Rather it was our reaction to September 11 that changed the world."[54]

Similarly, studies at Tufts University with which the author has been associated have underscored continuities across a series of ostensibly very different conflicts in the post-Cold War era. Examining settings such as Afghanistan, Iraq, Colombia, the Sudan, the Occupied Palestinian Territory, Sri Lanka, and Nepal, our research has concluded that the challenges faced by humanitarian organizations in maintaining access to people in need and in protecting their independence of action from politicization have been remarkably constant. Our studies suggest that in a fundamental sense, "no crisis is unique. As long as every crisis is perceived as wholly without precedent or parallel, there will be little scope for institutional learning."[55]

Early in the Obama administration, an approach was beginning to take shape that differed from the one that offered the Global War on Terror as the overarching response to threats to U.S. national security. While details had yet to crystallize, the alternative was clear and the implications far reaching. "As for our common defense," said the new president in his inaugural address, "we reject as false the choice between our safety and our ideals. Our founding fathers, faced with perils that we can scarcely imagine, drafted a charter to assure the rights of man, a charter expanded by the blood of generations. Those ideals still light the world, and we will not give them up for expedience's sake." [56]

Beyond the individual discontinuities and continuities identified, the commentary provided by veterans from Afghanistan and Iraq underscores the archetypal experiences of soldiering across the history of American wars. For all of the variations in particulars, these experiences involve recurring elements: uprooting from family and community pursuits, baptism by immersion into withering conflict, solidarity among those thus exposed, testing of principles and instincts by the unfamiliar and unknown, stresses of reentry, and challenges of fashioning a "new normal" after each particular conflict.

The observation made by Commander Kirk in the context of his own conversations with World War II veterans is particularly telling. Expressing the view that the similarities among conflicts outweigh the evident differences among them, he remarks that across the span of American wars, "The main similarity is that when you wear the uniform, it changes you. It's a statement that the success of the United States is your personal responsibility and that in some very basic way you are OK with losing your life if it is in defense of that country. It completely sets you apart from everyone else in the level of commitment that you've decided to make." [57]

■ ■ ■

The military service of veterans of the Afghanistan and Iraq conflicts provides them with an instructive perspective on earlier American wars. The importance of listening to their voices is the subject of the final chapter.

—TWELVE—

Listening to Veterans

One of the final questions in the Veterans History Project's field kit asks soldiers to reflect on the lessons they have learned from Afghanistan and Iraq and the wider meaning of their experience for their lives. Interviewers from the University of Arkansas participating in the VHP exercise conclude their own series of interviews with two additional queries: "Why do you think it is important for vets to share their stories?" and "How would you like to be remembered as a veteran of war?" Even veterans not specifically asked these questions have views on these matters to share.

WHAT ARE THEY SAYING?

From the experience of the two hundred-plus veterans consulted for this book, a number of themes emerge. First, veterans take an evident pride in having answered their country's call and in having done what was asked of them. Military service, said Marine SSgt. Brendon Bass of his time in Iraq, "really made me grow up and have a complete understanding of what the people before had gone through. My family fought in every war and I am proud to have fought for my country and continued that tradition." He took particular satisfaction in having proved himself to his father, who had said he would never amount to anything.[1]

Some began their tours with reservations about the U.S. undertakings in Afghanistan and particularly in Iraq but eventually became persuaded of the importance of what the United States was trying to do. Some whose trajectories took the opposite direction—from initial support for the missions to eventual cynicism about the results—nevertheless took pride in having done their part.

The challenges of serving in Afghanistan and Iraq took veterans on highly personal voyages of discovery. Johnny Torres, a corporal in an Army Ranger regiment, welcomed the discipline instilled during training and implemented in theater. "The training experience is tough and teaches you a lot about yourself." His time in the military "taught me a lot about life." In fact, he found himself wishing that he had enlisted a year earlier to reap the benefits of his new-found maturity sooner.[2]

Pictured in his battle gear elsewhere in the book, SSgt. Blake C. Cole, a troubled youngster and one of five children raised by a single mother, learned in boot camp "the proper mentality for combat" and went on to distinguish himself as a scout sniper platoon chief with the Marines in Fallujah. Despite the hardships involved for himself and his family, he sees the dividends as "huge" and is enrolled in courses that will enable him to make the Marines a lifelong career. His awards include the Iraqi Campaign Medal, the Global War on Terror Expeditionary Medal, the Global War on Terror Service Medal, and a Purple Heart.[3]

For all of the inconveniences and dangers encountered—one veteran counted twenty-six moves that his family had made in thirty-two years[4]—most of those interviewed, irrespective of their particular assignments and challenges, do not consider themselves heroes. "You're not there to be a hero," observed Army Sgt. E-5 Nicole Ferretti. "You're there to help the two people—the one in front of you and the one behind you."[5] In fact, relatively few were overjoyed to be deployed. Navy Third Class Petty Officer Philip Thomas Jr., who served on active duty for four years, concluded that few of his cohorts were happy to have been shipped out to Iraq. "At least 80 percent," he estimated, "were reluctant to be on his ship or in Iraq."[6] Happy or otherwise, however, most sought to make the best of a difficult situation and succeeded in doing so.

The pride most veterans express is in the performance of their colleagues and themselves rather than in the recognition they receive from others. The medals mentioned in response to an interviewer's question or brought along to interviews are often something of an embarrassment. "I didn't do anything spectacular," said Army 2nd Class Petty Officer Eric Heath. "'You know,' my dad said, 'You're a part of something that not many people get to say they're a part of. You did stuff that most people won't do for their country.' I don't see it as that. I did my job to the best of my ability. If someone was to look at this, I would like them to say, 'It's people like me and other people who sacrifice even more that paved the way for future things.'"[7]

"I'm just some guy that did his job," says Army Reserve Spec. Christopher Gamblin. "I don't think it's anything special. There's a lot of veterans from previous wars that we've had who did a lot more, and they went through a lot harder times than we did."[8] Army SSgt. Bradley Burd had a somewhat different take. "Anybody over there," in his estimation, "is performing some form of heroism just by being there."[9] "The real heroes," says Army Spec. Gonzalo Gonzalez, "are the ones at home praying for us, watching out for everything. Those are my heroes."[10]

Many veterans return to the States with a new appreciation of family, country, freedoms, and life itself. "Seeing how others live makes you appreciate what you have back home," says Air Force Sgt. 1st Class David Brown in a comment repeated by many others.[11] As noted earlier, many veterans upon returning become more involved than they had been in civic affairs, serving on town committees, participating in veterans' organizations and holiday celebrations, and even running for elective office. Life is precious, they say with a single voice, and needs to be savored and cherished each day.

"Some people say I don't get as upset or excited about things as before," mused Col. William Andrews, who was shot down and captured during Operation Desert Storm. ""Some things seem smaller than they might have before the war. You know, you're not sure if you're ever going to come home."[12] "Going away and having the possibility of dying on a daily basis changes you, and makes you realize what life is really about," said Ferretti.[13]

Many develop a new respect for the military service of earlier generations. "After watching the war in *Band of Brothers*," said Army Lt. Col. Maria Cochran on her return from the Middle East, "I wish I knew more about my uncle in the Navy in the Second World War in the Pacific. I wish I knew them, but they're gone now. I don't think my story is all that unique or special, but I think collectively there is such a unique American experience captured in these stories. I think it ain't about me. It's about the service. It's about the American experience. Get as many of these stories as you can," she urged her interviewer.[14] "I think it is important to have some record of the war," concurs Army Spec. Nicholas Fosholdt, a reservist with an engineering company in Iraq. Some of the events have lost their sharpness even in his own memory, he concedes. Even more so, he says, the World War II experience is in danger of being lost as veterans age and die.[15]

For all the positive aspects of their tours, many veterans were—and are—troubled by particular aspects of the experience. One has decided not to share his photographs from Iraq with his children until they are older and better able to understand. Others specify that while their experiences may be shared with readers, they themselves are to remain anonymous. Those who say, "I don't regret anything that I've done" in the line of duty are perhaps exceptions. However, such a categorical statement may be giving a broad assessment of the overall experience rather than an imprimatur on each specific action.

The ambivalence that many veterans feel often emerges from discussions about whether they would like their own children to follow them into the military. Few respond enthusiastically in the affirmative. Some equivocate; others express reservations. Army Lt. Col. Jude Ferran, a career professional with children ages eleven, nine, and six at the time of his interview, said that "America is a great country and it is the responsibility of its citizens to give back," whether through the military or in other ways. "I wouldn't discourage them from military service," he said, "but I would want to make sure they understand and choose with their eyes open."[16]

"I'm a firm believer that everybody—every young man and woman—ought to serve their country in some capacity, in some way, shape or form, at a minimum to do something to help humanity," says Army Lt. Col. Gregory Marinich. "I felt that the army provided me with a lot of possibilities in terms of serving not only country but others."[17] "The army is not for everybody," said Capt. Lynn Wagner. "There are other ways to do your duty."[18] After fifteen years in the military and two deployments to Iraq, SSgt. Shawn Stenberg is not anxious to have family and friends follow in his footsteps. While he identifies positive elements from his years in the Army, he thinks the Coast Guard might be a safer bet for his son.[19]

Many veterans convey a keen awareness of what they consider the privilege of having been personally involved in the making of history. Taking stock of his deployment in Iraq, Army Spec. James R. Welch of Toledo, Ohio, remarks that "I'm honored myself to have been a part of history."[20] "It's an honor to be able to serve and to be a part of history," says Army Chief Warrant Officer Two Jeffrey Beard, "and an honor to fight for freedoms my fathers and forefathers fought for and so many soldiers died for."[21]

"What was it like when you arrived in places like Abu Ghraib and the Sunni Triangle, Fallujah and Baghdad?" Marine SSgt. Brandon M. Bass was asked. Referring to L. Frank Baum's *Wizard of Oz* tale, he replied, "It was that feeling of when Dorothy said, 'We ain't in Kansas anymore.'"[22] Indeed, many who served in Afghanistan and Iraq described what Army Sgt. Jeremy Lima called the feeling of "Pinch me. It's real!" On arriving at Al Asad Air Base, where his security battalion would be based, Lima remembered saying to himself, "Wow! I can't believe I'm here."[23]

"I have been involved in so many historical events," reminisces Marine Lt. Col. Robert D'Amico in his Veterans History Project interview conducted by his daughter Becky Ann. He mentions specifically 9/11, the Gulf War, and the conflicts in both Afghanistan and Iraq. "Do you feel as though you've missed out on anything?" she asks. Yes, her father said, "I have missed out on birthdays and kindergarten graduations and the like which you can never get back. But everyone misses them. I've missed significant events but for the right reason. I've done things and been a part of history that I never would have imagined growing up."[24] Capt. Ryan Aument believes that he made the right selection among the military services because of his reading, as "a student of history," that the Army had produced the largest number of makers and shapers in American military history.[25]

Several vets express the view that their up front and personal involvement in these events was particularly irreplaceable. "Especially if you serve in a conflict," says Navy Commander Mark Kirk, "you have that realization that everyone else may read a book or see the History Channel and see how the story turned out while you were in it. You realize that nobody knew what the hell was going on, and how it would turn out was completely in doubt. No one had the big picture."[26] His comment offers a caution to historians of the conflicts not to let the wisdom of hindsight diminish the uncertain outcomes of events as they were being experienced.

The wars in Afghanistan and Iraq demonstrate service members at their best—or, in some instances, at their worst. Keeping both aspects in tension guards against tendencies to lionize—or demonize—the troops. "Instead of thinking of soldiers and veterans as 'warriors,'" counsels the Easter Seals organization in New Hampshire, "we must remind ourselves that they are fathers, mothers, coworkers, or the girl next door, who may be desperately struggling with Post Traumatic Stress Disorder, or living near poverty level in need of groceries, or who has just been fitted with a prosthetic limb."[27] That humanness emerges in a variety of ways as veterans recount their involvement.

While many veterans are anxious to share their experience with family and friends, community and country, some have no absolutely no inclination to do so. Army Sgt. Cody Allen kept a journal faithfully while in Iraq, only to leave it there when he left. "I don't want those types of memories," he explained.[28] Upon returning, some have resisted joining veterans' organizations because they do not want to keep the memories alive. Others have rejected therapy because the retelling of traumatic events forces those events to be relived. For some, the experience of Afghanistan and Iraq has been so raw and intense as to discourage sharing it even within the most intimate circle of family and friends. Some veterans identify guilt (for example, at having returned while others have remained in the fray), shame (over the effects of the violence on civilians) or fear (of the impacts of sharing their stories on their future careers) as inhibitors to telling their stories.

Veterans acknowledge the heterogeneity of their experiences and their reactions to what they encountered. "I think that it's good to have a kind of archive of people's views," observed Eric Heath. "My views probably differ from another veteran's views. More importantly, you have a completely different perspective from someone who has never experienced the military.

A veteran can give you a positive view of some of the good things that are going on over there. And maybe, if people are smart enough and intuitive enough to want to know both sides of the story, they can see the world and what's going on in it from a different light and maybe not so negatively. Even though it is a negative situation, you can still get a somewhat positive slant from hearing it from a veteran."[29]

If a veterans' perspective on events offers something not available otherwise, that perspective itself remains partial. "After we got hit the first time," said Sergeant Mayfield describing an ambush in Sadr City, "it was, you know, forget a bunch of understanding what we're doing over here and the big strategy, and let's just keep each other alive."[30] By contrast, given the preoccupation of the boots on the ground with their own safety, Jude Ferran stressed that "the importance of taking the 'big picture' view is key to understanding why we do things and what we need to do."[31]

The interviews confirm the observation of the DVA official quoted earlier: "Most people who have survived this experience will be changed by it, whether crossing some psychiatric threshold or not."[32] Whether or not they have shared their disquiet with others, most veterans now carry around within them a piece of Iraq or Afghanistan.

As we consider the road that unfolds before us, we remember with humble gratitude those brave Americans who, at this very hour, patrol far-off deserts and distant mountains. They have something to tell us, just as the fallen heroes who lie in Arlington whisper through the ages. We honor them not only because they are guardians of our liberty, but because they embody the spirit of service; a willingness to find meaning in something greater than themselves. And yet, at this moment—a moment that will define a generation—it is precisely this spirit that must inhabit us all.

*—President Barack Obama**

---

* President Obama's inaugural address, January20, 2009, http://www.whitehouse.gov/the-press-office/president-barack-obamas-inaugural-address

WHY LISTEN?

Why is it important to listen to the voices of veterans? The veterans themselves and the experiences they recount provide some answers.

First, we can learn a lot from them. Their perspective has something special to offer not available elsewhere. Veterans are an essential element in this country's social fabric and history, points out Marine Sgt. Dax Carpenter. "You will not have a country if you take away its veterans. If we don't have veterans that'll be there when America needs them, then we don't have a country. A veteran is a person who has put their life on the line and said, 'No matter what, come hell or high water, I will be there for whoever needs me whether it be at home like Katrina or afar like Iraq.'" Quite apart from any individual military contribution, veterans are an essential part of the country's collective national memory. "History is written by man," notes Carpenter. "But usually the person that does the writing wasn't there."[33]

The military itself, in posting its own historians on the ground among the troops and in its increasingly systematic debriefings and lessons learned exercises, is coming to appreciate the importance of the identifying and reflecting upon the experiences of veterans.[34] The New Hampshire National Guard, interviewing its troops returning from Afghanistan and Iraq, was rewarded with a rich collection of experience and recommendations upon which this narrative has drawn. The Veterans History Project offers a huge oral history resource from participants in the current and earlier wars.

Indeed, the recent upsurge of interest in oral history itself represents an important resource. Initiatives currently under way that examine particular groups of soldiers and particular issues—the views of reservists in a California unit called up to serve in Afghanistan and Iraq,[35] the experience of PTSD among selected veterans,[36] and the political activism of selected veterans returning from the field[37]—bode well for the larger task of pondering the experience of veterans and taking their perspectives into account.

Veterans offer a point of entry for Americans into a wider world about which they are often unaware. Spec. Gonzalo Gonzalez, a gunner in an Army escort unit, feels that people have difficulty understanding what the troops have gone through because "they've never seen things, they've never been anywhere."[38] Newspaper readers in northern Vermont were treated by one of their National Guard soldiers to a mini-tutorial on Islam. "People need to know what is going on and how everything impacts a soldier," observes Army Lt. Col. Rick Mayes. "The more knowledge that's out there, the better decisions can be made. All the information is just coming from single sources now. It's not coming from the soldiers themselves. It's not coming from what you'd call 'the other side.'"[39]

"A student who has a gunshot wound from a battle in Fallujah," observes Dartmouth College president James Wright, who undertook to enroll veterans in his school, "is going to bring something intangible to any classroom discussion."[40] Vietnam vets played a similar role in earlier classrooms. "Teaching a course on Vietnam with Vietnam vets in the classroom," recalls one professor at a state university, "brought a greater sense of reality to my teaching of the material and a greater level of engagement in the issues among the other students." Vietnam veterans can help broaden our own perspective and reduce what they themselves identify as the provincialism of the country. "The life experiences which Vietnam veterans have," observes Dax Carpenter, "are invaluable to us new generations of war veterans."[41]

Second, coming to terms with the experience of veterans represents an essential step in reclaiming our own sense of humanity as citizens. For many of the troops, the wars in Afghanistan and Iraq are being fought "off the screen, off the books, and off the radar." During the first eight months of 2008 alone, wrote Charles Pierce in a *Boston Globe Magazine* article, "The Forgotten War," ninety-three soldiers back from the war had taken their own lives, with precious little reaction from the body politic as a whole. "Taken as itself, the war seems to exist in another place. The war is something that happens to someone else. It almost seems as if the war has slipped the country's mind."[42] It rings hollow, veterans seem to be saying, for the public to profess to take service member needs seriously while exhibiting so little interest in the ongoing wars themselves.

At numerous points in recent years, national and local demonstrations against U.S. policy have gathered citizens, including some military personnel, spouses, parents, and other family members, behind signs reading "Not in our name." Demonstrators have specifically challenged the Bush administration's March 2003 declaration of war against Iraq; its abrogation of international laws, institutions, and processes; and its pursuit of strategies in Iraq and Afghanistan that have led to disproportionately high numbers of civilian casualties. Such demonstrations represent a reinvigoration of a sense of humanity among American citizens in the face of the prevailing lack of public engagement in the issues of the conflicts.

Indeed, with the Obama administration committed to reducing U.S. troop strength in Iraq but also to increasing the number of boots on the ground in Afghanistan, the time is ripe for a wide-ranging public debate. The systematic processing of the rich and diverse experiences of soldiers in these conflicts affords a vehicle whereby the American body politic may begin to come to terms with recent events. The advice offered by former Army paratrooper Stan Goff to his own son and his son's cohorts serving in Iraq might be directed as well to American civil society: "Don't surrender your humanity." Instead, begin the lengthy and necessarily painful process of reclaiming it.

What would a newly engaged public mean? The outcomes of informed and spirited public dialogue on the conflicts are not self-evident. Considerations of humanity might point in divergent directions. They might lead to phasing down the level of U.S. military involvement in Afghanistan and/or Iraq. Alternatively, however, concern for the safety and future well-being of Americans and Afghans alike might point toward continued or increased U.S. military presence in the region. Or again, considerations of humanity, the earlier discussion of hearts and minds activities suggests, might lead some to advocate increased levels of assistance by troops to local communities. By contrast, others interpret the experience to suggest that health and education programs carried out by soldiers draw such communities more deeply into the conflict.

Concern for the well-being of U.S. military personnel and of Afghan and Iraqi civilians does not necessarily dictate one set of policies over another. This fact underscores the reality that humanity is not the private preserve of peace activists. A *Times* (U.K.) article on Gen. David Petraeus, former commander of U.S. troops in Iraq and then head of the U.S. Central Command, is headlined, "It will take humanity as well as guns to beat the Taliban. The thinking man's soldier explains the limitations of shooting and killing."[43]

Finally, the viewpoints of veterans are essential for the nation to take into account as it reexamines its own priorities and policies. What can be learned from the decade of the Global War on Terror to guide U.S. preparation for and engagement in future conflicts? If the use of a Cold War framework has proved problematic for the United States in understanding and responding to the conflicts in Afghanistan and Iraq, what are the take-away lessons from these two conflicts for the framework of the future? What can be learned from the war in Iraq for the approach to Afghanistan? Many veterans consider their experience, however positive or negative, as a resource to future generations.

Broadly speaking, the experiences of veterans in Afghanistan and Iraq sound a cautionary note as the nation looks to the future. Many veterans express the view that their service has removed something of the mystique and allure from soldiering for them and, they hope, for future generations. Their accounts of the effects—on them no less than on their adversaries—of violence and destruction, injury and death, require pondering. "The experience makes me a whole lot more against war in general. It would be a last resort for me," concludes Marine Sgt. Adam Paulson. "The first-person perspective has definitely changed my life in thinking about that kind of thing. How big a responsibility it is for someone to declare war or wage war!"[44]

The heartfelt wish expressed by Jonathan McMaster, a Marine injured in Iraq in 2004, deserves pondering. "I wish that civilians and policymakers understood, at an emotional level, the tremendous toll and cost of war on those who actually experience it."[45] Specialist Robert Acosta notes that in addition to his Purple Heart, he carries with him a constant reminder of his experience in Iraq. "All the reasons we went to war, it just seems like they're not legit enough for people to lose their lives for and for me to lose my hand and use of my legs and for my buddies to lose their limbs."[46] It would be a loss to the country, observed Greg Mayfield, if veterans kept their experiences to themselves. "They need to share it, so that people know. Maybe people will understand eventually how traumatic it is, and that will keep other wars from being fought."[47]

Looking to the future, there are broad policy questions about the United States and its role in the world to be debated and resolved. Is waging a "global war on terror" the appropriate response to current threats to U.S. national security? Should the architects and implementers of U.S. policy be held accountable for the costs and consequences of the global war on terror and, if so, how? What should be the balance between hard power and soft power? Is there a continuing need for neutral humanitarian assistance, devoid of political agendas, or will hearts-and-minds activities by the military, approached as an integral element of counterinsurgency strategy, be adequate? What are the roles of international institutions and traditional canons of soldiering? Should the draft be reinstated? What should be the response of a modern Western military to a low-tech enemy? Are some conflicts so asymmetric and so hazardous to U.S. service members that they should not be joined?

Questions of a more programmatic nature also demand attention. How should the United States respond to adversaries who use tactics calculated to provoke bad behavior on the part of American soldiers, implicate them in abuses, rob them of their humanity, and diminish them in the eyes of the world? What is the accountability of senior civilian officials who encourage or countenance the torture of interrogation suspects? If the military is to play an expanded role in assisting civilian populations, how may their competence in such traditionally nonmilitary functions be enhanced? What should be the role of civilian contractors in formerly military tasks? What is the media's role and under what circumstances should journalists be embedded in military operations?

Finally, there are specific practical matters to be addressed. How can military personnel be better trained for the unfamiliar and dangerous environments in which they must function? Should the media be given or denied access to the process of repatriation of the remains of U.S. soldiers killed abroad? How should the increasingly high cost of treatment for modern battlefield injuries be met? Should U.S. community groups collect relief items for distribution by the troops? Should the coveted Purple Heart be awarded to those whose combat wound takes the form of PTSD rather than of a lost limb?[48] Should family caregivers whose ministrations make it possible to avoid institutionalizing the wounded be reimbursed for their labors?[49]

Paratroopers

Justin Thompson (AFC2001/001/43583), Photographs (PH98), VHP, AFC, LOC.

Justin Thompson was a member of the Army's Second Battalion, 20th Special Forces Group (Airborne), which was based at Bagram Airbase in Afghanistan from March to November 2003. His unit's mission within Operation Enduring Freedom was to search for and destroy weapons caches that could otherwise be used against coalition forces. Although the fighting was only sporadic, he found the conditions in Afghanistan "very rugged and dangerous." "The combat wasn't really combat," he recalls, describing it as "more them firing at a vehicle from about a mile away."

His Airborne Special Forces duties fulfilled a promise made by his recruiting officer—to find Thompson a post in the military where he could "jump out of airplanes." Thompson

Paratroopers continued

took the photograph just after landing during a Special Forces training mission in Karshi-Karabad ("K-2") in neighboring Uzbekistan. "I see that picture and think of all the exercises and training we did," he says. With the focus on Iraq, Thompson observed that, "It was basically a peaceful time." However he and fellow soldiers in his unit grew frustrated and angry "when we discovered and blew up the largest weapons cache yet found, and it didn't make the news." In more recent years, the tables have turned, he notes, with violence in Iraq largely limited to occasional suicide bombers while in Afghanistan the insurgents mount major campaigns. His Special Forces unit has already returned once to Afghanistan and is scheduled to make a third deployment.

Issues such as these, from macro to micro, may be reviewed and reassessed as the Obama administration settles in. Shortly after taking office, President Obama signaled a new approach toward defining and pursuing the threat of terrorism directed against the United States. Whether or not the changes that emerge over time signify "closing the door on the Bush administration's Global War on Terror," as some have suggested, remains to be seen.[50] Whatever the way forward, however, there is much to be learned from the front line experience of veterans over the past decade.

■ ■ ■

There are as many experiences of the wars in Afghanistan and Iraq as there are veterans. Each veteran takes us along on a very personal journey. Each journey represents a particular interaction between an individual soldier and the circumstances he or she confronts. Veterans interpret their experiences differently. At the same time, the process has certain archetypical elements, which connect these veterans to each other and to their predecessors in earlier conflicts. Few, if indeed any, of the two million plus veterans who have served in the Global War on Terror have emerged unscathed, few families unchanged, few communities unaffected.

The experience of veterans deserves to be understood and respected. There will be a time, in the aftermath of the wars, for critiquing the experience, probing the assumptions, challenging the assertions, and passing judgment on behavior, civilian and military alike. But the time is not now and the place is not here. The stories and the experiences are what they are and deserve respectful attention and thoughtful pondering in all of their commonalities and diversity.

NOTES

Introduction

1. Figures include casualties in non-hostile as well as hostile action. Source: DOD, Defense Manpower Data Center (DMDC), Data Analysis and Programs Division. Combined killed in action and wounded in action for OEF and OIF.
2. The figures used in the book's narrative are those that were available when the text was written in early 2009. This and later footnotes update the data. Thus by the end of 2009, more than two million U.S. military personnel had served in Afghanistan and Iraq. As of January 30, 2010, U.S. casualties in the Global War on Terror in its two major operations stood at 41,900. Source: DOD, Defense Manpower Data Center (DMDC), Data Analysis and Programs Division. Global War on Terror casualties by military service component, October 7, 2001 through January 30, 2010.
3. Medford, MA: Feinstein International Center, Tufts University (2007), http://www.fic.tufts.edu.
4. See Minear, *U.S. Citizen-Soldier,* Appendix 4, "Methodology," 84–86.
5. Robert D'Amico Collection (AFC2001/001/62471), DVD recording (MV01), Veterans History Project, American Folklife Center, Library of Congress (hereafter referred to as "VHP, AFC, LOC").
6. Telephone interview with the author, September 11, 2007. See also Shawn Stenberg Collection (AFC2001/001/41268), video recording (MV01), VHP, AFC, LOC.

Chapter1: The Global War on Terror

1. David Wood, "What's Missing in the War on Terrorism: An Overarching Strategy," Newhouse News Service, June 19, 2002, Newhouse.com.
2. Office of the Press Secretary, "President Holds Prime Time News Conference," October 11, 2001, http://www.globalsecurity.org/military/library/news/2001/10/mil-011011-usia01b.htm.

3. International Security Assistance Force website, http://www.nato.int/ISAF/ (accessed February 28, 2009).
4. President's Radio Address, March 20, 2003, www.whitehouse.gov/news/releases.
5. "President Bush Announces Major Combat Operations in Iraq Have Ended," May 1, 2003, http://georgewbush-whitehouse.archives.gov/news/releases/2003/05/20030501-15.html. Quoted in Catherine Dale, *Operation Iraqi Freedom: Strategies, Approaches, Results, and Issues for Congress,* Congressional Research Service (Damascus, MD: Penny Hill Press, December15, 2008), 37.
6. Department of Defense News Briefing with Secretary Rumsfeld and General Myers, June 30, 2003, available at http://www.defense.gov/Transcripts/Transcript.aspx?TranscriptID=2767. Quoted in Dale, *Operation Iraqi Freedom,* 52.
7. Dale, *Operation Iraqi Freedom*, 45.
8. Waleed Ibrahim and Tim Locks, "U.S. Forces under Iraq Mandate, Hand Over Green Zone," *Reuters*, January 1, 2009.
9. UN Security Council Resolution 1790, December 18, 2007.
10. UN Security Council Resolution 1483, May 22, 2003.
11. UN Security Council Resolution 1546, June 8, 2004.
12. Dale, *Operation Iraqi Freedom*, 44.
13. *Iraq Index: Tracking Variables of Reconstruction and Security in Post-Saddam Iraq*, February 5, 2009, 25, Brookings Institution, http://www.brookings.edu/iraqindex.
14. Helene Cooper, "Putting Stamp on Afghan War, Obama will Send 17,000 Troops," *New York Times*, February 18, 2009.
15. The twenty-eight countries were Afghanistan, Algeria, Armenia, Azerbaijan, Bangladesh, Colombia, Djibouti, Egypt, Ethiopia, Georgia, Hungary, India, Indonesia, Jordan, Kazakhstan, Kenya, Oman, Pakistan, Philippines, Poland, Russia, Saudi Arabia, Tajikistan, Tunisia, Turkey, Turkmenistan, Uzbekistan, and Yemen. For a discussion, see Larry Minear, "Colombia Country Study" in Antonio Donini et al., *Humanitarian Agenda 2015: Principles, Power, and Perceptions* (Medford, MA: Feinstein International Center, September 2006).
16. Eric Schmitt, "U.S. Training in West Africa Aims to Stave Off Extremists," *New York Times*, December 13, 2008.
17. Amy Belasco, *The Cost of Iraq, Afghanistan, and Other Global War on Terror Operations Since 9/11*, CRS Report for Congress, Congressional Research Service, updated October 15, 2008.
18. Linda J. Bilmes and Joseph E. Stiglitz, "The Iraq War Will Cost Us $3 Trillion, and Much More," *Washington Post,* March 9, 2008.
19. Updating the figures through the end of 2009, DOD reports that a total of 2,052,406 soldiers have been deployed in OEF and OIF. Of these, 809,612 have been deployed more than once. The total number of deployments for this period was 3,346,143. Source: DOD, DMDC, CTS, Deployment File for Operations Enduring Freedom and Iraqi Freedom as of December 31, 2009.
20. Executive Summary, *An Achievable Vision: Report of the Department of Defense Task Force on Mental Health.* Department of Defense Task Force on Mental Health (Falls Church, VA: Defense Health Board, 2007).

21. The global figures are taken from the Department of Defense's Contingency Tracking System, Profile of Service Members Currently Deployed as of November 30, 2008.
22. Thom Shanker, "Pentagon Rethinking Old Doctrine on 2 Wars," *New York Times*, March 15, 2009.
23. DOD CTS (Contingency Tracking System), Deployment File for Operations Enduring Freedom and Iraqi Freedom as of November 30, 2008. (Percentage calculations are by the author.)
24. Larry Minear, *The U.S. Citizen-Soldier and the Global War on Terror: The National Guard Experience* (Medford, MA: Feinstein International Center, Tufts University, 2007).
25. Damon DiMarco, *Heart of War: Soldiers' Voices from the Front Lines in Iraq* (New York: Citadel Press, 2007), xv.
26. DOD, DMDC, CTS, Operation Enduring Freedom, Military Deaths and Military Wounded in Action, October 7, 2001 through January 3, 2009.
27. DOD, DMDC, CTS, Operation Iraqi Freedom, Military Deaths and Military Wounded in Action, March 19, 2003 through January 3, 2009.
28. The numbers in Figure 4 have been calculated by the author from the source indicated in the two previous footnotes.
29. The percentages updated through January 2, 2010 are: active-duty personnel, 80.6%; National Guard, 6.9%; Reserves, 12.5%. Source: DOD, DMDC, Analysis and Programs Division.
30. The updated percentages are: Army, 71%; Navy, 2%; Marines, 25.5%; Air Force, 1.5%. Source: DOD, DMDC, Data Analysis and Programs Division.
31. DOD, "Operation Iraqi Freedom." DOD reports 1,841 casualties among persons whose ages were not known, with casualties for veterans of all ages totaling 38,399. By age, the updated percentages are: under age 22, 28.5%; ages 22 to 24, 26.1%; ages 25 to 30, 25.3%; ages 31 to 35, 10.2%; age 36 and over, 9.9%. Source: DOD, DMDC, Data Analysis and Programs Division.
32. Julia Preston, "U.S. Military Will Offer Path to Citizenship," *New York Times*, February 15, 2009. Thereafter, the slumping U.S. economy made for greater ease in meeting recruitment targets. See James Dao, "With Recruiting Goals Exceeded, Marines Toughen Their Ad Pitch." *New York Times*, September 18, 2009.
33. Veterans for America, *American Veterans and Servicemembers Survival Guide*, 2008, 25.
34. The updated figures for casualties according to gender are: male, 98.1%; female, 1.9%. As of January 2, 2010, 20 women had lost their lives in Afghanistan and 104 in Iraq. Source: DOD, DMDC, Data Analysis and Programs Division.
35. The updated casualty figures by race and ethnicity are: white, 77%; black, 8.2%; Hispanic, 6.6%; Asian/Pacific Islander, 2.3%; Native American/Alaskan, 1.1%; multi-racial, 4.8%. Source: DOD, DMDC, Data Analysis and Programs Division.
36. Anita U. Hattiangadi et al., "Non-Citizens in Today's Military," Center for Naval Analyses, Alexandria, VA, April 2005. A more recent estimate places

the number at 29,000. See Bryan Bender, "Foreigners Answer Call to U.S. Service," *Boston Globe*, March 1, 2009.

37. Veterans for America, *Survival Guide,* 575–76.
38. The figures cited in this paragraph come from Veterans for America, "Trends in Treatment of America's Wounded Warriors" (Washington, November 7, 2007): 3–4.

Chapter 2: Enlistment and Patriotism

1. Terrell Spencer Collection (AFC/001/57175), manuscript (MS01), VHP, AFC, LOC.
2. Jeremy Lima Collection (AFC2001/001/53039), transcript (MS01), VHP, AFC, LOC.
3. William Andrews Collection (AFC2001/001/42880), transcript (MS04), VHP, AFC, LOC.
4. Telephone interview, April 30, 2007.
5. Andrew Wells Collection (AFC2001/001/50457), video recording (MV01), VHP, AFC, LOC.
6. Lizette Alvarez, "More Americans Join Military as Jobs Dwindle," *New York Times*, January 19, 2009.
7. Brandon Bass Collection (AFC2001/001/62664), transcript (MS04), VHP, AFC, LOC.
8. Brian Coles Collection (AFC2001/001/41574), DVD (MV01), VHP, AFC, LOC. Photos taken by Coles during his two deployments are found in Chapter 6.
9. This quotation is taken from an interview in the collection of the Pryor Center at the University of Arkansas and is used with permission.
10. Matthew Neely Collection (AFC2001/001/29104), transcript (MS04), VHP, AFC, LOC.
11. Phillip Geiger Collection (AFC2001/001/30333), transcript (MS04), VHP, AFC, LOC.
12. Nicole Ferretti Collection (AFC2001/001/57083), transcript (MS04), VHP, AFC, LOC.
13. "Warriors: What It Is Really Like to Be a Soldier in Iraq," Public Broadcasting System, aired April 2007.
14. Brian Aria Collection (AFC2001/001/50457), video recording (MV01), VHP, AFC, LOC.
15. In Matthew Currier Burden, *The Blog of War: Front-Line Dispatches from Soldiers in Iraq and Afghanistan* (New York: Simon and Schuster, 2006), 10.
16. Basil Cofield Collection (AFC2001/001/60173), transcript (MS01), VHP, AFC, LOC.
17. Gregory Schulte Collection, (AFC2001/001/30235), video recording (MV01), VHP, AFC, LOC.
18. Jude Ferran Collection (AFC2001/001/30609), audio recording (SR01), VHP, AFC, LOC.
19. Interview, Concord, New Hampshire, April 25, 2007.
20. In Yvonne Latty, *In Conflict: Iraq War Veterans Speak Out on Duty, Loss, and the Fight to Stay Alive* (Sausalito, CA: PoliPointPress, 2006), 129.

21. Shawn Molloy Collection (AFC2001/001/46283), audio recording (SR01), VHP, AFC, LOC.
22. Patrick McGonigle III Collection (AFC2001/001/48161), video recording (MV01), VHP, AFC, LOC.
23. Mark Warnecke Collection (AFC2001/001/34941), video recording (MV01), VHP, AFC, LOC.
24. Timothy Rieger Collection (AFC2001/001/44622), video recording (MV01), VHP, AFC, LOC.
25. Jay Czarga's farewell letter to his family is reprinted in Burden, *Blog of War*, 20. His blog is located at www.themakahasurfreport.blogspot.com.
26. Joseph Medina Collection (AFC2001/001/28619) video recording (MV01), VHP, AFC, LOC.
27. Eric March Collection (AFC2001/001/43154) video recording (MV01), VHP, AFC, LOC.
28. PBS, "Warriors," in the PBS series "America at a Crossroads," 2007.
29. Interview, Concord, New Hampshire, April 26, 2007.
30. Christopher Buser Collection (AFC2001/001/51140), video recording (MV01), VHP, AFC, LOC.
31. Interview, Manchester, New Hampshire, May 9, 2007.
32. Interview, Brighton, Massachusetts, May 2, 2007.
33. Eric Giles Collection (AFC2001/001/58906), audio recording (SR01), VHP, AFC, LOC.
34. Travis Fisher Collection (AFC2001/001/34140), video recording (MV01), VHP, AFC, LOC.
35. Dana Canedy, *A Journal for Jordan: A Story of Love and Honor* (New York: Crown Publishers, 2008), 7.
36. Interview, Concord, New Hampshire, May 16, 2007.
37. Terrell Spencer Collection (AFC2001/001/57175), transcript (MS01), VHP, AFC, LOC.
38. Julia Preston, "Sharp Rise Seen in Applications for Citizenship," *New York Times*, July 5, 2007.
39. Ferretti Collection, VHP.
40. Latty, *In Conflict*, 178
41. Michael Gordon, "U.S. Command Shortens Life of 'Long War' as a Reference," *New York Times*, April 23, 2007.
42. Associated Press, "Audit Finds Flaws in Terror Statistics," *New York Times*, February 23, 2007. See also Lara Jakes Jordan, "FBI List on Terror Suspects Outdated, Incomplete, Audit Says," *Associated Press*, March 18, 2008.
43. Gordon, "U.S. Command Shortens Life."

Chapter 3: Politics and Professionalism

1. *Concord Monitor*, September 30, 2006.
2. Quotations from the New Hampshire National Guard Guard's unpublished *War on Terrorism History Project* (March–September 2005) are made without attribution to individual veterans under ground rules agreed to by the author.

3. Sarah Sewall and John P. White, "The Civil-Military Challenge," *Boston Globe*, January 29, 2009.
4. "Back from Battle: Student Veterans' Perspectives on the Iraq War," *Yale Journal of International Affairs* (Spring/Summer 2007): 137.
5. Joelle Farrell, "Veterans Divided over War's Politics," *Concord Monitor*, October 1, 2006.
6. Ralan Hill Collection (AFC2001/001/43145), transcript (MS01), VHP, AFC, LOC.
7. Craig Keys Collection (AFC2001/001/39063), audio recording (SR01), VHP, AFC, LOC
8. Matthew Smith Collection (AFC2001/001/52561), video recording (MV01), VHP, AFC, LOC.
9. Farrell, "Veterans Divided."
10. Holland Carter, "Words Unspoken Are Rendered on War's Faces," *New York Times*, August 22, 2007.
11. Ralph Riley Collection (AFC2001/001/43537), audio recording (SR01), VHP, AFC, LOC.
12. "Warriors: What It Is Really Like to Be a Soldier in Iraq," PBS, aired April 2007.
13. Andrew Carroll, ed. *Operation Homecoming: Iraq, Afghanistan, and the Home Front, in the Words of U.S. Troops and Their Families* (New York: Random House, 2006), 156.
14. Farrell, "Veterans Divided."
15. Quotations are taken from a transcript of *The War Tapes*, by Steve Pink, Zack Bazzi, and Mike Moriarty and used with their permission. The documentary, which aired in 2006, was directed by Deborah Scranton and produced by Robert May and Steve James (Senart Films, 2006).
16. Ibid.
17. Ibid.
18. Eric Cox Collection (AFC2001/001/52703), transcript (MS04), VHP, AFC, LOC.
19. In Damon DiMarco, *Heart of War: Soldiers' Voices from the Front Lines in Iraq* (New York: Citadel Press Books, 2007), 38.
20. Derek Sutton Collection (AFC2001/001/47344), audio recording (SR01), VHP, AFC, LOC.
21. Mark Warnecke Collection (AFC2001/001/34941), video recording (MV01), VHP, AFC, LOC.
22. Joshua Townsend Collection (AFC2001/001/39304), transcript (MS04), VHP, AFC, LOC.
23. Pink, Bazzi, and Moriarty, *The War Tapes.*
24. Carroll, *Operation Homecoming,* xxv.
25. Pink, Bazzi, and Moriarty, *The War Tapes.*
26. Farrell, "Veterans Divided."
27. In Matthew Currier Burden, *The Blog of War: Front-Line Dispatches from Soldiers in Iraq and Afghanistan* (New York: Simon and Schuster, 2006), 255.

28. Bradley Burd Collection (AFC2001/001/30269), video recording (MV01), VHP, AFC, LOC.
29. James Welch Collection (AFC2001/001/29065), audio recording (SR01), VHP, AFC, LOC.
30. Paul Gregory Mayfield Collection (AFC2001/001/60193), transcript (MS04), VHP, AFC, LOC.
31. Michael Kamber, "As Allies Turn Foe, Disillusion Arises among Some G.I.'s," *New York Times*, May 28, 2007.
32. Pink, Bazzi, and Moriarty, *The War Tapes*.
33. Ibid.
34. Ibid.
35. Interview, South Ryegate, Vermont, January 17, 2007.
36. Telephone interview, May 25, 2007.
37. An examination of the leadership provided by veterans from Iraq to antiwar efforts is the subject of Matthew Gutmann and Catherine Lutz, *Breaking Ranks: Iraq Vets Speak Out Against the War* (Berkeley: University of California Press, 2010, in press).
38. In Yvonne Latty, *In Conflict: Iraq War Veterans Speak Out on Duty, Loss, and the Fight to Stay Alive* (Sausalito, CA: PoliPointPress, 2006), 16.
39. Peter Slevin, "After War Injury, an Iraq Vet Takes on Politics." *Washington Post*, February 19, 2006.
40. "Kirk, Biggert Hearing on Improving Lives of Military Reservists," Press Release, U.S. Congressman Mark S. Kirk website, March 22, 2005.
41. Ryan Aument Collection (AFC2001/001/62372), video recording (MV01), VHP, AFC, LOC.
42. Anna Badken, "Volunteering for Duty: Veterans of the Iraq War Try to Complete Their Mission in a New Way: Charity," *Boston Globe*, February 15, 2009.
43. Latty, *In Conflict*, 62.
44. Irene Sege, "Veterans take their war views to the trail: N.H. campaigning could have impact," *Boston Globe*, October 17, 2008.
45. Thom Shanker, "Military Chief Warns Troops about Politics," *New York Times*, May 26, 2008.
46. Bryan Bender, "VWF, American Legion Back Iraq War," *Boston Globe*, August 16, 2007.
47. John McChesny, "Vets Groups Proliferate, along with Agendas," National Public Radio, *All Things Considered*, April 4, 2007.
48. www.ivaw.org.
49. VetsForFreedom.org, accessed March 10, 2007.
50. http://www.sldn.org/.
51. Leslie Laufman, "Veterans' Families Seek Aid for Caregiver," *New York Times*, November 12, 2008.
52. Telephone interview, Nancy Lessin, cofounder, Military Families Speak Out, August 21, 2007.
53. Anthony Swofford, Foreword, in *Iraq Veterans Against the War*, and Aaron Glantz, *Winter Soldier Iraq and Afghanistan: Eyewitness Accounts of the Occupations* (Chicago: Haymarket Books, 2008), ix.

54. Press Release, "Military Families Speak Out," July 28, 2007.
55. Veterans History Project, Field Kit, Library of Congress (undated).
56. Craig Keys Collection (AFC2001/001/39063), manuscript (MS04), VHP, AFC, LOC.
57. As reported by his mother, Carole Welch. Interview, South Ryegate, Vermont, January 17, 2007.
58. Roxana Tiron, "Huckabee, Dems, to Meet Retired Officers on Torture," *The Hill*, November 30, 2007. Also Holly Ramer, "Ex-Officers Brief Dems on Humane Tactics," Associated Press, April 13, 2007.
59. Randall Mikkelsen, "Ex-Generals to Urge Obama Action on Torture Issue," Reuters, December 2, 2008.
60. Sarah Sewall and John P. White, "The Civil-Military Challenge," *Boston Globe*, January 29, 2009.
61. Brian Aria Collection (AFC2001/001/50457), video recording (MV01), VHP, AFC, LOC.

Chapter 4: Coping with Unfamiliarity and Violence

1. Linda McHale Collection (AFC2001/001/47162), manuscript (MS04), VHP, AFC, LOC.
2. Julius Tulley in Yvonne Latty, *In Conflict: Iraq War Veterans Speak Out on Duty, Loss, and the Fight to Stay Alive* (Sausalito, CA: PoliPointPress, 2006), 112.
3. McHale Collection, VHP.
4. New Hampshire National Guard, *Global War on Terrorism History Project,* (March–September 2005, unpublished).
5. James Maddix Jr. Collection (AFC2001/001/30235), video recording (MV01), VHP, AFC, LOC.
6. Aubrey Shea Youngs Collection (AFC2001/001/41857), audio recording (SR01), VHP, AFC, LOC.
7. Travis Fisher Collection (AFC2001/001/34140), video recording (MV01), VHP, AFC, LOC.
8. Andrew Carroll, ed. *Operation Homecoming: Iraq, Afghanistan, and the Home Front, in the Words of U.S. Troops and Their Families* (New York: Random House, 2006), 108.
9. Jude Ferran Collection (AFC2001/001/30609), audio recording (SR01), VHP, AFC, LOC.
10. Michael Kamber, "As Allies Turn Foe, Disillusion Rises in Some G.I.'s," *New York Times*, May 28, 2007.
11. "Warriors," in "America at a Crossroads, PBS, aired April 2007.
12. Shawn Molloy Collection (AFC2001/001/46283), audio recording (SR01), VHP, AFC, LOC.
13. Pink, Bazzi, and Moriarty, *The War Tapes.*
14. New Hampshire National Guard, *Global War on Terrorism.*
15. Joelle Farrell, "Lessons of War," *Concord Monitor*, October 3, 2006.
16. Interview, Brighton, Massachusetts, May 2, 2007.
17. Pink, Bazzi, and Moriarty, *The War Tapes.*

18. Ralph Riley Collection (AFC2001/001/43537), audio recording (SR01), VHP, AFC, LOC.
19. Joelle Farrell, "The Forgotten Five," *Concord Monitor*, October 2, 2007.
20. New Hampshire National Guard, *Global War on Terrorism.*
21. Henry Lujan Collection (AFC2001/001/31394), audio recording (SR01), VHP, AFC, LOC
22. Jeffrey Bartling Collection (AFC2001/001/29443), manuscript (MS04), VHP, AFC, LOC.
23. Ryan Aument Collection (AFC2001/001/62372), video recording (MV01), VHP, AFC, LOC.
24. New Hampshire National Guard, *Global War on Terrorism.*
25. Elizabeth Jensen, "From Brownstone to Baghdad, TV Crew Armed with Ingenuity," *New York Times*, April 16, 2007.
26. Sabrina Tavernise, "In Life of Lies, Iraqis Conceal Work for U.S.: Desperate for Pay, but Fearing Reprisal," *New York Times*, October 7, 2008.
27. Ernesto Londoro, "Ban on Masks Upsets Iraqi Interpreters," *Washington Post*, November 17, 2008.
28. Dana Canedy, *A Journal for Jordan: A Story of Love and Honor* (New York: Crown Publishers, 2008), 96. For a description of a similar effort at Fort Polk, LA., see James Dao, "To Prepare for War, G.I.'s Get a Dress Rehearsal." *New York Times*, November 29, 2009.
29. Paul Gregory Mayfield Collection (AFC2001/001/60193), transcript (MS04), VHP, AFC, LOC.
30. David Rhode, "Army Enlists Anthropology in War Zones," *New York Times*, October 5, 2007.
31. Ibid.
32. Bryan Bender, "Efforts to Aid U.S. Roil Anthropology," *Boston Globe*, October 8, 2007.
33. Rhode, "Army Enlists Anthropology." Brown University academic Michael Bhatia lost his life in Iraq as a member of one such team. See Adam Geller, "One Man's Odyssey from Campus to Combat," Associated Press, March 7, 2009.
34. Julia Preston, "U.S. Military Will Offer Path to Citizenship: Temporary Immigrants Are Program's Focus," *New York Times*, February 15, 2009.
35. Bryan Bender, "Foreigners Answer Call to U.S. Service: Military Efforts to Recruit Specialists Gets Big Response," *Boston Globe*, March 1, 2009.
36. Julia Preston, "Thriving Military Recruitment Program Blocked," *New York Times*, January 22, 2010. Pentagon efforts to increase the troops' sensitivity to local mores were also undercut by its firing of scores of gay linguists from its own ranks. See Stephen Benjamin, "Don't Ask, Don't Translate," *New York Times*, June 8, 2007.
37. C. W. Hogue et al., "Combat Duty in Iraq and Afghanistan: Mental Health Problems and Barriers to Care," *New England Journal of Medicine* 351, no. 1 (July 1, 2004). With the conflict in Iraq still at an early stage, the study's sample involved more troops after duty in Afghanistan (1,962) than in Iraq (894).

38. Jay Craven and Robert Miller, *After the Fog: Interviews with Combat Veterans* (Barnet, VT: Kingdom County Productions, 2006). The portions quoted were transcribed and edited by the author and amplified in an interview with Pickett, and are used with permission.
39. Theresa Little Collection (AFC2001/001/57131), transcript (MS04), VHP, AFC, LOC.
40. John Little Collection (AFC2001/001/30295), video recording (MV01), VHP, AFC, LOC.
41. Pink, Bazzi, and Moriarty, *The War Tapes.*
42. Latty, *In Conflict,* 138.
43. Nicole Ferretti Collection (AFC2001/001/57083), transcript (MS04), VHP, AFC, LOC.
44. Gregg Zoroya, "Soldier's Death Reflects Impact of Stress in the Ranks: Incidents Increase as Pentagon Extends Time Many Spend in Combat," *USA Today*, January 13, 2009.
45. Mayfield Collection, VHP.
46. New Hampshire National Guard, *Global War on Terrorism.*
47. Mark Warnecke Collection (AFC2001/001/34941), video recording (MV01), VHP, AFC, LOC.
48. Latty, *In Conflict,* 76.
49. The focus group, convened by the author, was held in the Bradford, Vermont, armory on November 13, 2006.
50. Matthew C. Burden, *The Blog of War: Front-line Dispatches from Soldiers in Iraq and Afghanistan* (New York: Simon and Schuster, 2006), 125.
51. Christopher Walotka Collection (AFC2001/001/30268), video recording (MV01), VHP, AFC, LOC.
52. Trevor Bradna Collection (AFC2001/001/47553), audio recording (SR01), VHP, AFC, LOC.
53. Carroll, *Operation Homecoming,* 68.
54. Jonathan Trouern-Trend, *Birding in Babylon: A Soldier's Journal from Iraq* (San Francisco: Sierra Club Books, 2006): 9, 11, 12. His postings are archived at http://birdingbabylon.blogspot.com.
55. New Hampshire National Guard, *Global War on Terrorism.*
56. Carroll, *Operation Homecoming,* 128.
57. Sgt. Lorin T. Smith, "Texans Perform 'Duty Day with God,'" *On Guard*, 36, no. 3 (March 2007): 13.
58. Jeffrey Bitcon, "Letter from Afghanistan: Some Notes about Ramadan," *Caledonian Record*, October 3, 2005.
59. Carroll, *Operation Homecoming,* 337.
60. Ralan Hill Collection (AFC2001/001/43145), transcript (MS04), VHP, AFC, LOC.
61. Stephanie Corcoran, "Year in Review," November 20, 2006, correspondence with the author.
62. Ibid.
63. Latty, *In Conflict,* 47–48.

64. Eric Giles Collection (AFC2001/001/58906), audio recording (SR01), VHP, AFC, LOC.
65. New Hampshire National Guard, *Global War on Terrorism.*
66. Mayfield Collection, VHP.
67. Damian Budziszewski Collection (AFC2001/001/39092), transcript (MS04), VHP, AFC, LOC.
68. Rick Mayes Collection (AFC2001/001/57132), manuscript (MS01), VHP, AFC, LOC.

Chapter 5: Wrestling with Ethical Issues

1. Joelle Farrell, "In Combat Brian Shelton Comes of Age," *Concord Monitor*, October 1, 2006.
2. James Welch Collection (AFC2001/001/29065), audio recording (SR01), VHP, AFC, LOC.
3. Tyler Mueller Collection (AFC2001/001/15910), video recording (MV01), VHP, AFC, LOC.
4. Steve Pink, Zack Bazzi, and Mike Moriarty, *The War Tapes*. Directed by Deborah Scranton and produced by Robert May (Senart Films, 2006).
5. Ibid.
6. Derek Sutton Collection (AFC2001/001/47344), audio recording (SR01), VHP, AFC, LOC.
7. Pink, Bazzi, and Moriarty, *The War Tapes.*
8. Yvonne Latty, *In Conflict: Iraq War Veterans Speak Out on Duty, Loss, and the Fight to Stay Alive* (Sausalito, CA: PoliPointPress, 2006), 132.
9. Theodor A. van Baarda and Desirée E. M. Verweij, eds., *Military Ethics: The Dutch Approach—A Practical Guide* (Leiden and Boston: Brill Academic Publishers, 2006), xiv
10. Pink, Bazzi, and Moriarty, *The War Tapes.*
11. Travis Fisher Collection (AFC2001/001/34140), video recording (MV01), VHP, AFC, LOC.
12. Joelle Farrell, "Lessons of War," *Concord Monitor*, October 3, 2006,
13. James Maddix Jr. Collection (AFC2001/001/27736), video recording (MV01), VHP, AFC, LOC.
14. Ibid.
15. Welch Collection, VHP.
16. Eric Heath Collection (AFC2001/001/57086), transcript (MS04), VHP, AFC, LOC.
17. David Brooks, "A Million Little Pieces," *New York Times*, June 5, 2007.
18. Farrell, "War Stories: In Combat," A6.
19. James Nappier Collection (AFC2001/001/43525), video recording (MV01), VHP, AFC, LOC.
20. William Jones Collection (AFC2001/001/47486), transcript (MS04), VHP, AFC, LOC.
21. Bobby Lee Lisek Collection (AFC2001/001/60191), transcript (MS04), VHP, AFC, LOC.

22. Benedict Carey, "Stress on Troops Adds To U.S. Hurdles in Iraq," *New York Times*, May 6, 2007. The survey of troops noted in Chapter 3 found that 1 percent of those sampled with combat experience in Afghanistan and 7 percent in Iraq reported having been responsible for the death of at least one noncombatant.
23. Thomas Ricks and Ann Scott Tyson, "Troops at Odds with Ethics Standards: Army Also Finds More Deployment Means More Mental Illness," *Washington Post*, May 5, 2007.
24. Chris Hedges and Laila al-Arian, "The Other War: Iraq Vets Bear Witness," *The Nation*, July 30, 2007, http://www.thenation.com/doc/20070730/hedges.
25. Ibid.
26. Maddix Jr. Collection, VHP.
27. "Warriors: What It Is Really Like To Be a Soldier in Iraq," Public Broadcasting System, aired April 2007.
28. John McCary, "To the Fallen," in *Operation Homecoming: Iraq, Afghanistan, and the Home Front, in the Words of U.S. Troops and Their Families*, ed. Andrew Carroll (New York: Random House, 2006), 300.
29. Pink, Bazzi, and Moriarty, *The War Tapes*.
30. Jay Craven and Robert Miller, *After the Fog: Interviews with Combat Veterans*, (Barnet, VT: Kingdom County Productions, 2006).
31. William Schelhouse Collection (AFC/2001/001/47506), video recording (MV01), VHP, AFC, LOC
32. Blake Cole Collection (AFC2001/001/62554) video recording (MV01), VHP, AFC, LOC.
33. Maria Cochran Collection (AFC2001/001/62436) audio recording (SR01), VHP, AFC, LOC.
34. William Yardley, "Trial Starts for Officer Who Refused to Go to Iraq," *New York Times*, February 6, 2007. See also Jeremy Brecher and Brendan Smith, "Lt. Watada's War Against the War," *Nation*, June 26, 2006. On October 26, 2009, the Army allowed Watada to resign.
35. Latty, *In Conflict*, 169–170.
36. Ibid, 177. Mejía published a book in 2007 on his experiences, *Road from ar Ramadi: The Private Rebellion of Staff Sergeant Camilo Mejía* (New York: New Press), and has played a prominent role in the activities of veterans opposed to the Iraq war.
37. Bill Nichols, "8,000 Desert during the Iraq War," *USA Today*, March 7, 2006.
38. Hedges and al-Arian, "The Other War."
39. Paul Gregory Mayfield Collection (AFC2001/001/60193), transcript (MS04), VHP, AFC, LOC.
40. New Hampshire National Guard, *Global War on Terrorism History Project* (March to September 2005, unpublished).
41. Correspondence dated March 7, 2007, from Ryan T. McCarthy to Anne Miller, director, New Hampshire Peace Action.
42. Mayfield Collection, VHP.
43. Heath Collection, VHP.

44. Quoted in Seymour M. Hersh, "The General's Report: How Antonio Taguba, Who Investigated the Abu Ghraib Scandal, Became One of Its Casualties," *New Yorker*, June 25, 2007.
45. Ibid., 69.
46. Mark Mazzeti, "Rules Lay Out C.I.A.'s Tactics in Questioning," *New York Times*, July 21, 2007. Also Charlie Savage, "Bush Issues Orders on Interrogations," *Boston Globe*, July 21, 2007.
47. Bob Woodward, "Detainee Tortured, Says U.S. Official," *Washington Post*, January 14, 2009.
48. Carroll, *Operation Homecoming*, 292.
49. Pink, Bazzi, and Moriarty, *The War Tapes*.
50. Allison Steele, "After Suicide, Nothing but Questions," *Concord Monitor*, June 26, 2005.
51. Mark LaChance, "War Makes Monsters of Us All," in *Warrior Writers: Move, Shoot, and Communicate,* ed. Lovella Calica (Burlington, VT: Iraq Veterans Against the War, 2007), 14–15.
52. Latty, *In Conflict,* 157.
53. Charles White Collection (AFC2001/001/53770), video recording (MV01), VHP, AFC, LOC.

Chapter 6: Winning Hearts and Minds

1. Jeremy Krug Collection (AFC2001/001/28682), video recording (MV01), VHP, AFC, LOC.
2. Andrew Wells Collection (AFC2001/001/54819), video recording (MV01), VHP, AFC, LOC.
3. New Hampshire National Guard, *Global War on Terrorism History Project* (March to September 2005, unpublished).
4. Benjamin Braden Collection (AFC2001/001/30610), audio recording (SR01), VHP, AFC, LOC.
5. Dennis Harvey Collection (AFC2001/001/38625), video recording (MV01), VHP, AFC, LOC.
6. Rex Hendrix Collection (AFC2001/001/51205), audio recording (SR01), VHP, AFC, LOC.
7. New Hampshire National Guard, *Global War on Terrorism.*
8. Ibid.
9. Ibid.
10. Chris McCann, "Iraqi, U.S. Soldiers Bring Smiles to Schools," U.S. Central Command, April 4, 2007, dateline: Az Zaidon, Iraq.
11. Joelle Farrell, "Veterans Divided over War's Politics," *Concord Monitor*, October 1, 2006.
12. Shawn Molloy Collection (AFC2001/001/46283), audio recording (SR01), VHP, AFC, LOC.
13. James Machen Collection (AFC2001/001/21371), VHP, AFC, LOC.
14. Daniel Neville Collection (AFC2001/001/55035), video recording (MV01), VHP, AFC, LOC.

15. New Hampshire National Guard, *Global War on Terrorism.*
16. Jacqueline Mitchell, "The Major's Got Wings: It Takes a Tender Veterinarian to Fix Iraq's Poultry Industry," *Tufts Magazine* (Spring 2008): 12–13.
17. Andrew Carroll, ed. *Operation Homecoming: Iraq, Afghanistan, and the Home Front, in the Words of U.S. Troops and Their Families* (New York: Random House, 2006), 68–69.
18. http://www.operationiraqichildren.org.
19. Joelle Farrell, "The Forgotten Five," *Concord Monitor,* October 2, 2007, A6.
20. Eric March Collection (AFC2001/001/43154), video recording (MV01), VHP, AFC, LOC.
21. Telephone interview, March 20, 2009.
22. Metz Duites Collection (AFC2001/001/58571), video recording (MV01), VHP, AFC, LOC.
23. Linda McHale Collection (AFC2001/001/47162), transcript (MS04), VHP, AFC, LOC.
24. See, for example, *New York Times*, March 6, 2007, also August 15, 2007.
25. New Hampshire National Guard, *2006 Missions*, CD.
26. *Granite Guardian* (Summer/Fall 2007): 10, 18.
27. Gregory Schulte Collection (AFC2001/001/30235), video recording (MV01), VHP, AFC, LOC.
28. Joelle Farrell, "War Stories: In Combat Brian Shelton Comes of Age," *Concord Monitor*, October 1, 2006.
29. New Hampshire National Guard, *Global War on Terrorism.*
30. Paul Gregory Mayfield Collection (AFC2001/001/60193), transcript (MS04), VHP, AFC, LOC.
31. Farrell, "In Combat."
32. Petraeus and Amos, U.S. Army, Counterinsurgency Field Manual, 2006, A47.
33. New Hampshire National Guard, *Global War on Terrorism.*
34. Yvonne Latty, *In Conflict: Iraq War Veterans Speak Out on Duty, Loss, and the Fight to Stay Alive* (Sausalito, CA: PoliPointPress, 2006), 46–47.
35. For a detailed discussion of tensions between military and humanitarian actors in Afghanistan and Iraq, see Antonio Donini et al., *The State of the Humanitarian Enterprise: Humanitarian Agenda 2015,* Final Report (Medford, MA: Feinstein International Center, 2008). Also Greg Hansen, "Iraq: More Challenges Ahead for a Fractured Humanitarian Enterprise" (Feinstein International Center, January 2009), fic.tufts.edu.
36. In July 2007, agreement was reached between humanitarian and military actors following a two-year consultative process on "Guidelines for Relations between U.S. Forces and Non-governmental Humanitarian Organizations in Non-Permissive Environments." See Linda Poteat, "InterAction Member CEOs Launch Civil-Military Guidelines with DOD," InterAction *Monday Developments* 25, no. 8 (August 2007): 28.
37. After considerable discussion, President Obama committed an additional 30,000 troops to Afghanistan in December 2009. See "Inside the Situation Room: How a War Plan Evolved," Peter Baker, *New York Times*, December 6, 2009.

Chapter 7: Working with Private Contractors

1. Rick Mayes Collection (AFC2001/001/57132), video recording (MV01), VHP, AFC, LOC.
2. Rex Hendrix Collection (AFC2001/001/51205), audio recording (SR01), VHP, AFC, LOC.
3. Paul Gregory Mayfield Collection (AFC2001/001/60193), transcript (MS04), VHP, AFC, LOC.
4. Christopher Gamblin Collection (AFC2001/001/60182), transcript (MS04), VHP, AFC, LOC.
5. Jeremy Krug Collection (AFC2001/001/28682), video recording (MV01), VHP, AFC, LOC.
6. Terrell Spencer Collection, (AFC2001/001/57175), transcript (MS04), VHP, AFC, LOC.
7. Press Conference by Maj. Gen. Michael Eyre, commanding general, Gulf Region Division, and Richard Hancock, *Reconstruction Update,* January 25, 2009. Operation Iraqi Freedom website, http://www.mnf-iraq.com/index.php?option=com_frontpage&Itemid=1 (accessed January 29, 2009).
8. Jackie Northam, "The Impact of War: Contract Businesses Thrive during Wartime," *Morning Edition*, National Public Radio, June 25, 2007.
9. For a more extended discussion, see P. W. Singer, *Corporate Warriors: The Rise of the Privatized Military Industry* (Ithaca and London: Cornell University Press, 2008, updated edition), 254.
10. Shangraw in Steve Pink, Zack Bazzi, and Mike Moriarty, *The War Tapes*. Directed by Deborah Scranton and produced by Robert May (Senart Films, 2006).
11. Brandon Wilkins, in Pink, Bazzi, and Moriarty, *The War Tapes*. Cheney left DOD in 1995 to become chief executive officer of Halliburton, serving as board chair from 1996 to 1998 and again in 2000. In August 2000, he left Halliburton to run for the vice presidency on the ticket of George W. Bush. He served as U.S. vice president from January 2001 to January 2009. Halliburtonwatch.org (accessed August 16, 2007).
12. Joelle Farrell, " 'Risking My Life for Kitty Litter': Halliburton Raises the Ire of Some Soldiers," *Concord Monitor*, October 3, 2006.
13. Interview, Brighton, Massachusetts, May 2, 2007.
14. Pink, Bazzi, and Moriarty, *The War Tapes*.
15. Correspondence with the author, March 12, 2009.
16. Spencer Collection, VHP.
17. Samuel Main Collection (AFC2001/001/56467), transcript (MS04), VHP, AFC, LOC.
18. Eric Schmitt and Thom Shanker, "Pentagon Sees One Authority over Guards," *New York Times*, October 17, 2007.
19. IAVA, "Veterans Demand Answers from KBR," press release, January 8, 2009.
20. See, for example, James Glanz, C. J. Chivers, and William K. Rashbaum, "Inquiry on Graft in Iraq Focuses on U.S. Officers: Contracting at Issue," *New York Times*, February 15, 2009.

21. James Glanz and Sabrina Tavernise, "Security Firm Faces Criminal Charges in Iraq," *New York Times,* September 23, 2007.
22. Janine R. Wedel, "The Shadow Army," *Boston Globe,* September 30, 2007.
23. David M. Herszenhorn, "House's Iraq Bill Applies U.S. Laws to Contractors," *New York Times*, October 5, 2007.
24. Waleed Ibrahim and Tim Cocks, "U.S. Forces under Iraq mandate, hand over Green Zone," Reuters, January 1, 2009.
25. Jeremy Scahill, "Iraq: A Very Private War," *Guardian*, August 1, 2007. See also Scahill, *Blackwater: The Rise of the World's Most Powerful Mercenary Army* (London: Serpent's Tail, 2007).
26. Valerie Bailey Grasso, "Defense Contracting in Iraq: Issues and Options for Congress," Congressional Research Service Report for Congress (updated May 16, 2007), summary page.
27. James Risen, "Use of Contractors in Iraq Costs Billions, Report Says," *New York Times*, August 11, 2008. In mid-2009, an independent wartime contracting commission reported major abuses in performance and accounting by KBR and other private contractors. See Richard Lardner, "Panel Cites Billions in Wasteful Spending on War Contractors." *Boston Globe*, June 8, 2009.

Chapter 8: Dealing with the Media and Public Opinion

1. Bobby Lisek Collection (AFC2001/001/60191), transcript (MS04), VHP, AFC, LOC.
2. Mark Kaplan Collection (AFC2001/001/57488), video recording (MV01), VHP, AFC, LOC.
3. Andrew Carroll, ed. *Operation Homecoming: Iraq, Afghanistan, and the Home Front, in the Words of U.S. Troops and Their Families.* (New York: Random House, 2006), xxv.
4. Brian Clousen Collection (AFC2001/001/16248), audio recording (SR01), VHP, AFC, LOC.
5. In Carroll, *Operation Homecoming*, 127.
6. James Maddix Jr. Collection (AFC2001/001/27736), video recording (MV01), VHP, AFC, LOC.
7. Justin Thompson Collection (AFC2001/001 /43583), audio recording (SR01), VHP, AFC, LOC.
8. Derek Sutton Collection (AFC2001/001/47344), audio recording (SR01), VHP, AFC, LOC.
9. Nathan Fegan Collection (AFC2001/001/53077), audio recording (SR01), VHP, AFC, LOC.
10. Daniel Neville Collection (AFC2001/001/55035), video recording (MV01), VHP, AFC, LOC.
11. Yvonne Latty, *In Conflict: Iraq War Veterans Speak Out on Duty, Loss, and the Fight to Stay Alive* (Sausalito, CA: PoliPointPress, 2006).
12. Steve Pink, Zack Bazzi, and Mike Moriarty, *The War Tapes*. Directed by Deborah Scranton and produced by Robert May (Senart Films, 2006).
13. This comment was made in an off-the-record conversation.

14. New Hampshire National Guard, *Global War on Terrorism History Project* (March to September 2005, unpublished).
15. Ibid.
16. Mark Kaplan Collection, VHP.
17. "Back from the Battle: Student Veterans' Perspectives on the Iraq War: Roundtable," *Yale Journal of Alumni Affairs* 2, no. 2 (2007): 112.
18. Jude Ferran Collection (AFC2001/001/30609), audio recording (SR01), VHP, AFC, LOC.
19. Brian Turner, "War in the Present Tense," *New York Times* website, June 5, 2007.
20. Benjamin Braden Collection (AFC2001/001/30610), audio recording (SR01), VHP, AFC, LOC.
21. Quincy Boggan Collection (AFC2001/001/31460), video recording (MV01), VHP, AFC, LOC.
22. Samuel Main Collection (AFC2001/001/56467), transcript (MS04), VHP, AFC, LOC.
23. *Rutland Herald*, "On the Guard's Return," June 25, 2006.
24. Katherine Q. Seelye, "Coffins' Arrival from War Becomes an Issue Again as Photo Ban is Reviewed," *New York Times*, February 22, 2009.
25. Pauline Jelinek and Anne Gearan, "Pentagon Clears Way for Photos of Soldiers' Coffins," Associated Press, February 27, 2009. Also Seelye, "Coffins' Arrival."
26. Carroll, *Operation Homecoming*, 155.
27. Lizette Alvarez, "For Troops in Iraq and Loved Ones at Home, an Internet Lifeline," *New York Times*, July 8, 2006.
28. Ibid.
29. Terry Bruns Collection (AFC2001/001/57032), transcript (MS04), VHP, AFC, LOC.
30. Robert D'Amico Collection (AFC2001/001/62471), video recording (MV01), VHP, AFC, LOC.
31. New Hampshire National Guard, *Global War on Terrorism.*
32. Ryan Aument Collection (AFC2001/001/62372), video recording (MV01), VHP, AFC, LOC.
33. Alvarez, "Internet Lifeline."
34. Todd Walton Collection (AFC2001/001/38931), audio recording (SR01), VHP, AFC, LOC.
35. Rick Mayes Collection (AFC2001/001/57132), transcript (MS04), VHP, AFC, LOC.
36. Main Collection, VHP.
37. New Hampshire National Guard, *Global War on Terrorism.*
38. Tyler Mueller Collection (AFC2001/001/15910), video recording (MV01), VHP, AFC, LOC.
39. "The Fresh Smell of Paint," in Carroll, *Operation Homecoming*, 261, 265.
40. The new regulation is quoted in Matthew C. Burden, *The Blog of War: Front-Line Dispatches from Soldiers in Iraq and Afghanistan* (New York: Simon and Schuster, 2006), 257.

41. Ed Pilkington, "Iraq Veteran Wins Blog Prize as U.S. Military Cuts Web Access," *Guardian*, May 15, 2007.
42. Catherine Foster, "Battlegrounds: A Trinity Reproduction Joins a Growing List of Plays that Look at the Iraq War," *Boston Globe*, April 16, 2006. As of January 30, 2010, 1 Rhode Islander had been killed and 8 wounded in OEF; 10 had been killed and 109 wounded in OIF. Source, DMD, DMDC.
43. John Moore, "Denver: War from 8 Angles," *American Theatre Magazine*, April 1, 2006.
44. "Boston University School of Theatre Presents David Hare's *Stuff Happens*," Boston University Media Relations website, April 10, 2008, http://www.bu.edu/phpbin/news/releases/display.php?id=1560.
45. Noah Adams, "Homebody/Kabul: New Play a Timely Examination of East/West Understanding," *All Things Considered*, National Public Radio, December 3, 2001.
46. Mike O'Sullivan, "Hollywood Films Look at Impact of Wars in Iraq, Afghanistan," *Voice of America*, September 20, 2007. In January 2010, *The Hurt Locker*, a movie featuring a trio of veterans involved in defusing IEDs in Iraq, was nominated for nine Academy Awards and was awarded six Oscars, including Best Picture. A.O. Scott, "Apolitics and the War Film," *New York Times*, February 7, 2010.
47. Nicholas Kristof, "The Poets of War," *New York Times*, June 11, 2007.
48. A private theater group, Theater of War, is collaborating with the Defense Centers of Excellence for Psychological Health and Traumatic Brain Injury to present one hundred performances at military installations and gatherings. Patrick Healy, "The Anguish of War for Today's Soldiers, Explored by Sophocles." *New York Times*, November 17, 2009.
49. Holland Cotter, "Words Unspoken Are Rendered on War's Faces," *New York Times*, August 22, 2007.
50. Quoted in Foster, "Battlegrounds."

Chapter 9: Reestablishing Normalcy

1. "National Guard Troops Get Tearful, Enthusiastic Welcome across Nebraska," Nebraska StatePaper.com, April 28, 2004.
2. Michael A. Thomas, "Personal Narrative," in *Operation Homecoming: Iraq, Afghanistan, and the Home Front, in the Words of U.S. Troops and Their Families*, ed. Andrew Carroll (New York: Random House, 2006), 320–321.
3. Yvonne Latty, *In Conflict: Iraq War Veterans Speak Out on Duty, Loss, and the Fight to Stay Alive* (Sausalito, CA: PoliPointPress, 2006), 141, 147.
4. Samuel Main Collection (AFC2001/001/56467), transcript (MS04), VHP, AFC, LOC.
5. Nathan Fegan Collection (AFC2001/001/53077), audio recording (SR01), VHP, AFC, LOC.
6. Todd Walton Collection (AFC2001/001/38931), audio (SR01), VHP, AFC, LOC.
7. Nancy Montgomery, "A General Battles Post-Combat Stress," *Stars and Stripes*, Mideast Edition (January 11, 2009): 1.

8. "Enthusiastic Welcome," Nebraska.Statepaper.com, June 24, 2007.
9. Dana Canedy, *A Journal for Jordan: A Story of Love and Honor* (New York: Crown Publishers, 2008), 189.
10. Christopher Gamblin Collection (AFC2001/001/60182), transcript (MS04), VHP, AFC, LOC.
11. Ryan Aument Collection (AFC2001/001/62372), video recording (MV01), VHP, AFC, LOC.
12. Gamblin Collection, VHP.
13. Gonzalo Gonzalez Collection (AFC2001/001/60176), transcript (MS04), VHP, AFC, LOC.
14. Robert D'Amico Collection (AFC2001/001/62471), video recording (MV01), VHP, AFC, LOC.
15. Paul Gregory Mayfield Collection (AFC2001/001/60193), transcript (MS04), VHP, AFC, LOC.
16. Andrew Wells Collection (AFC2001/001/54819), video recording (MV01), VHP, AFC, LOC.
17. Ryan Aument Collection (AFC2001/001/62372), video recording (MV01), VHP, AFC, LOC.
18. "Acknowledging the Psychological Cost of War," *New England Journal of Medicine* 351, no. 1 (July 1, 2004).
19. "The Hardest Letter to Write," in Carroll, *Operation Homecoming*, 369.
20. Joelle Farrell, "Lessons of War," *Concord Monitor*, October 3, 2006.
21. Leslie Kaufman, "After War, Love Can Be a Battlefield," *New York Times*, April 6, 2008.
22. Steve Pink, Zack Bazzi, and Mike Moriarty, *The War Tapes*. Directed by Deborah Scranton and produced by Robert May (Senart Films, 2006).
23. Main Collection, VHP.
24. New Hampshire National Guard, *Global War on Terrorism.*
25. Latty, *In Conflict,* 49.
26. Dax Carpenter Collection (AFC/2001/001/57035), transcript (MS04), VHP, AFC, LOC.
27. Jeffrey D. Barnett, "The New Normal," from Opinionator: Exclusive Online Commentary from the Times, *New York Times*, June 1, 2007. Barnett was also author of a blog, "The Midnight Hour."
28. Jay Craven and Robert Miller, *After the Fog: Interviews with Combat Veterans* (Barnet, VT: Kingdom County Productions, 2006). The portions quoted were transcribed and edited by the author and amplified in an interview with Pickett, and are used with permission.
29. Joelle Farrell, "Bringing it Home," *Concord Monitor*, October 4, 2006.
30. Joelle Farrell, "In Combat Brian Shelton Comes of Age," *Concord Monitor*, October 1, 2006.
31. Matthew Gutmann and Catherine Lutz, *Breaking Ranks: Iraq Vets Speak Out Against the War* (Berkeley: University of California Press, 2010, in press).
32. Nicole Ferretti Collection (AFC/2001/001/57083), transcript (MS04), VHP, AFC, LOC.

33. Gutman and Lutz, *Breaking Ranks.*
34. Rick Mayes Collection (AFC2001/001/57132) Manuscript (MS01), VHP, AFC, LOC.
35. Interview, Bradford, Vermont, January 16, 2007.
36. Carpenter Collection, VHP.
37. Travis Fisher Collection (AFC2001/001/34140), video recording (MV01), VHP, AFC, LOC.
38. Gamblin Collection, VHP.
39. Mayfield Collection, VHP
40. Gonzalez Collection, VHP.
41. Wells Collection, VHP.
42. Teresa Little Collection (AFC/2001/001/57131), transcript (MS04), VHP, AFC, LOC.
43. Carpenter Collection, VHP.
44. Jack Van Zanten Collection (AFC2001/001/62027), video recording (MV01), VHP, AFC, LOC.
45. In Matthew Currier Burden, *The Blog of War: Front-Line Dispatches from Soldiers in Iraq and Afghanistan* (New York: Simon and Schuster, 2006), 245.
46. The National Guard units in Bradford and elsewhere around Vermont were mobilized for another tour—this time to Afghanistan—in early 2010.
47. Ferretti Collection, VHP.
48. Nicholas Fosholdt Collection (AFC2001/001/60174), transcript (MS04), VHP, AFC, LOC.
49. Name withheld under ground rules of the interview conducted by the author.
50. Pink, Bazzi, and Moriarty, *The War Tapes.*
51. Ibid.
52. Carpenter Collection, VHP.
53. Stephanie Corcoran, "Year in Review," November 20, 2006, correspondence with the author.
54. Pink, Bazzi, and Moriarty, *The War Tapes.*
55. Ibid.
56. Stan Goff, "Hold on to Your Humanity: An Open Letter to GIs in Iraq," *Counterpunch* (November 14/23, 2003).
57. Gonzalo Gonzalez Collection (AFC2001/001/60176), transcript (MS01), VHP, AFC, LOC.
58. Bobby Lee Lisek Collection (AFC/2001/001/60191), transcript (MS04), VHP, AFC, LOC
59. Zoroya, "Soldier's Death."
60. The website of the group, which is sponsored by Iraq Veterans Against the War, is http://www.combatpaper.org
61. Sharon Webster, "Review: Combat Paper," March 6, 2009, at www.combatpaper.org (accessed March 10, 2009).
62. Quoted in testimony by Nancy Lessin, co-founder of Military Families Speak Out, in *Winter Soldier Iraq and Afghanistan: Eyewitness Accounts of the Occupations*, by Iraq Veterans Against the War and Aaron Glantz (Chicago: Haymar-

ket Books, 2008), 171.
63. Interview, Veterans Center, White River Junction, Vermont, November 13, 2006.
64. Jeremy Lima Collection (AFC2001/001/53039), transcript (MS04), VHP, AFC, LOC.
65. Jeffrey Bartling Collection (AFC2001/001/29443), video recording (MV01), VHP, AFC, LOC.
66. Pink, Bazzi, and Moriarty, *The War Tapes*.
67. In March 2009, the Obama administration announced its intention to reduce to an absolute minimum the number of veterans affected by stop-loss arrangements. Since such arrangements were instituted in September 2001, 120,000 troops had been affected. As of early 2009, 13,000 soldiers were prohibited from leaving the ranks. *New York Times*, "Stopping Stop-Loss," (editorial), March 22, 2009.
68. For an examination of the particularly significant impacts of repeated deployments on the Army's Brigade Combat Teams, see Veterans for America, "The Consequences of Churning," April 2008.
69. Gamblin Collection, VHP.
70. Lisek Collection, VHP
71. Lynn Wagner Collection (AFC2001/001/60931), video recording (MV01), VHP, AFC, LOC.
72. Farrell, "Lessons of War."
73. D'Amico Collection, VHP.
74. William Andrews Collection (AFC2001/001/42880), video recording (MV01), VHP, AFC, LOC.
75. Trevor Bradna Collection (AFC2001/001/47553), video recording (MV01), VHP, AFC, LOC.
76. Name withheld on request.
77. In Carroll, *Operation Homecoming*, 297.
78. http://www.us-army-info.com/pages/enlist.html (accessed January 31, 2009).
79. Nancy A. Youssef, "Guardsman Would Rather Face Taliban than U.S. Economy," McClatchy Newspapers, January 6, 2009.
80. Bryan Bender, "Down Economy Boosts Military, *Boston Globe,* March 1, 2009.
81. "A Letter to the Republic for Which We Stand," in Burden, *Blog of War,* 247–248.

Chapter 10: Accessing Institutional Resources

1. Paul Gregory Mayfield Collection (AFC2001/001/60193), transcript (MS04), VHP, AFC, LOC.
2. Terrell Spencer Collection (AFC2001/001/57175), transcript (MS04), VHP, AFC, LOC.
3. Bobby Lee Lisek Collection (AFC2001/001/60191), transcript (MS04), VHP, AFC, LOC.
4. Ibid.
5. Dax Carpenter Collection (AFC/2001/001/57035), transcript (MS04), VHP, AFC, LOC.

6. Veterans for America, "Fort Drum: A Great Burden, Inadequate Assistance" (Washington, D.C., February 13, 2008), 2, 3.
7. Philip Thomas Collection (AFC2001/001/52496), video recording (MV01), VHP, AFC, LOC.
8. Robert Pear, "Military Medical Care Panel Hears Frustrations of Wounded Soldiers," *New York Times*, April 15, 2007.
9. Nicole Ferretti Collection (AFC/2001/001/57083), transcript (MS04), VHP, AFC, LOC.
10. Interview, Concord, New Hampshire, May 16, 2007.
11. Telephone interview, May 25, 2007.
12. One study of noncommissioned officers suffering from PTSD symptoms following duty in Iraq put the incidence at 12 percent after one deployment, 18.5 percent after a second deployment, and 27 percent after a third. The Brookings Institution, "Iraq Index: Tracking Variables of Reconstruction and Security in Post-Saddam Iraq" (February 5, 2009), 28, http:///.www.brookings.edu/iraqindex.
13. Maya Schenwar, "Two Wars, 400,000 VA Patients," *Truthout,* January 29, 2009, http://www.truthout.org/012909J. See also Maya Schenwar, "A Lease on Her Life," *Truthout*, January 25, 2008.
14. Lizette Alvarez and Dan Frosch, "A Focus on Violence by GIs Back from War," *New York Times*, January 1, 2009.
15. A mass shooting at Fort Hood on November 5, 2009, in which thirteen people were killed and thirty wounded—traumatic enough in its own right—also highlighted unmet mental health needs at the largest military base in the U.S., an installation which "for years . . . has been an emblem of an overstretched military." James Dao, "At Fort Hood, Reaching Out to Soldiers at Risk." *New York Times*, December 24, 2009.
16. Lolita C. Baldor, "Kentucky Base Braces for Soldiers' Return," *Boston Globe*, November 30, 2008. In mid-2009, Fort Campbell, Kentucky, held a three-day stand down for stock-taking purposes after eleven soldiers on the base committed suicide during the course of the year. See "Fort Campbell Holds 'Suicide Stand-Down.'" UPI, May 27, 2009.
17. Mental Health Advisory Team-IV, Final Report, November 17, 2006, Office of the Surgeon, Multinational Force-Iraq and Office of the Surgeon General, U.S. Army Medical Command.
18. Executive Summary, *An Achievable Vision: Report of the Department of Defense Task Force on Mental Health,* Department of Defense Task Force on Mental Health (Falls Church, VA: Defense Health Board, 2007).
19. Mental Health Advisory Team-V, Report, March 6, 2008.
20. Leslie Kaufman, "New York City Bolsters Effort to Shelter Homeless Veterans," *New York Times*, December 16, 2008.
21. Erik Eckholm, "Surge in Number of Homeless Veterans is Anticipated, *York Times*, November 7, 2007.
22. Veterans for America, *The American Veterans and Servicemembers Survival Guide,* 2008 edition, 295, http://veteransforamerica.org.

23. Anna Badken, "Shelters Take Many Vets of Iraq, Afghan Wars," *Boston Globe*, August 7, 2007.
24. Paul Rieckhoff, executive director, Iraq and Afghanistan Veterans of America, "President Obama: Make Veterans a Priority in the First 100 Days," January 20, 2009.
25. Paul Sullivan, executive director of Veterans for Common Sense, quoted in Maya Schenwar, "Two Wars."
26. Telephone interview, Dr. Andrew Breuder, chief of staff, Veterans Administration Medical Center, Manchester, New Hampshire.
27. Pia Malbran, "VA Staffer Discourages PTSD Diagnoses: The Department of Veterans Affairs Condemns 'Inappropriate' E-mail," CBS News, May 15, 2008. Circulated by VoteVets Political Action Committee.
28. Art Shapiro, "Army Blocks Disability Paperwork Aid at Fort Drum," National Public Radio, January 29, 2008. For follow-up story, see NPR, February 7, 2008.
29. Charles M. Sennott, *Boston Globe*, February 11, 2007.
30. Metz Duites Collection (AFC2001/001/58571), video recording (MV01), VHP, AFC, LOC.
31. Nevertheless, the figures for U.S. troops deployed to either Iraq or Afghanistan deemed medically unfit for combat were striking: 10,854 (2003), 8,996 (2004), 5,397 (2005), 8,672 (2006), and 9,140 (2007). Brookings Institution, *Iraq Index*.
32. David Zucchino, "New Battle for Injured Vets: Benefits," *Los Angeles Times*, November 27, 2008.
33. Associated Press, "Study Suggests Mental Health Crisis Looming," April 17, 2008.
34. Lizette Alvarez, "Nearly a Fifth of War Veterans Report Mental Disorders, a Private Study Finds, *New York Times,* April 18, 2008.
35. Bob Roehr, "High Rate of PTSD in Returning Iraq Vets," *Medscape Medical News*, November 6, 2007, http://www.medscape.com/viewarticle/565407 (accessed February 23, 2009).
36. "If current trends continue, suicide will eventually surpass the civilian rate of 19 suicides per 100,000 people. The Army thinks, unlike previous wars, that multiple redeployments may be a factor, along with failed relationships and financial problems." Betty Ann Bowser, "Military, VA Confront Rising Suicide Rates Among Troops," *The News Hour*, Public Broadcasting System, November 10, 2008.
37. Ronald Glasser, "A Shock Wave of Injuries," *Washington Post*, April 8, 2007.
38. President's Commission on Care for America's Returning Wounded Warriors, *President's Commission on Care for America's Returning Wounded Warriors Issues Six Groundbreaking Patient and Family Centered Recommendations to Serve, Support and Simplify Care*, July 25, 2007.
39. Laura Colarusso, "Concerns Grow about War Veterans Misdiagnoses: Brain Injuries Can Defy Easy Detection," *Boston Globe*, June 10, 2007. One account estimates the lifetime cost of treating a single TBI patient at $17 million.

40. Deborah Warden, national director of the Defense and Veterans Brain Injury Center, quoted in Susan Okie, "Traumatic Brain Injuries in the War Zone," *New England Journal of Medicine* 352 no. 20 (May 19, 2005): 2043. For a review of the status of efforts to diagnose and treat PTSD and TBI, see Veterans for America, "Trends in Treatment of America's Wounded Warriors: Psychological Trauma and Traumatic Brain Injuries: The Signature Wounds of Operation Iraqi Freedom and Operation Enduring Freedom," November 7, 2007.
41. Interview, White River Junction, Vermont, November 13, 2006.
42. Charles M. Sennott, "New Generation's War Rekindles Earlier Horrors," *Boston Globe*, June 18, 2007.
43. President's Commission on Care, *America's Returning Wounded Warriors.*
44. Interview with Jo Moncher, bureau chief, Community-Based Military Programs, New Hampshire Department of Health and Human Services, January 8, 2009.
45. Minnesota National Guard, "Beyond the Yellow Ribbon pilot program established to help National Guard soldiers with Reintegration," *In the News* (undated), http://MinnesotaNationalGuard.org (accessed March 17, 2009). A comparable correlation was confirmed among Army wives by a study released in 2010 based on a 250,000-person sample during the years 2003–2006. See A. J. Mansfield et al., "Deployment and the Use of Mental Health Services among U.S. Army Wives," *New England Journal of Medicine* 362, no.2 (January 14, 2010), 101.
46. New York State Health Foundation, "New York State Health Announces RFP Seeking First Comprehensive Needs Assessment of New York's Returning Veterans and Their Families," http://NYSHealthFoundation.org (accessed March 17, 2009).
47. Jude Ferran Collection (AFC2001/001/30609), audio recording (SR01), VHP, AFC, LOC.
48. Among the 190 members of a military police company from Massachusetts sent to Iraq in July 2007, at least thirty left posts in law enforcement and other emergency services agencies. Bryan Bender, "Guard Deployments Weaken Public Safety Forces," *Boston Globe*, July 14, 2006.
49. Brian MacQuarrie, "For Self-Employed, Guard Duty Has a Price: Many Struggle to Reclaim Jobs after Service Tours, *Boston Globe*, August 7, 2005.
50. Pam Belluck, "After Duty, New Chance for Old Job: Ex-Serviceman Wins Case against Employer," *New York Times*, June 21, 2008.
51. Eric Heath Collection (AFC2001/001/57086), transcript (MS04), VHP, AFC, LOC.
52. "Bases Brace for Surge in Stress-Related Disorders," November 29, 2008, http://www.msnbc.msn.com/id/27968227/.
53. Telephone interview, January 15, 2007. *After the Fog* has been adapted for use by the DVA.
54. Paul Rieckhoff, executive director, Iraq and Afghanistan Veterans of America, "President Obama: Make Veterans a Priority in the First 100 Days," January 20, 2009.

55. Leslie Kaufman, "New York City Bolsters Effort to Shelter Homeless Veterans," *New York Times*, December 16, 2008.

Chapter 11: The Global War on Terror and Earlier Wars

1. Mark Kirk Collection (AFC2001/001/38582), video recording (MV01), VHP, AFC, LOC.
2. Jude Ferran Collection (AFC2001/001/30609), audio recording (SR01), VHP, AFC, LOC.
3. Benjamin Braden Collection (AFC2001/001/30610), audio recording (SR01), VHP, AFC, LOC.
4. Ralan Hill Collection (AFC2001/001/43145), transcript (MS04), VHP, AFC, LOC.
5. Jeremy Lima Collection (AFC2001/001/53039), transcript (MS04), VHP, AFC, LOC.
6. "The All-Volunteer Army: Can We Still Claim Success?" *Military Review* (July–August 2008): 102.
7. Paul Gregory Mayfield Collection (AFC2001/001/60193), transcript (MS04), VHP, AFC, LOC.
8. Benjamin Braden Collection (AFC2001/001/30610), audio recording (SR01), VHP, AFC, LOC.
9. Samuel Main Collection (AFC2001/001/56467), transcript (MS04), VHP, AFC, LOC.
10. Mark Kirk Collection (AFC2001/001/38582), video recording (MV01), VHP, AFC, LOC.
11. Metz Duites Collection (AFC2001/001/58571), video recording (MV01), VHP, AFC, LOC.
12. Larry Bond Collection (AFC2001/001/43890), video recording (MV01), VHP, AFC, LOC.
13. Robert D'Amico Collection (AFC2001/001/62471), video recording (MV01), VHP, AFC, LOC.
14. Gregory Marinich Collection (AFC2001/001/54920), video recording (MV01), VHP, AFC, LOC.
15. Michael Daake Collection (AFC2001/001/44668), audio recording (SR01), VHP, AFC, LOC.
16. William Andrews Collection (AFC2001/001/42880), transcript (MS04), VHP, AFC, LOC.
17. Todd Walton Collection (AFC2001/001/38931), audio recording (SR01), VHP, AFC, LOC.
18. Marinich Collection, VHP.
19. New Hampshire National Guard, *Global War on Terrorism.*
20. Ibid.
21. Marinich Collection, VHP.
22. Ibid.
23. For an extended discussion on National Guard duties and performance, see Larry Minear, "A New National Guard?" in *The U.S. Citizen-Soldier and the Global War on Terror* (Medford, MA: Feinstein International Center), 61–65.

24. Mark Warnecke Collection (AFC2001/001/34941), video recording (MV01), VHP, AFC, LOC.
25. In Yvonne Latty, *In Conflict: Iraq War Veterans Speak Out on Duty, Loss, and the Fight to Stay Alive* (Sausalito, CA: PoliPointPress, 2006), 126.
26. Mark Benjamin, "Medical Evacuations in Iraq War Hit 18,000," *Washington Times*, March 31, 2004, available at www.VeteransforCommonSense.org (accessed March 8, 2009).
27. Christopher Haug, "Aeromedical Process Key to Saving Lives in Iraq," available at http://www.globalsecurity.org/military/library/news/2005/07/mil-050729-afpn01.htm (accessed March 7, 2009).
28. Maria Cochran Collection (AFC2001/001/62436), audio recording (SR01), VHP, AFC, LOC.
29. Mayfield Collection, VHP.
30. New Hampshire National Guard, *Global War on Terrorism.*
31. John Cencich Collection (AFC2001/001/48508), video recording (MV01-c.1), VHP, AFC, LOC.
32. His experience ran counter to the findings of a survey which concluded that the rate of PTSD among U.S. troops in Somalia during the years 1992–1994 was about 8 percent, or roughly half of that in Afghanistan and Iraq.
33. David Paxson Collection (AFC2001/001/35232), video recording (MV01), VHP, AFC, LOC.
34. Latty, *In Conflict*, 185.
35. Ryan Aument Collection (AFC2001/001/62372), video recording (MV01), VHP, AFC, LOC.
36. Mark Kaplan Collection (AFC2001/001/57488), video recording (MV01), VHP, AFC, LOC.
37. New Hampshire National Guard, *Global War on Terrorism.*
38. Dr. Matthew J. Friedman, "Diagnosis and Assessment of PTSD: A Report to the Institute of Medicine," PowerPoint presentation (undated).
39. Interview with the author by a chaplain requesting anonymity.
40. David Dobbs, "The Post-Traumatic Stress Trap," *Scientific American,* April 2009, 64–69.
41. "Warriors: What It Is Really Like to Be a Soldier in Iraq," Public Broadcasting System, aired April 2007.
42. For an update, see Lizette Alvarez, "G.I. Jane Stealthily Breaks the Combat Barrier," *New York Times*, August 16 2009. (This article is part of the Women at Arms series.) Also, See Paula Broadwell, "Women Soldiers Crucial to U.S. Mission," *Boston Globe*, August 26, 2009.
43. Jay Craven and Robert Miller, *After the Fog: Interviews with Combat Veterans* (Barnet, VT: Kingdom County Productions, 2006).
44. Bob Roehr, "High Rate of PTSD in Returning Iraq Vets," November 6, 2007, Medscape Medical News. The DVA official quoted is Dr. Evan Kanter, staff psychiatrist in the PTSD Outpatient Clinic of the VA Puget Sound Health Care System.
45. DOD, Defense Manpower Data Center, Contingency Tracking Service, Op-

eration Enduring Freedom, Military Deaths and Military Wounded in Action, October 7, 2001 through January 3, 2009.

46. Interview, Concord, New Hampshire, April 26, 2007.
47. Joelle Farrell, "Female Soldiers Face their Own Challenges," *Concord Monitor*, October 4, 2006. By 2010 the term *military sexual abuse* was in use.
48. Mayfield Collection, VHP.
49. Maria Zambrana Collection (AFC2001/001/ 44402), video recording (MV01), VHP, AFC, LOC.
50. Ralan Hill Collection (AFC2001/001/43145), transcript (MS04), VHP, AFC, LOC.
51. Sarah Abbruzze, "Iraq War Brings Drop in Black Enlistees," *New York Times*, August 22, 2007.
52. Elisabeth Bumiller, "Building on Campaign Effort, Obama Carefully Cultivates the Military, *New York Times*, January 31, 2009. Also Bryan Bender, "Obama Seeks Assessment on Gays in Military," *Boston Globe*, February 1, 2009.
53. Strobe Talbott and Nayan Chanda, eds., *The Age of Terror: America and the World After September 11* (New York: Basic Books, 2001), x.
54. Louise Richardson, *What Terrorists Want: Understanding the Enemy, Containing the Threat* (New York: Random House, 2006), 140, 167.
55. Larry Minear, "Learning the Lessons of Coordination," in *A Framework for Survival: Health, Human Rights, and Humanitarian Assistance in Conflicts and Disasters*, ed. Kevin M. Cahill (New York and London: Routledge, 1999), 310.
56. "Barack Obama's Inaugural Address," transcript, *New York Times* (January 20, 2009), http://www.nytimes.com/2009/01/20/us/politics/20text-obama.html?pagewanted=1&_r=1.
57. Kirk Collection, VHP.

Chapter 12: Listening to Veterans

1. Brandon Bass Collection (AFC2001/001/62664), transcript (MS04), VHP, AFC, LOC.
2. Johnny Torres Collection (AFC2001/001/53414), audio recording (SR01), VHP, AFC, LOC.
3. Blake Cole Collection (AFC2001/001/62554), video recording (MV01), VHP, AFC, LOC.
4. Benjamin Braden Collection (AFC2001/001/30610), audio recording (SR01), VHP, AFC, LOC.
5. Nicole Ferretti Collection (AFC2001/001/57083), transcript (MS04), VHP, AFC, LOC.
6. Philip Thomas Jr. Collection (AFC2001/001/52496), video recording (MV01), VHP, AFC, LOC.
7. Eric Heath Collection (AFC2001/001/57086), transcript (MS04), VHP, AFC, LOC.
8. Christopher Gamblin Collection (AFC2001/001/60182), transcript (MS04), VHP, AFC, LOC.
9. Bradley Burd Collection (AFC2001/001/30269), video recording (MV01), VHP, AFC, LOC.

10. Gonzalo Gonzalez Collection (AFC2001/001/60176), transcript (MS04), VHP, AFC, LOC.
11. David Brown Collection (AFC2001/001/29450), video recording (MV01), VHP, AFC, LOC.
12. William Andrews Collection (AFC2001/001/42880), transcript (MS04), VHP, AFC, LOC.
13. Ferretti Collection, VHP.
14. Maria Cochran Collection (AFC2001/001/62436), transcript (MS04), VHP, AFC, LOC.
15. Nicholas Fosholdt Collection (AFC2001/001/60174), transcript (MS04), VHP, AFC, LOC.
16. Jude Ferran Collection (AFC2001/001/30609), audio recording (SR01), VHP, AFC, LOC.
17. Gregory Marinich Collection (AFC2001/001/54920), video recording (MV01), VHP, AFC, LOC.
18. Lynn Wagner Collection (AFC2001/001/60931), video recording (MV01), VHP, AFC, LOC.
19. Shawn Stenberg Collection (AFC2001/001/41268), audio recording (SR01), VHP, AFC, LOC.
20. James Welch Collection (AFC2001/001/29065), audio recording (SR01), VHP, AFC, LOC.
21. Jeffrey Beard Collection (AFC2001/001/30470), audio recording (SR01), VHP, AFC, LOC.
22. Bass Collection, VHP.
23. Jeremy Lima Collection (AFC2001/001/53039), transcript (MS04), VHP, AFC, LOC.
24. Robert D'Amico Collection (AFC2001/001/62471), video recording (MV01), VHP, AFC, LOC.
25. Ryan Aument Collection (AFC2001/001/62372), video recording (MV01), VHP, AFC, LOC.
26. Mark Kirk Collection (AFC2001/001/38582), video recording (MV01), VHP, AFC, LOC.
27. Easter Seals New Hampshire, "Veteran and Family Support Services: A Concept Paper" (undated).
28. Cody Allen Collection (AFC2001/001/28652), video recording (MV01), VHP, AFC, LOC.
29. Heath Collection, VHP.
30. Paul Gregory Mayfield Collection (AFC2001/001/60193), transcript (MS04), VHP, AFC, LOC.
31. Ferran Collection, VHP.
32. Interview, White River Junction, Vermont, November 13, 2006.
33. Dax Carpenter Collection (AFC/2001/001/57035), transcript (MS04), VHP, AFC, LOC.
34. Elisabeth Bumiller, "At an Army School for Officers, Blunt Talk about Iraq Strategy," *New York Times*, October 14, 2007.

35. Michael Musheno and Susan M. Ross, *Deployed: How Reservists Bear the Burden of Iraq* (Ann Arbor: University of Michigan Press, 2008).
36. Crosby Hipes, "The Framing of PTSD: Narratives of Mental Health Workers and Veterans," Master's Thesis, University of Arkansas, 2009.
37. Matthew Gutmann and Catherine Lutz, *Breaking Ranks: Iraq Vets Speak Out Against the War* (Berkeley: University of California Press, 2010, in press).
38. Gonzalo Gonzalez Collection (AFC2001/001/60176), transcript (MS04), VHP, AFC, LOC.
39. Rick Mayes Collection (AFC2001/001/57132) manuscript (MS01).
40. Alex Kingsbury, "From Combat to the Campus: A new program helps recently wounded soldiers attend college," *U.S. News and World Report*, September 24, 2007, 71.
41. Carpenter Collection.
42. Charles Pierce, "The Forgotten War," *Boston Globe Magazine*, November 2, 2008.
43. *The Times*, January 4, 2009, http://www.timesonline.co.uk/tol/news/world/iraq/article5437950.ece.
44. Adam Paulson Collection (AFC2001/001/52541), transcript (MS04), VHP, AFC, LOC.
45. Quoted in Conrad Mulcahy, "Outward Bound Looking In," *New York Times*, August 24, 2007.
46. Benjamin Genocchio, "Photographs That Speak Quietly of War and Grief," *New York Times*, December 24, 2006.
47. Paul Gregory Mayfield Collection (AFC2001/001/60193), transcript (MS04), VHP, AFC, LOC.
48. Lizette Alvarez and Erik Eckholm, "Purple Heart is Ruled Out for Traumatic Stress," *New York Times*, January 8, 2009.
49. Leslie Kaufman, "Veterans' Families Seek Aid for Caregiver," *New York Times*, November 12, 2008.
50. Howard LaFranchi and Gordon Lubold, "Obama Redefines War on Terror: The President Focuses on Al Qaeda and on Repairing America's Image in the Muslim World," *Christian Science Monitor*, January 29, 2009. For a more recent appraisal, see Jane Meyer, "The Trial: The Right's War on the Attorney General," *The New Yorker*, February 15 and 22, 2010.

BIBLIOGRAPHY

The following list is comprised primarily of works about the Iraq and Afghanistan experience, written by veterans and their family members.

Burden, Matthew Currier. *The Blog of War: Front-Line Dispatches from Soldiers in Iraq and Afghanistan*. New York: Simon and Schuster, 2006.

Calica, Lovella, ed. *Warrior Writers: Move, Shoot and Communicate: A Collection of Creative Writing by Members of Iraq Veterans Against the War.* Burlington, VT: Green Door Studio, 2007.

———. *Warrior Writers: Re-making Sense: A Compilation of Writings and Art Works by Iraq Veterans Against the War.* Barre, VT: Iraq and Afghanistan Veterans Against the War, 2008.

Canedy, Dana. *A Journal for Jordan: A Story of Love and Honor.* New York: Crown Publishers, 2008.

Carroll, Andrew, ed. *Operation Homecoming: Iraq, Afghanistan, and the Home Front in the Words of U.S. Troops and Their Families.* New York: Random House, 2006.

Craven, Jay. *After the Fog: Interviews with Combat Veterans*. www.kingdomcounty.com. Barnet, VT: Kingdom Productions, 2006.

Davenport, Christian. *As You Were: To War and Back with the Black Hawk Battalion of the Virginia National Guard.* Hoboken, NJ: John Wiley & Sons, 2009.

Diaz, Sue. *Minefields of the Heart: A Mother's Stories of a Son at War*. Washington, DC: Potomac Books, 2010.

DiMarco, Damon. *Heart of War: Soldiers' Voices from the Front Lines in Iraq*. New York: Citadel Press, 2007.

Gutmann, Matthew and Catherine Lutz. *Breaking Ranks: Iraq Vets Speak Out Against the War*. Berkeley: University of California Press, *at press*.

Henderson, Kristin. *While They're at War: The True Story of American Families on the Home Front.* Boston and New York: Houghton Mifflin, 2006.

Hipes, Crosby. "The Framing of PTSD: Narratives of Mental Health Workers and Veterans." Master's Thesis. University of Arkansas, 2009.

Iraq Veterans Against the War and Aaron Glantz. *Winter Soldier Afghanistan and Iraq: Eyewitness Accounts of the Occupation.* Chicago: Haymarket Books, 2008.

Jamail, Dahr. *The Will to Resist: Soldiers Who Refuse to Fight in Iraq and Afghanistan.* Chicago: Haymarket Books, 2009.

Latty, Yvonne. *In Conflict: Iraq War Veterans Speak Out on Duty, Loss, and the Fight to Stay Alive.* Sausalito, CA: PoliPointPress, 2006.

Minear, Larry. *The U.S. Citizen-Soldier and the Global War on Terror: The National Guard Experience.* Medford, MA: Feinstein International Center, Tufts University, 2007. (fic.tufts.edu)

Minear, Larry and Philippe Guillot. *Soldiers to the Rescue: Humanitarian Lessons from Rwanda.* Paris: Organisation for Economic Co-operation and Development, 1996.

Murphy, Patrick. *Taking the Hill: From Philly to Baghdad to the United States Congress.* New York: Henry Holt, 2008.

Musheno, Michael, and Susan M. Ross. *Deployed: How Reservists Bear the Burden of Iraq.* Ann Arbor: University of Michigan Press, 2008.

Pieslak, Jonathan. *Sound Targets: American Soldiers and Music in the Iraq War.* Bloomington: University of Indiana Press, 2009.

Rieckhoff, Paul. *Chasing Ghosts: Failures and Facades in Iraq: A Soldier's Perspective.* New York: New American Library, 2007.

Scranton, Deborah. *The War Tapes.* New York: SenArt Films [DVD], 2006.

Sherman, Nancy. *The Untold War: Inside the Hearts, Minds, and Souls of Our Soldiers.* New York: W.W. Norton, 2010.

Trouern-Trend, Jonathan. *Birding Babylon: A Soldier's Journal from Iraq.* San Francisco: Sierra Club Books, 2006.

Veterans for America. *The American Veterans and Servicemembers Survival Guide: How to Cut Through the Bureaucracy and Get What You Need—and Are Entitled To.* www.veteransforamerica.org, 2008.

Wilder, Andrew. "Losing Hearts and Minds in Afghanistan," in *Afghanistan, 1979–2009: In the Grip of Conflict,* Viewpoints Special Edition. Washington, DC: The Middle East Institute.

INDEX OF VETERANS

NG	National Guard
USA	United States Army
USAF	United States Air Force
USCG	United States Coast Guard
USMC	United States Marine Corps
USN	United States Navy
I	served in Iraq
A	served in Afghanistan
U.S.	served on the home front in Operation Noble Eagle

*Denotes veterans whose collections in the Veterans History Project of the Library of Congress are available in digitized form over the Internet at http://www.loc.gov/vets/.

■ ■ ■

INDEX

ABOUT THE AUTHOR

Larry Minear is a researcher and writer on international humanitarian and military institutions in armed conflicts around the world. Co-founder and director of the Humanitarianism and War Project, he has been associated since 1989 with research groups at Brown University's Watson Institute for International Studies and Tufts University's Feinstein International Center. His publications include *The U.S. Citizen-Soldier and the Global War on Terror: The National Guard Experience* (2007); *The Humanitarian Enterprise: Dilemmas and Discoveries* (2000); with Ian Smillie, *The Charity of Nations: Humanitarian Action in a Calculating World* (2004); and with Philippe Guillot, *Soldiers to the Rescue: Lessons from Rwanda* (1996). He retired from Tufts in 2006 and lives with his wife, Beth, on Cape Cod.